SHYLOCK'S RIGHTS:
A GRAMMAR OF LOCKIAN CLAIMS

The existence of human rights has been compared with the existence of unicorns, but a more apt comparison would be with the existence of the world proletariat. And while the world proletariat may be going the way of unicorns, human rights are present in the world, as unicorns are not, as a mode of discourse justifying the empire of commerce. But the language of rights is not the only grammar to articulate the demands of justice, even if human rights has bested the world proletariat, if not by a knockout at least by a unanimous decision.

Edward Andrew locates the source of rights-talk in the conceptual separation of justice and charity, or in opposition to imperial Christian charity as expounded in Aquinas' *Summa Theologica*. Thomistic natural law restricts commercial enterprise, particularly usury, enjoins a duty to assist the needy that supersedes property right, and demands that unbelievers be coerced, with penalty of death, into true belief. All rights advocates stand in opposition to imperial charity.

Andrew's interpretation of *The Merchant of Venice* presents Shylock as the prototypical rights-claimant (representing Grotius, Selden, Hobbes, Spinoza, Pufendorf, Locke) in opposition to Antonio as the embodiment of Thomistic natural law. *Shylock's Rights* champions Hobbes and Spinoza, the philosophic exponents of Shylockian doctrine, but deprecates Locke, who shied away from the boldness of Hobbesian egoism and covered Hobbesian rights with the veneer of natural law.

The English-speaking world has inherited the confusion in Locke's shying away from Hobbes, in his grounding rights in a rationally untenable natural law. The basic confusion to which Andrew draws attention is the error of equating rights with what is right. Rights permit, right obliges. Right (whether Thomistic natural law or Kantian moral law) directs us to what is morally choiceworthy whereas rights protect choices or options. In rights-based doctrines, the rights claimant is not obliged to use his right for morally justifiable purposes. Shylock has a right to do wrong, to claim his pound of flesh, although the exercise of his right is morally unattractive.

EDWARD ANDREW is Professor of Political Science at the University of Toronto.

EDWARD ANDREW

Shylock's Rights

A Grammar of Lockian Claims

University of Toronto Press
Toronto Buffalo London

© University of Toronto Press 1988
Toronto Buffalo London
Printed in Canada

ISBN 0-8020-2611-7 (cloth)
ISBN 0-8020-6660-7 (paper)

Canadian Cataloguing in Publication Data

Andrew, Edward, 1941–
Shylock's rights

Includes bibliographical references and index.
ISBN 0-8020-2611-7 (bound) ISBN 0-8020-6660-7 (pbk.)

1. Locke, John, 1632–1704. 2. Natural law.
3. Liberalism. I. Title.

B1297.A5 1988   192   c87-094344-8

PICTURE CREDITS

Rembrandt's *King Uzziah* (p x): Devonshire Collection, Chatsworth, reproduced by permission of the Chatsworth Settlement Trustees; photo courtesy of the Courtauld Institute of Art.
Portraits of John Locke by M. Dahl (p 2), Thomas Hobbes by J.M. Wright (p 66), and John Stuart Mill by G.F. Watts (p 168): reproduced by permission of the National Portrait Gallery, London.
Portrait of Pufendorf by Carl Peter Mörth after David Klöcker Ehrenstrahl (p 60): reproduced by permission of the Nationalmuseum, Stockholm.
Portraits of David Hume by Allan Ramsay (p 134) and Adam Smith by Muir (p 152): reproduced by permission of the Scottish National Portrait Gallery.
Portrait of Edmund Burke (p 158): Picture Collection, the Branch Libraries, the New York Public Library.

To Geoffrey Clement Andrew
educator, liberal, and lover of poetry
who hit me only once —
for an adolescent anti-Semitic exclamation.
And to Donna Trembowelski Andrew
who failed to convert me entirely
to the American persuasion.

CONTENTS

ACKNOWLEDGMENTS ix

Introduction 3

1 The Circumcision of the Heart 25

2 The Opposition of Rights-Based Justice and Christian Charity 53

3 Contractualism and Promise-Keeping: The Bond of Civil Society 67

4 Inalienable Right and Alienable Properties: Rights as Properties 81

5 Inalienable Right, Rebellion, and Revolution 99

6 Rights as the Personalization of Right 119

7   The Historicization of Right as Civil Rights:
Old Property, New Money, and Potential Wealth
of One's Person   135

8   The Right to Be Offensive:
Rights and Manners in Liberal Doctrine   169

9   Conclusion   193

NOTES   201
INDEX   221

ACKNOWLEDGMENTS

Ronald Replogle and Patrick Neal first stimulated my interest in the subject with their intelligent insistence that rights-talk is the only moral discourse appropriate to the modern world. My friend Barry Cooper has been most supportive of this book, despite our lack of agreement on anything political. Barbara Holst has been unsnarlingly competent in her typing and retyping of this manuscript. Stan Draenos has provided useful suggestions in his copy editing, and thanks are due to R.I.K. Davidson, who initiated the editorial labours.

This book has been published with the help of a grant from the Social Science Federation of Canada, using funds provided by the Social Sciences and Humanities Research Council of Canada.

Rembrandt's portrait bodies forth Jewish nobility:
the Dutch source of English liberalism

SHYLOCK'S RIGHTS
A Grammar of Lockian Claims

Shy Locke: the father of English liberalism

INTRODUCTION

The title, *Shylock's Rights*, may give the misleading impression that the book is devoted to an interpretation of *The Merchant of Venice*. Indeed, the first chapter interprets *The Merchant* in an unorthodox manner, but with the purpose of establishing a framework for understanding the subsequent tradition of liberal political thinking, articulated through the language of rights. The subtitle, *A Grammar of Lockian Claims*, conveys more clearly the subject-matter of the book. Indeed, I demonstrate the similarity between Shakespeare's Shylock and the acknowledged progenitor of liberal doctrine, John Locke.

Shylock's Rights is a grammar of Lockian claims in that its subject-matter is words, and their correct usage. The meaning of the word 'rights' is to be illuminated by its philosophic usage in the progenitors of the liberal tradition, and in the less thoughtful or common usage of rights that has been handed on to us. It is a grammar also in the sense of a primer, an ABC of rights-discourse. To reach the prime or primary sense of rights, I explore some common themes in seventeenth-century thinkers where the fundamental structure of rights-discourse is explored. The fundamental characteristic of all seventeenth-century rights-advocacy is an opposition to imperial Christian charity. The image of Shylock is a composite of Grotius, Hobbes, Spinoza, Pufendorf, and Locke in the way that the mighty Leviathan, the artificial man, is composed of a number of natural men.

Shylock personates liberalism. Rembrandt's *Portrait of an Oriental* embodies my conception of Shylock (and liberalism). The portrait displays the nobility of countenance, grasp of life, and humane wisdom evident in portraits of Hobbes and Spinoza. But the grasping hands command attention as well. The portrait of Locke lacks the evidence of the Oriental's grasp. However, it corresponds more closely to an anti-Semite's image of Shylock than the Rembrandt portrait. The difference between the portraits indicates my view that liberalism has a dignity and stature lacking in Locke. Shylock has received a bad press while Locke has enjoyed a good press. *Shylock's Rights*, under the guidance of Aristotle's golden mean, aims to rectify this injustice by emphasizing Shylock's nobility (or that of Hobbes and Spinoza) and Locke's ignobility (and that of his followers).

Shylock is 'a possessive individualist,' the term that C.B. Macpherson in his celebrated work applied to Hobbes and Locke.[1] Shylock is, of course, a fictional embodiment of heartless greed, limitless acquisitiveness, the Elizabethan spirit of capitalist individualism.[2] However, Shylock is more than a grasping usurer. He is a Jew who wishes to retain his religious identity, whose deepest desire is to see his daughter, Jessica, married to a Jewish husband, whose religion is persecuted by the Christians in *The Merchant*, and who is ultimately compelled to convert to Christianity. Just as Shylock's persecutors ignore any non-economic motivations to Shylock's actions, C.B. Macpherson ignores the religious dimension of British liberalism. Liberalism is not exhausted in the term 'possessive individualism' but includes religious freedom. By abstracting from the religious dimension of the English civil war, the Glorious Revolution and the political theories attendant on these events, Macpherson unduly narrows the focus of the founders of liberal doctrine. Grotius, Hobbes, Spinoza, and Locke, just as Shylock opposed compulsive Christian charity for reasons which included but transcended a desire to remove barriers to commercial acquisition. *Shylock's Rights* attempts to add a dimension of religious liberty, tolerance, and plurality to Macpherson's *The Political Theory of Possessive Individualism*. That is, it attempts to establish the connection between religious toleration and an individualist market morality. Locke's *Letter Concerning Toleration* is the key to Shylockian doctrine; namely, 'if any man err from the right way, it is his own misfortune, no injury to thee.'[3]

The title of the book might have been *Shy Locke's Rights*, if such a title did not appear obscure and precious, in that Locke lacked the boldness of Hobbes' systematic egoism. Scholars are agreed that there is an apparent incongruity between the sensationalism and egoism of Locke's philosophy in *An Essay Concerning Human Understanding* and Locke's use of Christian natural law in his political writings.[4] Leo Strauss, Richard Cox, and C.B. Macpherson have argued that Locke's use of Christian natural law was mere camouflage to disguise an essentially Hobbesian egoism, to make it more palatable to Locke's contemporaries.[5] More recent scholarship, such as that of James Tully or John Dunn, emphasizes the importance of natural law, and its irreducibility to the natural right of commodious self-preservation, in Locke's political doctrine.[6] Dunn points out that Locke explicitly shied away from the boldness of Hobbesian philosophy. Locke wrote: 'The original and foundation of all Law is dependency. A dependent intelligent being is under the power and direction and dominion of him on whom he depends and must for the ends appointed him by that superior being. If men were independent, he could have no will but his own will, no end but himself. He would be a god to himself and the satisfaction of his own will the sole measure and end of all his action.'[7]

Thus, for Locke, individuals are not autonomous beings, ends in themselves, but creatures or instruments of God. A curious feature of contemporary liberal thought is the rejection of the foundations of Locke's thought in heteronomous natural law, while accepting the edifice that is constructed without any solid basis. That is, Locke is widely regarded as the most authoritative figure in the liberal pantheon, although his political teaching is acknowledged to lack a philosophic foundation. Robert Nozick, for example, finds Lockian natural law unacceptable but espouses Lockian natural rights as the core of his own thought.[8] John Rawls, while deriving his conception of procedural justice from the Lockian framework of individual rights and contracts, supplements Lockian fare with a Kantian diet of moral autonomy.[9] Rawls could have derived his 'moral constructivism,' that is, moral doctrine that is not dependent on natural facts or divine commandments,[10] from the boldest exponent of Shylockian doctrine, Thomas Hobbes. However, Rawls endows, from Kant's patrimony, Lockian doctrine with a moral dignity and a philosophic stature thought to be lacking in Hobbes, as in Locke. The title *Shy Locke's Rights* would more accurately convey the subject-matter of the book if the reader were to understand not only the affinity between Locke and Shylock but also the fact that Locke shied away from the boldness of Hobbesian philosophy.

Locke is the central figure in our account of rights because he embodies what I would call the 'amoral moralism' of rights-discourse, namely, the combination of raw Hobbesian egoism and processed Kantian moralism. The combination is manifest in the typical 'I have the right to *x*' claim. It is less obvious that 'she has a right to *y*' or 'they have a right to *z*' is more than a disinterested appeal to impersonal justice.

The basic confusion in the grammar of rights pertains to the relationship between rights and morality, between what are one's rights and what is right, between what one is permitted to do and what one is morally obliged to do. Rights-discourse is, in English usage, 'permissive' rather than 'forbidding.' While positive law proscribes and moral duty prescribes, rights (whether 'legal' or 'moral') permit or allow opportunities to exercise choice. In continental Europe, 'Recht,' 'droit,' and 'diretto' signify both right and law. Thus the English distinction between rights and laws has to be expressed on the continent as the distinction between subjective and objective right. Thus one must be careful in translating Kant's

'Rechtslehre' or Hegel's 'Rechtsphilosophie' into the language of rights.

Within the tradition of liberal theory, our obligations are delineated by the laws of nature or the Kantian moral laws (which define what is right, which are categorical in character, but which are only binding on conscience or intention as distinct from action in the external world). Moral laws, as Hobbes had it, are binding 'in foro interno,' not 'in foro externo.' The standards of what is right (rectitude, righteousness, rightness) are articulated by laws, not rights. *The* right is not the sum total of right*s* but the sum total of moral laws. Laws serve to guide conduct or to indicate what is choiceworthy; rights serve to protect choices or secure liberties. That is, *the* right is conceptually distinct from *my* rights, *her* rights, *our* rights, *their* rights (right*s* as the possessions of individuals or groups, rights in the plural, modified by some possessive pronoun).

Rights are the right personalized, privatized, and relativized. Rights become the possessions of individuals whereas the law is always a collective possession (*our* laws and *their* laws but not *my* laws and *her* laws). The privatization of what is common (the law or the right) alters its character. To use an analogy, a publicly owned enterprise or utility, for better or worse, is different in character from one that is privately owned, even if each member of society has an equal equity in the privatized corporation. The privately owned corporation is still ours, but ours in a different way than it is as a publicly owned corporation. To be sure, so-called conservatives cannot conceive how the Canadian Broadcasting Corporation or PetroCanada can be considered 'ours.' This inability to conceive of one's own in a common possession or public property is the psychological accompaniment of the transition from common law to individual rights.

The transition from the right to rights could be understood as the conceptual separation of charity from justice, or imperfect from perfect obligations, of what is morally binding from what is legally binding. One might think that charity and justice have always been conceptually distinct in that the former is a Christian virtue and the latter is a pagan virtue. However, St Thomas Aquinas explicitly argued against the separation of charity and justice in that he thought that charitable compulsion of unbelievers into the Christian communion is right or just[11] and also that providing the needy with the means of subsistence is not only charitable but also just.[12] Proprietors do not have a title to property that overrides the claims of the needy; they are stewards of God's property, obliged in justice to provide for the needy. If the wealthy do not provide for the needy poor, then a poor man may justly take, either secretly or openly, whatever property is necessary for his own, his family's, or his neighbour's subsistence.[13] St Thomas explicitly argued against the view that 'in succouring the needy we give them what is not theirs but ours.' He wrote: 'Since justice is a cardinal virtue, other secondary virtues, such as mercy, liberality and the like, are connected with it ... Wherefore to succor the needy, which belongs to mercy or pity, and to be liberally beneficent, which pertains to liberality, are by a kind of reduction ascribed to justice as to their principal virtue.'[14]

The argument of *Shylock's Rights* is that the separation of charity and justice is historical rather than transhistorical, that rights are born precisely from this separation of charity and justice, that rights emerge with the expansion of commerce, are contemporaneous with the dissolution of Thomistic strictures against usury and with the triumph of property right over the Christian idea of possession as a trust for the common good. Shylock is harassed for his un-Christian commercial practices by Antonio who personates Christian natural law in *The Merchant of Venice*. The charitable bleeding heart Antonio ultimately compels Shylock to convert to Christianity. The entire liberal tradition is opposed to compulsory conversion. In addition, Shylock's views on usury were shared by all rights-advocates. However, his view that property right (his pound of flesh) is to prevail over neediness or necessity only triumphed, albeit ambiguously, with Pufendorf and Locke. *Shylock's Rights* situates the birth of rights-discourse in the opposition of Shylock (liberal rights) and Antonio (Christian law). The book appears to champion the psychological nobility of Shylock over the sociological nobility of Antonio, Shylock's doctrine (thoughtfully presented by Grotius, Hobbes, and Spinoza) over Antonio's doctrine (presented in canonical law and Aquinas' *Summa Theologica*). However, my purpose of clarifying rights-discourse is not served by estimating the relative stature of Shylock (Hobbes) and Antonio (Aquinas), but by describing differences. We will never understand the meaning of rights if we forget that they were born in opposition to imperial charity, and flourish in conjunction with the imperatives of 'sweet commerce.' Rights then are born in the conceptual separation of justice and charity, or through the opposition of Shylock and Antonio.

Natural rights are to be distinguished from Graeco-Roman natural justice or Christian natural law. Indeed, as we shall see in chapter 1, the ancient Greeks, Romans, and medieval Christians had no word for rights. 'Diké' and 'jus' or 'ius' cannot be readily translated into the language of rights. While my concern is words not things, I am concerned to show how the transformation of political words implicates political things. An example might be found in the work of John Finnis, who translates (inappropriately in my view) Thomistic natural law into the language of human rights. Yet Finnis is aware of some of the difficulties involved in dressing up Thomas in the latest fashion. Finnis writes: 'One could say that for Aquinas "jus" primarily means "the fair" or "the what's fair"; indeed, if one could use the adverb "aright" as a noun, one could say that his primary account is of "arights" (rather than rights).'[15] The difficulty with translating natural law as human rights is that an intrinsically common property (the law) becomes private property (my rights or her rights). The grammar of 'the fair,' 'the what's fair,' or 'arights' is necessarily different from that of rights. 'The fair' is not susceptible to being possessed or borne by persons. Personal pronouns cannot modify 'the what's fair' or 'arights.' We cannot say my or her 'arights' as we can say my or her rights.

Finnis is by no means alone in mistranslating an ancient idiom into the modern language of rights. Aristotle's natural justice or Leo Strauss' natural right cannot be translated into the language of Lockian natural rights, despite the practice of most of the North American epigones of Strauss. Also a continental idiom cannot be translated into English without the greatest caution. The Rousseauan principle of right and the Kantian moral law do not differentiate law and moral liberty or right, whereas the antithesis of law and liberty is inherent in the Anglo-Saxon rights-tradition. Yet John Rawls or Alan Gewirth readily transcribe the principle of right or the moral law into the language of rights, obliterating what is distinctive about a right – namely, its conceptual antithesis to law. The subject matter of *Shylock's Rights* is the relationship of rights to the right, a relationship usually unexamined and always obliterated by those who identify rights with what is morally right. Rights-doctrines, from their initial conception, were predicated on the separation of rights from what is morally right, a separation that derives from the privatization or personalization of right.

To repeat, the transition from 'jus naturale' to natural rights can be understood as the conceptual separation of charity and justice, of imperfect and perfect obligations, or of the morally binding from the legally binding. However, the difference between moral obligations (what is morally binding) and legal obligations (what is legally binding) does not correspond to the difference between moral rights (what ought to be permitted) and legal rights (what is permitted by law). For the rights-advocate typically wishes to keep moral obligations distinct from legal obligations but wishes to convert moral rights into legal rights wherever feasible (that is, where no particular circumstances or special relationships prevent the generalization of moral rights into universally binding rules or enforceable laws). Thus there is a tendency for rights to move away from the right (the natural or moral law) and to approach positive laws. Indeed, the greater capacity of rights doctrines (relative to doctrines based on virtue, honour, utility, equity, or humanity) to be readily translated into positive laws is one of the major reasons for the breadth of its acceptance. As David Hume observed, virtues and vices admit gradations but rights and properties have the precision required by law. 'Half rights ... are perfect absurdities in their tribunal' and thus 'a man has either a full and perfect property, or none at all.'[16] But the proximity of, and relative harmony between, rights and positive laws has, as a solemn complement, a distancing of, and increasing opposition between, rights and morality. Morality here encompasses both historically changing manners (standards of decency or propriety) as well as relatively invariant and universal ideas of justice (such as not punishing someone innocent of crime, not making judgments until the evidence is in, not inflicting, or allowing to be inflicted, unnecessary misery).

The basic confusion in the grammar of rights to which I am opposed is 'she has a right to x' with 'it is right that she have x.' For, as we have seen, what is right is articulated by means of natural or moral laws, not by means of natural or moral rights. Rights are closer to what is not wrong rather than to what is right. As Hugo Grotius put it, 'right signifies nothing more than what is just, and that, more in a negative than a positive sense; so that *right* is that which is not unjust.'[17] Or, as Thomas Hobbes stated, rights are that which are not forbidden by the laws of nature (which can be encapsulated in a negative form of the golden rule). 'Do not unto others as you would not have them do unto you' is Jesus' commandment without the injunction of charity or love for one's neighbour.[18]

But the sentence 'she has a right to an abortion' is not equivalent to 'it is not wrong for her to have an abortion,' althought it is closer than 'it is right for her to have an abortion.' Rather the claim to an abortion means 'it is not wrong for women to have the choice to carry their child to term or to terminate its existence, even if the choice entails the option of doing wrong.' Choices entail the power of doing wrong, unless one takes the nihilist position that choices define what is right for the individual. Rights are like properties: they imply the capacity to use or abuse them; they are subject to the will of the individual possessing them. One might justify the right to an abortion while thinking abortion morally wrong, just as one could justify private property while thinking some of its uses morally wrong, on John Stuart Mill's grounds that the development of 'moral muscles' depends on their exercise, that a sense of responsibility and care is enhanced by moral choices, that vitality and variety depend on securing a sphere of individual choice, and so forth. Mill's championship of the right of national self-determination in *Representative Goverment* is not a declaration that it is always the right policy for small nationalities to secede from large empires. His defence of the Mormons' right to polygamous marriages coexists, in *On Liberty*, with his view that polygamy is morally wrong. Thus we cannot conclude from our intuition that Shylock's claim to his pound of flesh is morally unattractive that he did not have a right to his pound of flesh.

The right to do wrong is the moral core of liberalism. However, liberals may prefer to call Shylock's right to do wrong an abuse of rights. This phrase presumably means that rights as a general rule are good things but, when used by Mormons or other extremists, they may have occasional adverse consequences. (We might compare 'abuse of rights' with the now popular phrase 'drug abuse.' Presumably drugs, like rights, are good things except when overdoses occasion unwanted consequences.) That rights entail the right to do wrong is clear from a comparison of 'the abuse of rights' with 'the abuse of law' or 'the abuse of justice.' An abuse of law refers to people taking unforeseen advantages of the loopholes in the law. Such abuses are to be rectified by revising the law. Rights-advocates, however, usually foresee what are dismissed as mere abuses and they defend such rights in spite of known abuses; they defend choice in full awareness that some choices will be unworthy. One cannot refer to an abuse of justice as one can to an abuse of rights in spite of the fact that many claim that the language of rights is our only means to express the demands of justice. One can refer to an abuse of the justice system, but that is considered a failure of justice, not an abuse of justice. The natural right to the best lawyer, accountant, or lobbyist money can buy may engender not only the (occasional) abuse of rights but also the (occasional) failure of justice. If this is so, then upholding rights is different from upholding right or justice.

The use of 'I have the right to x' as meaning 'it is right that I am / have / feel x' could be construed as 'I have a reason for x (but I am bloody well not going to tell you)' or 'I have a reason for x (but I will not tell you because it is my reason).' This hermeneutic of rights as reasons collapses into rights as properties inasmuch as the person who stands on his rights is not usually willing (or even expected) to provide the reasons justifying his stand. Normally the rights-claimant just indicates the rights he possesses, or perhaps asserts that he belongs to a class of persons who are expected to possess what he claims. The rights-claimant typically offers and withholds a rational justification of his conduct. He takes his stand with Shylock:

> You'll ask me why I rather choose to have
> A weight of carrion flesh, than to receive
> Three thousand ducats: I'll not answer that!
> But say it is my humour, – is it answer'd?
> (IV.1.40–3)[19]

Shylock compares his right with the Christians' right to their bought slaves.

> you will answer
> 'The slaves are ours,' – so do I answer you:
> The pound of flesh which I demand of him
> Is dearly bought, 'tis mine and I will have it:
> (IV.1.97–100)

Shylock here manifests not only what I have called the amoral moralism of the rights-claimant but also what I should like to call the unreasonable rationalism of the rights-claimant. Shylock stands on the Law, and reasons within it but does not provide a rational justification of Law, just as Lockian natural law is given no rational foundation. For Shylock and Locke, rights are properties, personal possessions subject to the overlordship of Law (the authority of which is beyond human understanding).

It is precisely because rights are personal properties that Mill argues that voting is a trust or a public responsibility rather than a right. 'If it is a right, if it belongs to the voter for his own sake, on what ground can we blame him for selling it, or using it to recommend himself to any one whom it is his interest to please? A person is not expected to consult exclusively the public benefit in the use he makes of his house, or his three per cent stock, or anything else to which he really has a right.'[20] That is, for Mill, *a right is that for which no public accounting is necessary.* The possessor of a right is morally indignant if pressed to give reasons for the exercise of his or her right. My concern here is not to support Mill's views about the secret ballot but to indicate his grammatically correct (Shylockian) usage of the concept of a right.

The moralized amoralism and rationalized unreason of rights-discourse is manifest in such phrases as 'the legitimate rights of Catholics' or 'the justifiable rights of Palestinians.' Such phrases may strike many as absurd or redundant, although they are used in common speech, albeit not in the intellectual heart of the liberal world. If rights were understood solely as entitlements, then the words 'legitimate rights' would appear patently redundant. But 'rights' are understood to be 'claims' as much as 'entitlements,' and 'claims' can signify 'pretense of entitlement' as well as 'entitlements.' 'Valid claims,' like 'justifiable rights,' is in a sense a redundancy and in another sense (as demands, assertions, or pretensions of interest) is not a redundancy. John Locke's 1690 preface to *Two Treatises of Goverment* serves 'to justifie to the World' the 'Just and Natural Rights' of English Whigs. The qualification 'just' with respect to 'rights' may well not be a redundancy. But if it is not a thoughtless redundancy, we must seriously question whether the language of rights is adequate to articulate the demands of justice.

The apparent redundancy of rights-discourse, which illustrates the amoral moralism and rationalized unreason in the usage of rights, is manifest even at the intellectual heart of the liberal world, if not in such obvious form as 'the legitimate rights of Catholics.' Herbert Hart writes: 'Rights are typically conceived as *possessed* or *owned by* or *belonging to* individuals, and these expressions reflect the conceptions of moral rules as not only prescribing content but as forming a kind of moral property of individuals to which they are as individuals entitled; only when rules are conceived in this way can we speak of rights and wrongs, as well as right and wrong actions.'[21] To be sure, Hart is here referring to moral or natural, as distinct from legal or positive, rights. Referring to positive rights elsewhere, Hart says: 'Nor need rules which confer rights be just or morally good rules.'[22] Thus the idea of rights as individual moral properties seems not to be redundant because the addition of the word 'moral' seems necessary to distinguish natural rights from positive rights (or legal rights for which there is no moral justification). But Maurice Cranston considers 'moral properties' to contain an absurd redundancy 'for the simple reason that the word "property" by definition implies a right.'[23]

By 'moral properties,' Hart does not mean that rights are invisible qualitites as distinct from visible features, such as hair colour or size. By 'moral properties,' he does not intend to exclude material property from human rights or moral entitlements. Rather, the claims to moral things (such as equal respect) are modelled on our claims to tangible assets. But if something is an individual's property, the proprietor is not obliged to use it for moral purposes. Natural rights are no more subject to rules of justice and morality than are positive rights, when they are conceived as the private property of individuals. Justice or the right is not owned by individuals, whereas rights are commonly conceived to belong to individuals. Thus Hart misleadingly conflates rights with what is right when he defines rights as moral properties.

Hart obscures the essential connection between rights and properties by defining rights as individual moral properties. The moralizing of properties into rights seems to be inherent in rights-discourse, whether or not 'moral property' is recognized as a redundancy. By adding 'moral' to 'property,' Hart seems to be distinguishing between rights and properties, or separating individual rights from private properties, while at the same time presupposing that private property is morally justifiable and that entitlements to intangible possessions are patterned on material holdings.

The confusion about the meaning of the word 'rights' is more fundamental than disagreement about the content or substance of human rights. This confusion is so extreme that one might say that there is no significant proposition about rights the negation of which is not equally valid. We have touched upon the propositions 'one has a right to do wrong' and 'no one has a right to do wrong' and we shall continue to explore these propositions throughout *Shylock's Rights*. Similarly, we shall explore the propositions that human rights are, and are not, inalienable. The inalienability of rights would seem to be a condition of their being possessed by all human beings but, at the same time, they are commonly conceived to be personal properties, the value of which pertains to their alienability or their facility at being used in a bargaining-game model of justice, the very stuff of negotiations, compromises, or contracts. Further, we shall examine the propositions that rights are, and are not, privileges just as persons (the bearers of rights) are, and are not, privileged. Rights-discourse is based on a respect for persons (the abstract subject of rights) which is not a respect for persons (as distinctive individuals or individuals of distinction). If one maintains the common view that rights are not privileges and that the bearers of rights are not the privileged, then the words 'equal rights' contain a redundancy which is rarely avoided in common usage. If one consults thoughtful individuals, such as Herbert Hart, John Rawls, or Ronald Dworkin, as to whether 'equal rights' is a redundancy or not, whether it merely elaborates what is entailed in the concept of rights or adds something substantial to the idea of a right, one gets no clear guidance. In short, we may say that substantial confusion abounds in the literature on rights. What we are suggesting is that the confusion about rights is not attributable to the stupidity of writers on this topic but is rather the result of the contradictory significations borne by the word 'rights.'

Two centuries ago, Adam Ferguson observed: 'Every peasant will tell us, that a man has his rights; and that to trespass on those rights is injustice. If we ask him farther, what he means by the term *right*? We probably force him to substitute a less significant, or less proper term, in the place of this ...'[24] Two centuries of literature on rights have added to Ferguson's observation only that it is not only peasants who are confused about rights. I am following in the grand and vain tradition of trying to eliminate confusion about rights by substituting the word 'properties' for the less significant term 'rights.' The chief aim of the thinker, as Hobbes declared, is to avoid 'insignificant speech.'

The substitution of 'properties' for 'rights' may explain the contradictory significations borne by the word 'rights.' Thus while the proposition that one has the right to do wrong seems paradoxical, the proposition that one may put one's property to a good or bad use appears unproblematic. Further, the mist surrounding the relation of equality and right does not hang over the relation of equality and property. As proprietors (as a substitute for persons or bearers of rights) we are both equal and unequal, formally equal and substantially unequal. We are equal with respect to the absence of legal disability to acquire property, equal with respect to the legal power to oblige the state to secure our property, no matter of what kind and of what amount, and equal with respect to the most fundamental of human rights, namely, the ability to hire the best lawyer money can buy.

There are only two propositions which command near unanimous assent in the literature on rights. The first is that most people, other than the author advancing his thesis, are highly confused about rights. The second is that rights, whatever they are, are good things. I dissent only from the second proposition.

The grounds of my dissent are illustrated in the inadequacy of Herbert Hart's rejection of Ronald Dworkin's view that rights exist only in relation to social prejudices. Hart finds Dworkin's view to be paradoxical, for if rights exist only to safeguard heterodox opinions and conduct of which a majority disapproves, it follows that 'the more tolerant a society is, the fewer rights there will be ...'[25] If Hart is thought to have refuted Dworkin, it could only be that rights are held to be good things. The more rights, the better the society. But why? The more lawyers, the better the society. Why is this proposition less evident than the former? Why could we not simply accept Hart's consequence as non-paradoxical and say, yes, the more tolerant the society, the fewer the rights? Why not a utopia where no rights (and no lawyers) exist?

The position adopted in this book is that rights are necessary evils, not positive goods. In a utopia (whether Plato's *Republic*, Augustine's *Civitas Dei*, or Marx's communist society), no rights exist. In our world, rights exist to the extent we are like Shylock and rights are necessary to the extent that there is an antagonism between Shylock and Antonio. It is better that Shylock has rights than his having no rights, but it would be better still if there were no Shylocks (produced by the bigotry and bad faith of the Antonios) or no need for Shylock to demand his rights. I am adopting the Marxian perspective advanced in *On the Jewish Question* that rights are to be understood as necessary evils, as claims against others that are necessary to societies based on conflict and competition, as the properties of individuals in societies based upon private property in the means of production, and as the equal entitlement to things (objects of desire or possession, either material or symbolic) based on unequal access to things. Thus Marx thought that a society which could take the absence of racial or religious discrimination for granted would have no need of a right to employment or public office regardless of race, religion, or creed. Now one might quite properly insist that one could never take such a utopian condition for granted, and that rights are necessary precisely because such a utopian condition will never come to be, at least not without constant vigilance and political art. But such an objection does not vitiate the assertion that rights are necessary evils rather than positive goods.

If one cannot take for granted the absence of racial or religious bigotry, one perhaps can take for granted in particular parts of the earth's surface an absence of foot-binding and genital mutilation. In countries without a tradition of these abhorrent practices, women do not claim the right to unimpaired feet and genitals. Herbert Hart might very well grant that more civilized and tolerant societies have less need for rights and less occasion for demanding, asserting, or claiming rights. Perhaps it is one thing to enjoy and exercise rights and quite another thing to claim them. The more civilized societies have greater exercise and enjoyments of rights, even if their members do not claim them or even if they are unaware of the rights they exercise. However, Hart makes clear that having rights depends upon the capacity to choose; to have a right implies the option of exercising or waiving one's right.[26] Option-rights seem to entail the capacity for conscious choice. Thus the proposition that a western girl exercises her right to unbound feet without being aware of her right is inconsistent with Hart's concept of rights. If the proposition that civilized individuals exercise rights without consciousness of doing so is problematic, the proposition that people could have rights without claiming them raises other problems. For, as Maurice Cranston says: 'A right presupposes a claim; if the claim is not made, the question of a right does not arise.'[27]

Hart might well concede that the degree of civilization is not precisely measured by the clamour of claims. But his proposition that the degree of civilization is gauged by the extent of rights depends on the existence of a class of unclaimed rights. Unclaimed entitlements appear less paradoxical than unclaimed claims. However, the activity of claiming something that is disputed seems to be integral to our undertstanding of rights. Joel Feinberg states that '*having a claim consists in being in a position to claim, that is to make claims to* or *claim that*. If this suggestion is correct it shows the primacy of the verbal over the nominative forms.'[28] If rights presuppose claims, and claims presuppose something contentious or disputed, then we would be using language idly if we were to say that North American girls are exercising their right to unbound feet. And if we are using language idly, then we can understand the Marxian position that rights are necessary evils, rather than positive goods.

Claiming rights is perhaps a transitional condition between feeling too oppressed to make claims and taking for granted an unquestioned, uncontended, and unclaimed good. To assert a right to clean air and water would seem to token the existence of pollution or inability to take clean air and water for granted. If one were to read that some country provided the constitutional right of equal opportunity to all persons, independent of height, sex, race, religion, and creed, one would probably think that in fact height matters more in this country than in those countries which omit a constitutional guarantee to short people. For the Marxist, the realm of right is an abstraction from the real social differences which in fact give some social groups more power and prestige than others.[29] Thus the constitutional right of short people would be necessary only where there is real discrimination on the basis of height (as well as sex, race, religion, and social class).

Shylock's Rights advances the Marxian thesis that rights are to be understood as individual properties (as distinct from *the* right or *the* law which is the common property of those bound by it). Rights as properties are to be conceived more as claims *against* others rather than as joint entitlements constituting a moral community. We have rights *against* others as we have duties *towards* one another. Rights as properties are option-rights rather than welfare-rights; they function to secure choice rather than direct us to what is choiceworthy. For example, compulsory retirement at the age of sixty or sixty-five may be an eminently sensible policy. Indeed, it may be the only means to enable corporations that wish to avoid litigation on 'agism' to continue to employ late middle-aged workers whose attention span is beginning to slip. However, when spokesmen for mandatory retirement as the means of decent retirement income use the language 'a right to retire,' they undermine their case. A right, as distinct from a duty, to retire implies the option of retiring or of not retiring if one can command a good price at the market. A right to retire strengthens those with a commanding position in the market and weakens those without economic or social power. Similarly the language of rights is inappropriate to promote policies such as compulsory education or universal immunization. If individuals lack the option of exercising or waiving their right, then the language of rights should be replaced by one based on need, and the duties to meet these needs.

These assertions on the appropriate use of the language of rights are in no sense to be taken as critical of the substance of so-called welfare rights. My concern is with political words, not political things. It will be shown that the language of rights belongs in the domain of the mighty Leviathan whose blood is money, namely, a commercial society with a representative form of government. To fight for social justice against the mighty Leviathan may entail that one disavow the language of rights. Prudence dictates that one be able to swim as well as the mighty Leviathan or else stay on dry land.

Canadians received the new Charter of Rights and Freedoms as if it were a welfare cheque sent to them from the Trudeau government. The argument of *Shylock's Rights* is that they were mistaken in this expectation. As the courts rule on the charter's provision of freedom of expression in favour of the advertisers and other whores, Canadians may begin to ask who profits from a rights-based polity.

Introduction

Rights are appropriately the means to express a tolerant market morality. Shylock is presented as the personification of the typical rights-claimant in that his objectives are both religious and economic, but combine in opposition to imperial Christian charity, personified by Antonio in *The Merchant of Venice*. The destination of complete clarity about rights-discourse may not be achieved by *Shylock's Rights*. But, for fellow travellers to that distant destination, there is fun along the way.

Our voyage will begin with an interpretation of Shakespeare's *The Merchant of Venice* in order to establish a conceptual framework for our exploration of seventeenth-century rights-discourse. The thesis of *Shylock's Rights* is that rights-discourse was most clearly articulated in the writings of Grotius, Hobbes, and Spinoza and then ossified into authoritative doctrine in the writings of John Locke. Although, in chapters 7 and 8, I describe the evolution of Lockian natural rights into historical manners (or changing estimates of what is useful and agreeable) in the eighteenth and nineteenth centuries, I argue that nothing fundamental (or comparable to the Hobbesian break with Christian natural law) has been added to Anglo-American rights-discourse since the seventeenth century (and perhaps some thought has been subtracted). The confusions we have enumerated in contemporary rights-discourse (with respect to rights and the right, with respect to rights as claims or entitlements and thus the questionable redundancy of 'equal rights,' 'legitimate rights,' 'moral properties,' and the like, with respect to what I have called the amoral moralism and the unreasonable rationalism of rights-talk) are to be dispelled by 'archeology.' By the elimination of the sedimented accretions to Lockian doctrine, I hope to liberate the Hobbesian philosophy contained therein to revivify the thought of our time.

Hobbes is the political philosopher of the English-speaking world; he is to thought what Shakespeare is to poetry. In saying that rights-discourse has lost the sunny clarity it enjoyed with Hobbes, I do not mean to depreciate the practical application of rights-discourse. Practical progress is compatible with theoretical regress. Liberalism, in my view, has not only relieved the estate of mankind but also has ennobled many inhabitants on that estate. However, as liberalism has evolved to contemporary liberal democracy, it has been increasingly challenged at home and abroad. Russian communism, National Socialism, various forms of socialist or fascist nationalism, and most recently, Khomeinism and other modes of religious fundamentalism have emerged to challenge liberal democracies. Perhaps liberal democrats should continue to denounce human rights violations, and increase the budgets for internal security and for the armed forces to police the empire of human rights. But blind denunciations of the evil rivals to the empire of human rights do not clarify the meaning of rights in general, let alone specific rights under contention. Seeing is a good in itself, and is often effective in the achievement of practical objectives. Theory is a seeing of the physically sightless; it is a listening to the essence of things, a hearing of the grammar of words.

Alleged ritual murder of St Simon:
what Shylock intended for Antonio

CHAPTER ONE

The Circumcision of the Heart

THE PLOT OF THE MERCHANT OF VENICE

The plot of *The Merchant of Venice* might be summarized for those not familiar with Shakespeare's play. The noble merchant Bassanio, having lost his money in unprofitable ventures, lacks funds to venture forth to win the heart and 'golden fleece' of the rich and fair heiress Portia, who resides at Belmont. Bassanio's great and good friend Antonio, saddened by the new direction of Bassanio's heart, is unable to lend Bassanio money (as he had frequently done before) because all of Antonio's fortune is tied up in his merchant fleet at sea. However, because Antonio's credit is better than Bassanio's, Antonio offers to stand surety for any loan Bassanio can make in Venice. Bassanio approaches the Jewish usurer Shylock, who offers to lend money free of interest on Antonio's promise to repay the loan, with the forfeit of an unprofitable pound of flesh if Antonio cannot repay Shylock within three months.

In Act II, Shylock's daughter, Jessica, elopes with Lorenzo, a friend of Bassanio and Antonio, assisted by other friends of the noble Christians. At the time, Shylock had been summoned to dine with Bassanio and Antonio to celebrate the bond of friendship between the Jew and the Christians.

In Act III, Shylock declares a public revenge against Antonio. At the time, Bassanio, because he is willing to 'give and hazard all he hath,' becomes the successful suitor of Portia. Portia gives her heart and property to Bassanio with a ring which Bassanio promises not to part with until he is dead. Portia's maid, Nerissa, falls in love with Bassanio's friend, Gratiano, and gives Gratiano her ring. Lorenzo and Jessica come to Belmont and tell Bassanio and Portia of Shylock's desire for revenge, coupled with the unexpected inability of Antonio to repay Shylock. The lovers depart for Venice to help Antonio, leaving Jessica and Lorenzo in the romantic utopia of Belmont.

Act IV is devoted to a judgment of Shylock's claim against Antonio. Nerissa, dressed as a law clerk, presents Portia, disguised as Balthasar, a Doctor of Laws, to adjudicate the suit. Portia tries to persuade Shylock to temper his just claim by the higher virtue of mercy. When Shylock refuses, Portia rules that Shylock may have his pound of flesh but not 'one drop of Christian blood.' Portia then rules that, for his attempt on Antonio's life, one half of Shylock's property is to go to Antonio and the other half to the state. Shylock's life is also forfeit, unless he successfully begs the Duke of Venice to be merciful. Antonio nobly refuses to take Shylock's property on condition that Shylock be converted to Christianity and that his property be turned over to Lorenzo, 'the gentleman that lately stole his daughter' (IV.i.383–4). (I have watched this play in England, the United States, and Canada. On every occasion, the audience has enthusiastically applauded what has justly been called the 'mercifixion'[1] of Shylock.) Then the disguised Portia and Nerissa, for services to the noble Antonio, demand and receive the rings that Bassanio and Gratiano swore would be inalienable during their lifetimes.

The final act is a thoroughly happy ending which adds, if possible, to our joy in the judgment against Shylock. All lovers return to the romantic setting of Belmont where Portia and Nerissa quiz their men about the lost rings, pretend to be angry about their breach of promise, then reveal their identities as Balthasar and the law clerk. Erotic harmony is restored and Antonio, as well as Lorenzo, is enriched.

THE SETTING OF THE MERCHANT

The site of Shakespeare's *The Merchant of Venice* was a commercial republic. Shakespeare's Venice was a republic of a completely different character than the ancient republics of Plato and Aristotle. The difference is of crucial importance to the understanding of *The Merchant*. The dramatic tension in the play pertains to attitudes towards usury, which derived from the ancient republics, that lived on, despite the growth of commercial activity. To understand *The Merchant*, we must first examine the economic practices and moral vocabulary of classical antiquity, then of the Christian middle ages, before returning to Renaissance commercialism and the nascent vocabulary of rights.

For both Plato and Aristotle, a prime condition for political life was the subordination of commerce to political and ethical goals. Economic life was a means to a political end, and was to be limited in terms of that end. The end of economic life was the reproduction of good citizens, that is, of soldiers capable of holding the citadel and of civilians capable of deliberating upon, and speaking to, matters of public policy. The emancipation of commerce, Aristotle thought, would undermine the self-sufficiency of the state, the solidarity of its citizens, and the possibility of a life of moral and intellectual excellence.

Commercial enterprise, Aristotle thought, was unnatural, and nothing more so than the life of the usurer who makes money breed.[2] (Aristotle's imagery of the unnatural offspring of usury, and of money's self-generative capacity, pervades *The Merchant of Venice*.) A natural economy, for Aristotle, was based on the exploitation of the soil, of animals, and of those human beings deemed incapable of contributing to political life (natural slaves, women and resident aliens in democratic regimes, and day-labourers and merchants as well in aristocratic regimes). A commercial economy was unnatural in that acquisition was made at the expense of fellow citizens. Plundering foreigners at war and hunting natural slaves were, in Aristotle's view, more just and honourable occupations than engaging in profitable exchanges with one's fellow citizens.[3]

Exchange in the form of barter was an honourable and useful addition to the household economy, supplementing the produce of the slaves, women, and productive citizens. But money, first introduced to facilitate exchange, comes to invert the proper relationship between economics and politics, mere life and the good life. Monetary acquisition becomes the goal of life. Economic life ceases to be a means to, and limited by, the end of life, namely the reproduction of good citizens.[4] There is no end to the pursuit of wealth and no end to the exploitation of fellow humans. The unlimited exploitation of the slaves in the mines and manufacturers replaces the exploitation of the household slave, limited by the domestic requirements of his master. The unlimited pursuit of wealth dissolves the bounds of the polis, disrupts its internal harmony, and transforms the pursuit of civic virtue into the pursuit of apolitical liberty and happiness.

Ancient political thought differs from modern political thought in that 1) the demands of justice or 'diké' are not expressed in terms of personal or subjective rights – indeed the Greeks had no word for rights – and 2) the former discouraged and the latter encouraged the emancipation of commerce. The two differences are interrelated. That is, there is an essential connection between the emancipation of commerce and the respect of individual rights.

Aristotelian hierarchy is overturned in the Christian Baptism: St Paul asserts (Gal. 3:20) 'There is neither Jew nor Greek, there is neither slave nor free, there is neither male nor female; for you are all one in Christ Jesus.' And when commerce sweetens this bitter vale of tears, she whispers, 'There is neither Greek nor barbarian, Jew nor gentile, male nor female, bond nor free; for you are all one at the marketplace.' Thus, one might say, the Greeks had no word or idea for human rights because of the different value they assigned to citizens and non-citizens.

But the ancient Greeks had no word or concept corresponding to the idea of positive or legal rights. Not only non-citizens but also citizens lacked rights as we understand them. This 'defect,' J.R. Pennock asserts, was the result of a 'lack of clear conceptualization' since 'the *idea* of "a right" was at least implicit and potential among the Greeks.'[5] However, Pennock goes on to imply that the Greeks lacked more than 'clear conceptualization' in that 'the implied right was not the same as would be the case in modern Anglo-American law, and that from our point of view it would be less satisfactory. If a court adjudged that the land belonged to A, it would take no steps to enforce its judgment. A must depend on self-help.'[6] However, the Greek popular courts were, according to J.W. Jones, 'primarily concerned to patch up a dispute and to re-establish the peace rather than to recognize and give effect to existing rights.'[7] That is, Jones realizes that Greek justice had different objectives than modern rights-based justice; it was not merely a primitive attempt to achieve modern objectives, as Pennock implies.

To be sure, the Greek system of justice had critics then as now. Plato viewed the popular courts as catering to vulgar passions, partisan interest, bribery, and rhetoric. Plato's view of Athenian justice, although it did not derive from a belief in rights which the courts did not recognize, was perhaps as warranted as the current disesteem of Cuban popular courts by advocates of human rights. But judicial decisions in Greek antiquity, besides expressing biases or arbitrary preferences, attempted to provide judgments of equity in particular cases rather than establishing universal rules. The procedural justice, the legalism and formalism (what Hegel called the spiritlessness) of systems of rights, was doubtless absent. Jones attributes this absence of rights to the lack of a specific term for possession and ownership, and the lack of distinction between materially possessing something and having a proprietary title to it, or a right of ownership.[8] Complementing Jones' interpretation, J.G.A. Pocock understands rights (or proprietary claims against others) to emerge with the decline of civic virtue or the demands of active citizenship. Pocock writes: 'Since law is of the empire rather than the republic, its attention is fixed on *commercium* rather than *politicum*. As the *polis* and *res publica* declined toward the level of municipality, two things happened: the universe became pervaded by law, the locus of whose sovereignty was extra-civic, and the citizen came to be defined not by his actions and virtues, but by his rights to and in things.'[9] Rights, or claims *against* the community, replace virtues or contributions *to* community.

The expansion of commerce was incompatible with the conditions of civic virtue in Aristotle's sense. The city-state gave way to the nation-state, citizens' armies gave way to professional armies, a participatory system of politics gave way to a representative system of government, and popular courts adjudicating a rough and unsystematic justice evolved into a judicial system based on developments in commercial law, civil codes of property and contract, and more clearly defined property title and civil rights.

Between world-views organized by the ancient principle of civic virtue and the modern principle of natural rights lay the tradition under the sway of Christian charity. Saint Thomas shared some of Aristotle's views on commerce. Trade, while not sinful, is not honourable. Profit gained through trade is ignoble in itself, unless directed to a higher purpose.[10] Thomas added a theological dimension to the Aristotelian prohibition of usury. 'The Jews were forbidden to take usury from their brethren; i.e. from other Jews. By this we are given to understand that to take usury from any man is evil simply, because we ought to treat every man as our neighbor and brother, especially in the state of the Gospel, where to all are called.'[11] John Locke, who charged interest on loans to his closest friends and who participated in the founding of the Bank of England, carried on the spirit of Christian universalism, while departing from the letter of the Thomist strictures on usury.

Christian charity, throughout the medieval period, was deemed to be incompatible with an absolute right to property, or a proprietary entitlement which overrides the needs of the poor. Brian Tierney writes: 'The *Decretum* and its *Glossa Ordinaria* bristle with phrases like this: "Feed the poor. If you do not feed them, you kill them." "Our superfluities belong to the poor." "Whatever you have beyond what suffices for your needs belongs to others." "A man who keeps for himself more than he needs is guilty of theft."'[12] Thomas cited St

Basil: 'It is the hungry man's bread that you withhold, the naked man's cloak that you have stored away, the shoe of the barefoot that you have left to rot, the money of the needy that you have buried underground: and so you injure as many as you would help.'[13] Later Thomas cited St Ambrose's somewhat more terse formulation: 'It is the hungry man's bread that you withhold, the naked man's cloak that you store away, the money that you bury in the earth is the price of the poor man's ransom and freedom.'[14] Thus St Thomas argues that not only charity but also justice demands that we provide property to those in need;[15] if the rich fail to perform their charitable duty, the poor may justly take what they need from them.[16] Although private possession is natural, and not born of sin as St Augustine had it, the proprietor is more a steward or trustee of the common goods than an owner with an absolute and clear title to exclude others from his possession.

Christian charity, throughout the Middle Ages, also entailed that unbelievers be forced into the Christian communion. St Thomas argued against the proposition that 'we should not even wish unbelievers should be put to death.' '*On the contrary*, It is written (Luke xiv.23): *Go out into the highways and hedges and compel them to come in.* Now men enter into the house of God, i.e. into Holy Church, by faith. Therefore some ought to be compelled into that faith.'[17] We shall see that this parable justifying compulsory conversion is crucial to an understanding of *The Merchant of Venice* but has been systematically ignored by all of Shakespeare's commentators, most of whom assume that Shakespeare thought Christian charity is unquestionably superior to Jewish justice.

All rights-advocates from Shakespeare's day to ours are opposed to charitable compulsion into religious communion. Hugo Grotius interprets Jesus' parable 'jesuitically' so as to exclude Christian imperialism. Grotius writes that 'the term, *compel*, here signifies nothing more than an earnest entreaty' because 'from the kind of evidence on which Christianity rests, it is plain that no force should be used with nations to promote its acceptance.'[18] Shakespeare's compatriot, and Grotius' rival in maritime law, John Selden, opposed the Thomistic strictures against usury and unbelief.[19] Moreover, Selden pointed out the injustice of the Imperial Constitutions whereby 'if a man Converted a Christian to be a Jew, he was to forfeit his Estate, and lose his life.'[20] – the very punishment Portia levies on Shylock before Antonio charitably insists that he be compelled to convert to Christianity.

Shakespeare's Venice was then in a transitional stage between a non-commercial city-state and a commercial nation-state. The Aristotelian and medieval Christian distaste for usury remained, but was joined to an entirely un-Aristotelian admiration for commerce, for noble merchant adventurers. Indeed, the hazards of commerce are presented not only as a form of noble gambling and adventure but also as a form of Christian love in contrast to the ignoble and unchristian security of the usurer. Bassanio wins Portia's heart and her wealth because he is willing to 'give and hazard all he hath.' The Christian merchant Antonio is willing to give and hazard his heart and his wealth, free of worldly interest. The unloving Shylock seems unwilling to give or hazard anything, and thus loses everything to the ungrasping Christians. The noble aspects of commercial enterprise are embodied in the Christians, the base aspects in the Jew. A characteristic feature of anti-Semitism is the tendency to abstract the unsavoury aspects, from other integral aspects, of commerce and to attribute them to the Jews.

Shakespeare's Venice and Belmont appear cosmopolitan in contrast to the closed and uncosmopolitan polises of classical antiquity. I say Shakespeare's Venice because *The Merchant of Venice* does not attempt an accurate historical portrait of Venice. As W. Cohen writes:

Venetian reality during Shakespeare's lifetime contradicted almost point for point its portrayal in the play. Not only did the government bar Jewish usurers from the city, it also forced the Jewish community to staff and finance low-interest, non-profit lending institutions that served the Christian poor. Funding was primarily derived from the involuntary donations of Jewish merchants in the Levantine trade. The Jews of Venice thus contributed to the early development of capitalism not as usurers but as merchants involved in an international, trans-European economic network.[21]

33 The Circumcision of the Heart

Shakespeare's Venice was then not so much a representation of historical Venice as it was a site to stage ideals of moral economy. 'Shylock the Jew was merely exotic local color; Shylock the usurer was a commentary on London life.'[22] Scholars have portrayed Shylock as 'the embodiment of capitalism' and Venice as 'a more advanced stage of the commercial development' that the English were themselves experiencing.[23] Indeed Shylock represents the very portrait of an Elizabethan puritan who 'portrays the worst side of the new capitalist individualism born in Shakespeare's time. He is the spirit of that economic self-seeking which is indifferent to the welfare of others ...'[24] My interpretation of Shylock, which complements more than competes with the interpretations above, sees him as an archetypical rights-claimant.

In 1571, a quarter-century before Shakespeare wrote *The Merchant of Venice*, all legislation against usury had been repealed in England. Indeed, by Elizabeth's reign, 'members of parliament ... regarded the usury laws as an antiquated remnant of popery.'[25] Protestant reformers, such as Martin Luther, Philipp Melanchthon, Huldreich Zwingli, Martin Bucer, and Jean Calvin, had removed the Thomist blanket condemnation of usury.[26] However, the debate about the legitimacy of usury continued after the repeal of laws against usury. In 1572, Thomas Wilson published *A Discourse uppon Usurye*. Following Wilson's attack on the practice, Thomas Rogers translated Philippus Caesar's *A General Discourse against the Damnable Sect of Usurers* in 1578. In 1595, *The Death of Usurie, or the disgrace of usurers* continued the attack on usury, a tradition carried on by Roger Fenton's *A Treatise of Usurie* in 1612 and by *Usurie Araigned and Condemned* in 1625. However, by 1653 Sir Robert Filmer, dismissing the criticism of usury, stated that 'this point of usury, as it is at this day contraverted, is a mere popish question ...'[27]

Francis Bacon wrote: 'Usury is a *concessum propter duritiem cordis* [a thing allowed by reason of the hardness of men's hearts]: for since there must be borrowing and lending, and men are so hard of heart as they will not lend freely, usury must be permitted.'[28] Bacon here articulated the message of *Shylock's Rights*: rights-discourse is a 'concessum propter duritiem cordis'; a right is a concession, not a moral principle, something which is permitted, not intrinsically noble. Bacon recommended a legislated maximum of 5 per cent interest for the general borrower, and a 9 per cent rate for merchant investors, so that 'the tooth of usury be grinded, that it bite not too much.'[29]

Thus, by Shakespeare's time, usury flourished in England despite condemnation by ecclesiastical and secular writers. English usurers were not Jews. Indeed, the fair daughter of commercial expansion, the representative system of government, was born in England with the expulsion of the Jews. G.L. Haskins asserts that the grant of taxes to Edward I in the first parliament of 1290 was conditional on the expulsion of the Jews from England.[30] The Jews, as a group, were not to return to England until Cromwell's rule, the late adolescence of the commercial and representative system, although individual Jews were resident in England during Shakespeare's time (such as Roderigo Lopez unjustly hanged in 1594 for his participation in English politics on behalf of the Portuguese pretender, Don Antonio).[31] England, as well as being less commercially developed, was less cosmopolitan than Venice. Elizabethan England had anti-Semitism without Jews.

The commercial, cosmopolitan site of Venice is central to the play in so far as its theme is religious as well as economic conflict. *The Merchant of Venice* not only portrays an English conflict between merchant and loan capital, or between equity and common law, but also presents a conflict between the Old and the New Testament, between law and love, between natural justice and supernatural charity, or Jewish vengeance and Christian mercy. Venice is the site for a confrontation between Christian and Jew.

RELIGIOUS ANTAGONISM, COMPULSORY CONVERSION, AND TOLERATION

I interpret *The Merchant of Venice* as if it were presenting the arguments for and against human rights. Rights, we have said, emerge from the distinction between charity and justice, represented in the play by the unity of opposites, Antonio and Shylock, 'matched as two gelded users of money.'[32] Natural rights in the person of Shylock confront Christian duties in the person of Antonio.

Allan Bloom suggests that *The Merchant of Venice* contains a covert message of religious tolerance. Religious intransigence can only be overcome by the powerful passion of greed. 'The commercial spirit causes men to moderate their fanaticism; men for whom money is the most important thing are unlikely to go off on Crusades. Venice was above all a commercial city and had indeed succeeded in bringing together in one place more types of men than any other city.'[33] To be sure, Venice brought men together, but not as friends, not with the ties of Aristotelian citizens, but as strangers, as bearers of rights, as citizens of a modern commercial state, a civil society which contains the opposition of Christian and Jew. Antonio admits (III.iii.26–31):

> The duke cannot deny the course of law:
> For the commodity that strangers have
> With us in Venice, if it be denied,
> Will much impeach the justice of the state,
> Since that trade and profit of the city
> Consisteth of all nations.

This equation of equal rights with commodious living, 'justice of the state' with 'trade and profit of the city,' anticipates the great founders of rights-doctrines in the century following Shakespeare. Yet justice means that everyone is to be treated as a stranger and not a friend. The drama of *The Merchant* depends on the tension of friendship and enmity.

Christians do not charge interest to fellow Christians and Jews do not charge interest to fellow Jews. The Torah (Lev. 25:36–7; Deut. 23:19) forbids the practice of usury amongst Jews but 'To a foreigner you may lend upon interest, but to your brother you shall not lend upon interest' (Deut. 23:20). Shakespeare makes clear that Shylock can borrow without interest from 'Tubal (a wealthy Hebrew of my tribe)' (I.iii.52) while Antonio 'lends out money gratis' to fellow Christians (I.iii.39). Antonio, who has spat upon Shylock and called him a 'misbeliever, cut-throat dog' for his usurious practices, offers to stand bond for his friend, Bassanio, who wants to borrow money to win 'the golden fleece' of Portia. Antonio asserts that since he will continue to scorn and spit on Shylock, the latter should not lend money 'As to thy friends, for when did friendship take / A breed for barren metal of his friend? / But lend it rather to thine enemy' (I.iii.127–9), that is, at interest. But Shylock responds 'I would be friends with you, and have your love' (I.iii.134). He will lend money to a friend, that is, free of interest, but should it happen that the loan is not repaid within three months, Antonio is to forfeit a useless pound of flesh. Although Bassanio suspects Shylock, Antonio agrees, and refers to Shylock as a 'gentle jew' (I.iii.173), that is, a gentile-man, and avers 'The Hebrew will turn Christian, he grows kind' (I.iii.174).

From Shylock's point of view, a happy ending to the comedy would not be the ideal harmony of Belmont where everyone is united in love (which contrasts not only with the conflict of Venice but also with the ubiquity of 'Jewish' usury in the real world of Christian commerce). A comic ending for Shylock would reflect the real historical world, of the coming-to-be of societies based on a respect for human rights, without the excesses of friendship or enmity, with the cool co-operation of competitors. From Shylock's point of view, an ideal conclusion, in contrast to the harmony of Belmont, would involve Shylock marrying off Jessica to a Jewish husband and carrying on his usurious business by converting the bachelor gentile-man Antonio to sensible commercial practices. The most economical way of accomplishing Shylock's ideal may lead us to question the precise place where Shylock wished to cut Antonio's flesh. But ideals or utopias are incompatible with respect for human rights. Shylock would have to dispense with utopian ends or ideal endings if he is to be the prototypical rights claimant.

We know that in the play Shylock did not accomplish his aims and, for punishment, was subjected to Christian 'mercifixion.' Antonio charitably insists that Shylock be compelled to become a Christian and that his property be turned over on his death 'unto the gentleman [gentile man] that lately stole his daughter' (IV.i.377–86). Poetic justice demands that the superhuman charity of the Christian be equivalent to the subhuman justice of the Jew and the supernatural Christian mercy be just retribution for unnatural Jewish cruelty.

What distinguishes Jew from Gentile is the rite of circumcision of the male descendants of Abraham. As rings in *The Merchant of Venice* symbolize the bonds of love, the ring of flesh in the Torah symbolizes the Jewish bond or covenant with God. The Torah (Deut. 10:16; see also 30:6; Lev. 26:41; Jer. 4:4 and 9:26; Ezek. 44:9) declares the divine command: 'Circumcise therefore the foreskin of your heart, and be no longer stubborn.' The flesh that the stiff-necked Shylock is to cut off the stubbornly Christian Antonio is 'nearest the merchant's heart' (IV.i.299, 250). In the New Testament, baptism replaces circumcision as a sign of one's covenant with God. Yet the link between Law and Love is that baptism is understood as a circumcision of the heart. St Paul explains: 'For he is not a real Jew who is one outwardly, nor is true circumcision something external and physical. He is a Jew who is one inwardly, and real circumcision is a matter of the heart, spiritual and not literal' (Rom. 2:28–9; also 3:27–31; 4:11; 1 Cor. 7:19; Gal. 5:6; 6:15; Col. 2:11; 3:11). Since 'real circumcision is a matter of the heart,' we should perhaps take Shylock's claim to Antonio's heart spiritually and not literally. The transcendence of the enmity between Antonio and Shylock depends upon one or other of them undergoing a circumcision of the heart.

But why should Shylock or Antonio wish to convert the other to his religion? From Antonio's point of view, Shylock's circumcised heart made the organ less sensitive, for he says (IV.i.78–80) there is nothing 'harder' than Shylock's 'Jewish heart.' A true inner circumcision would transform Shylock into a bleeding heart, and a source, elsewhere unobtainable, of interest-free loans. Shylock's interest in Antonio's conversion would be to eliminate an unbusinesslike competitor who undercuts his usurious trade. Also Shylock's profoundest desire is to see his daughter Jessica married to a Jew (IV.i.291–4). H.B. Charlton accepts as sincere Shylock's profession of friendship for Antonio. He points out that Antonio stands out as the most serious, understanding, and compassionate of the aristocratic Venetian youth. 'On every count, he is the one member of Venetian society who might understand deep suffering.'[34] Charlton does not add that Antonio also stands out as the only eligible bachelor in the play, and would be infinitely preferable to the poor, wasteful, and music-loving Lorenzo as a son-in-law. Although the relationship of Antonio and Bassanio would not bear close scrutiny to an illiberal father-in-law, Shylock is a tolerant man who respects human diversity (IV. i. 40–66). Besides, Antonio is very rich. Converted to more businesslike commercial practices, Antonio would be an ideal son-in-law for Shylock.

Shylock's forced conversion appears, as Barbara Lewalski notes, 'a gratuitous addition made by Shakespeare to the source story in *Il Pecorone*.'[35] By 'gratuitous,' Lewalski means a voluntary contribution to the source story, a contribution that is not integral to the original plot. However, Lewalski insists, correctly in my view, that any addition Shakespeare made should not be understood as gratuitous, in the sense of an unnecessary complication that is not essential to Shakespeare's purpose, and that Shakespeare's seemingly gratuitous addition can be understood as integral to *The Merchant*, when it is interpreted in the light of the meanings Shakespeare drew from the Biblical context. However I cannot accept Lewalski's assumption that Shakespeare shared her view of the unambiguous superiority of the New Testament to the Old, her assumption that Shakespeare's addition of Shylock's forced conversion is a necessary deliverance from the Law that 'leads only to death and destruction.'[36] As with every Shakespeare scholar, Lewalski conveniently ignores Jesus' parable justifying forced conversion.

The parable in question comes from Luke 14: 15–24. Jesus provides an allegory (as in Matt. 22: 1–14) of divine communion in a rich man's feast. The master sends his servant to invite his neighbours to a feast. When they decline, the servant is commissioned to bid 'the poor, the halt, the blind and the lame' to the banquet. After the servant has done this, the Lord sees that there remains some room at His banquet, and instructs his servant to find people lurking in the hedgerows and 'compel them to come in.' This story of the compulsory communion in the Christian feast became the scriptural warrant for imperial Love from the time of the early church fathers to Shakespeare's time.[37] Lewalski's interpretation that *The Merchant of Venice* expresses Shakespeare's view of the

39 The Circumcision of the Heart

demonstrable superiority of Christian Love to Jewish Law overlooks Jesus' justification of loving compulsion. That Shakespeare may have been sceptical of imperial love is manifest in *Measure for Measure*, set in the centre of the Holy Roman Empire. The extreme decadence and hypocrisy that characterize Shakespeare's Vienna indicate the poet's view of the results of imperial love.

Shylock's downfall dates from the time when he deserts his exclusivist (Jewish) principles for a feast of Love, celebrating his bond with Antonio and Bassanio. Shylock had earlier told Bassanio (I. iii. 30–3): 'I will buy with you, sell with you, talk with you, walk with you, and so following: but I will not eat with you, drink with you, nor pray with you.' Yet after making his bond with Antonio, Shylock shares a common communion with the Christians. In a direct parallel with Jesus' parable, Shylock is summoned by a servant to his lord's feast. The servant is Launcelot Gobbo, who deserted the service of Shylock for the better-rewarded service of Bassanio. During the feast, Shylock is robbed of his fortune and his daughter, his past and his future, his wife's jewels and his manhood ('and jewels, two stones, two rich and precious stones' (II. viii. 20), his means of carrying on the religion of Abraham, Isaac, and Jacob or his means of worldly immortality. Until this time, according to my interpretation, Shylock wished to be friends with Antonio. Following the banquet, Shylock has good reason to believe that Antonio conspired in the elopement of Jessica, thus shattering all of Shylock's fondest hopes.

To repeat, Antonio wanted Shylock to lend him money as an enemy (at interest) rather than as a friend (free of interest). But Shylock said that he wanted to be friends with Antonio and appears to lend him money free of interest, with the forfeit of a useless pound of flesh. To lend money free of interest is to relate as Christian to Christian or as Jew to Jew. Antonio thinks 'the Hebrew will turn Christian.' But perhaps Shylock wants the Christian to turn Hebrew. If so, then the pound of flesh is the equivalent of the Christian communion feast. Shylock's compulsory conversion to Christianity, on this interpretation, is the just response to his attempt to convert Antonio against his will. Shylock is deprived of his rights because he is an imperfect rights-claimant. He is too paternalist –

not only in the specific sense of wanting Antonio as a son-in-law but also in the general sense, which all rights-theorists use to stigmatize their opponents, of wanting to impose his morality on others. He is rightly dispossessed of his rights not because he is Jewish but because he is too 'Christian,' too full of the spirit of imperial love. Forsaking the exclusivist principles of his 'sacred tribe,' Shylock is punished for reaching out beyond his own.

Thus Shylock wished to be friends with Antonio not by becoming as Christian as Antonio but by Antonio becoming as Jewish as he. While the forfeit on the bond may be an unlikely prospect, Shylock does not venture anything. If Antonio repays the interest-free loan, he is indebted to Shylock as a friend. Shylock would then be in a better position to persuade Antonio of the greater reliability of business partners within the Jewish faith. (Indeed, there is no Christian upon whom Antonio could rely, when he is in desperate straits – that is, from the time when Shylock announces publicly his desire for revenge upon Antonio [III. i. 42–66] until the expiry date of the bond.) Alternatively, if Antonio is incapable of repaying the loan, Shylock thinks he has the means of ensuring the death of Antonio as Christian and his rebirth as Jew. He has the right to the flesh of whatever part of Antonio's body he wants. That is, Shylock thinks he has acquired the right by contract to circumcise Antonio.

Thus the compulsory conversion of Shylock is just, if and only if he had forfeited his right to be immune from compulsory conversion. Shylock's circumcision of the heart (baptism) is just punishment for his attempt to circumcise Antonio, as well as an expression of Christian charity or mercy. Shylock deserves 'mercifixion' not because he is too 'Jewish' but because he is too 'Christian,' too 'paternalist,' too full of the spirit of imperial love. A circumcision of the heart for a circumcision of the heart. Even Shylock's hatred of Antonio is born of thwarted love.

THE TRANSFORMATION OF LOVE INTO HATE

The traditional reading of *The Merchant of Venice* is to dismiss Shylock's profession of love and friendship as diabolical or Machiavellian cunning; the Jew, according to conventional estimates, could

41 The Circumcision of the Heart

not want the friendship of gentile men and himself become a gentleman. Moreover there is textual support for the traditional reading or against the view that Shylock genuinely wanted the love or friendship of Antonio; namely, Shylock's initial appraisal of Antonio as a 'fawning publican' (I. ii. 36) and his subsequent statement to Jessica, before going off to the festive communion celebrating the bond between Shylock and Antonio, that he will 'go in hate, to feed upon the prodigal Christian' (II. v. 14–15).

Shylock has two grievances against Antonio: he lends out money free of interest, thus lowering the rate of usury in Venice, and he has spat upon Shylock and called him a faithless dog for practising usury (I. iii. 125–6). Indeed, Shylock must have a marked propensity to turn the other cheek for friendship with Antonio to be possible. However the opposition between Shylock and Antonio is not personal but based on the religious difference, and thus disappears without the religious difference, and the usury which presupposes that difference.

However, the description of Antonio as a 'fawning publican' is curious in that it is an apparent appraisal of Antonio's person which has 'no apparent application to Antonio.'[38] Publicans (tax-farmers, imposters, escheaters) were, for the Jews of the New Testament, the lowest of the low, classed with prostitutes, as the dregs of society. Jesus tells (Luke 18: 10–14) of a Pharisee and a publican praying next to one another in a temple; the self-righteous Pharisee who looks down on the humble publican is less close to God than the praying sinner. Shylock's judgment that Antonio is a fawning publican seems to say more about himself than Antonio (who is not fawning, except on Love). Shylock is a Pharisee, one who adheres to the strict letter of the law, and particularly the law of circumcision (Acts 15: 1–5). However, Pharisees and publicans pray together. The opposition of Pharisees and publicans is a major theme of Luke 14–18. Dining at a Pharisee's house, Jesus teaches that the exalted will be humbled and the humble exalted (14: 11) and then tells the parable of how those invited to God's banquet (the Jews) will not taste of the feast, and so 'the poor, the halt, the blind and the lame' (the Gentiles) are bidden, and then those lurking in the hedgerows (the heretics) are compelled to come in (or forced to convert) to partake of the Christian feast (14: 15–24). Then Jesus says that unless one is like Antonio and hates all family, property, and 'even his own life,' he cannot be a true Christian (14: 25–33). Luke 15 recounts another occasion when 'publicans and other bad characters' crowded around Jesus and the Pharisees grumbled at his lack of propriety in consorting with sinners. So Jesus tells them of the prodigal son whom his father forgives and feeds on the fatted calf while the resentful elder son (the Pharisee) gets nothing of the fatted calf. The description of Christians as prodigal pervades *The Merchant of Venice*. Luke 16 tells of Jesus preaching against worldly wealth, and when he said 'You cannot serve God and Money,' 'The Pharisees, who loved money ... scoffed at him.' The Pharisaical rights-claimant scoffs at the Christian teaching of the gospel of Luke. Then the Pharisees ask when the Kingdom of Heaven will come and Jesus responds that 'the Kingdom of God is among you' and that 'whoever seeks to save his life will lose it; and whoever loses it will save it, and live.' Luke 18 tells of the righteous Pharisee and the lowly publican praying, and Jesus repeats the message that the exalted will be humbled and the humble exalted. Scholars agree that chapters 14 to 18 of the gospel of Luke are crucial to an understanding of *The Merchant of Venice*.[39] However, the parable of the servant compelling wayfarers to come to the Christian feast is not mentioned by commentators on *The Merchant*. Perhaps doing so would question the orthodox interpretation that the play exhibits the demonstrable superiority of Christianity to Judaism, or charity to justice.

Shylock offers friendship in making the interest-free loan. But this friendship is surely feigned, for when summoned to dine with Antonio and Bassanio by his former servant, Shylock says to Jessica that he will 'go in hate, to feed upon the prodigal Christian' (II. v. 14–15). H. B. Charlton understands this to be Shakespeare deferring to the mob's Shylock rather than the dramatist's Shylock. That is, the conventional portrait of the Jew who is too mean to provide adequate food for his household and wishes to dine at someone else's expense is merged with the Jew as a diabolical werewolf who feeds on human flesh. However, Shylock surely did not think he could bankrupt Bassanio with his belly. Also the diabolic werewolf eating human flesh is symbolically taking the bread of the Christian communion. Shylock unwittingly anticipates his conversion to Christianity.

However, the text reveals that Shylock says that he will go in hate precisely because he thinks he is 'not bid for love' (II. v. 13). Unlike the merchant venturers in love, Shylock wants security; not prodigal, he is not going to give his heart away without some guarantee of reciprocation. To avoid being made into a fool, giving away his principles of not dining with Gentiles on the wild gamble of obtaining friendship at dinner, Shylock tells Jessica that he will go in hate. Shylock is reluctant to go but friendship requires his attendance – so he goes, telling his daughter that he is nobody's fool.

Indeed, Shylock's foreboding is warranted. During the masque at suppertime, Jessica elopes with Lorenzo aided by the masked friends of Bassanio. Antonio cuts short the dinner of friendship (was Shylock even given any bread or wine?) because the wind is favourable for Bassanio's sailing to fortune at Belmont. Let us consider Shylock's chagrin at being so ill considered that the dinner of friendship is unceremoniously terminated, at returning home and finding his property stolen, his daughter and means of carrying on the religion of Abraham, Isaac, and Jacob vanished. Indeed, Shylock thinks he is the butt of a Christian conspiracy to destroy him.

> SOLANIO 'The villain Jew with outcries rais'd the duke,
> Who went with him to search Bassanio's ship.
> SALERIO He came too late, the ship was under sail,
> But there the duke was given to understand
> That in a gondola were seen together
> Lorenzo and his amorous Jessica.
> Besides, Antonio certified the duke
> They were not with Bassanio in his ship.
> (II. viii. 4–11)

Antonio's ability to certify that Jessica was not aboard Bassanio's ship depends upon his being party to the conspiracy against Shylock, and to the evidently false story that Jessica, disguised as a page boy, and the masked Lorenzo were recognized inside a covered gondola.

Shylock is enraged to distraction at the loss of his fortune and his daughter, his present and his future. Then Jessica violates his past. Shylock is tortured to hear that his daughter traded the ring her mother, Leah, had given Shylock – for a monkey (III. i. 108–12). Jessica has desecrated the Jewish family and dishonoured him. His deepest wish to see his daughter married to a Jew (IV. i. 291–4) is destroyed by her elopement and conversion. Jessica is dead to him. Shylock will revenge himself on the man who prevented Shylock from stopping the elopement.

But not in the low, sneaking cretin (chretien) manner of his adversaries. Well before the bond is due, Shylock, who is bemoaning the 'death' of his 'flesh and blood,' is provoked by Salanio and Solerio to announce publicly his desire for revenge on Antonio (III. i. 42–66). Where is the low cunning of the Jew in providing advance warning that he will no longer be trifled with? But the Christians apparently did not think highly enough of Shylock to think him capable of fulfilling the bond or of Antonio to lend him the money to release him from the bond. Where, one might ask, was the noble generosity or the Christian charity?

From Shylock's point of view a potential son-in-law has become a mortal enemy. The flesh which would have spelled Antonio's death as a Christian and rebirth as a Jew, if cut differently and more deeply, can mean Antonio's death as a man.

The book of Genesis (34) recounts a cruel and ignoble revenge of the violation of Leah's daughter, Dinah. Leah's daughter, Jessica, is twice referred to, in *The Merchant of Venice*, as Diana (v. i. 66; v. i. 109). The prospective husband of Dinah, Schechem, and all his kinsmen, were all circumcised as a condition of the marriage of Dinah and Schechem, and while the newly circumcised were writhing in agony, Dinah's brothers exacted a hideous revenge. Shylock's revenge, while cruel, is neither deceitful nor blasphemous as with the revenge of Dinah. Shylock's revenge for the daughter of Leah is frank, open, and consonant with the law in Venice.

My interpretation that Shylock's revenge takes the form of the

45 The Circumcision of the Heart

biblical account of the revenge of Leah's daughter (or of the illustration of the ritual murder of St Simon) seems to conflict with repeated statements (IV. i. 242, 248, 298) that the flesh is to be taken from Antonio's breast, rather than his foreskin. But could one stage the death of St Simon with propriety? In *Il Pecorone*, the source story for *The Merchant*, on being told to take a pound of flesh from any part of the Christian's body, 'the Jew ordered him to be stripped naked, and took a razor in hand which he had got for the purpose.'[40] In another source, Declamation 95 of *The Orator*, the Jew thinks he would kill the Christian 'if I should cut of his priuie members, supposing that the same would altogether weigh a iust pound.'[41] The exigencies of staging Antonio's peril explain why the Torah's 'foreskin of the heart' becomes the literal heart.

THE UNJUST JUDGMENT

I shall not comment here on the judgment against Shylock except to say that 'flesh and blood' belong together, as is evident in Shakespeare's use of the phrase. J.L. Palmer writes that 'Shylock was defrauded of his rights by a quibble which no court of law could in decency accept: ... since the right to perform a certain act, in this case the cutting of a pound of flesh, confers a right to the necessary incidents of the act, in this case the shedding of blood' just as the right to a pound of watermelon confers a right to the juice spilled during the cutting.[42] However, philosophers of rights would qualify Palmer's assessment of injustice depending on the source of the pound of flesh. If the foreskin of the heart signifies the spiritual death of Antonio (compulsory conversion by circumcision), then all rights-advocates would think Shylock gets his just deserts. If the pound of flesh would occasion the literal death of Antonio, some rights-advocates would think the bond between Shylock and Antonio to be invalid and thus the judgment should go against Shylock (although not with the provision that Shylock must convert to Christianity). A more detailed examination of the justice or injustice of taking another's soul or life is the subject of subsequent chapters.

However, we might note here that the judge, Portia as Daniel/Balthazar, is an interested party. Superficially, because the duke orders Antonio to reward the 'learned' and 'upright judge' for his favourable verdict (IV. i. 402–3). More deeply, Portia delivers Antonio from his bond to Shylock because she wants to free her beloved Bassanio of his bonds (of finance and of love) to Antonio.[43] Antonio has given his heart away for Bassanio, and until the bond between Bassanio and Antonio is broken, Bassanio cannot consummate his marriage to Portia. Shylock is the victim of Portia's love for Bassanio. Antonio, just before Shylock claims the foreskin of his heart, calls for the hand of his 'bosom lover,' Bassanio, and tells him (IV. i. 271–7):

> Say how I lov'd you, speak me fair in death:
> And when the tale is told, bid her be judge
> Whether Bassanio had not once a love:
> Repent but you that you shall lose your friend
> And he repents not that he pays your debt.
> For if the Jew do cut but deep enough,
> I'll pay it instantly with all my heart.

Bassanio responds (IV.i.278–83):

> Antonio, I am married to a wife
> Which is as dear to me as life itself,
> But life itself, my wife, and all the world,
> Are not with me esteem'd above thy life.
> I would lose all, ay sacrifice them all
> Here to this devil, to deliver you.

No wonder that we applaud Portia's intervention to destroy Shylock, if only to deliver us of the 'greater love hath no man' or to liberate Bassanio from his unseemly and sentimental bond with Antonio. Martin Luther was made of sterner stuff than Portia and her applauding audience. Luther approved of King Solomon's dictum that the man who stands surety for another should be slain. Luther wrote: 'It serves the surety right when he is caught and has to pay, for he acts thoughtlessly and foolishly in standing surety. Therefore it is decreed in Scripture that no one shall become surety for another unless he is able and entirely willing to assume the debt and pay it. Standing surety is a work that is too lofty for a man; it is unseemly for it is presumptuous and an invasion of God's rights.'[44] Antonio's imitation of Christ, like the Thomist prohibition of usury, is, for the Protestant, presumptuous for mere men.

JEWISH FIDELITY AND CHRISTIAN INFIDELITY

After he has been delivered from Shylock's bond by the judge, Portia-Balthasar, Antonio insists that Bassanio give his ring (which he has promised to part with only when he is dead) to the judge. Then Gratiano gives away Nerissa's ring to Nerissa disguised as a law clerk. The Christians all commit the cardinal sin of Hobbes and Kant; their word is not their bond. Fidelity in contracts, keeping promises, honouring one's word is the heart and soul of the contractarian doctrine of the philosophers of rights. The Christians, the prodigal sons of God, give their word lightly, expecting to be forgiven for breach of promise, unlike Shylock, Hobbes, and Kant whose word is their bond. The centrality of promising to the loveless doctrine of rights or to the doctrine of the incommensurability of goods (of, say, the Christian and the Jewish God) will be analysed in Chapter 3.

Of the Christians, no one gives his word more lightly than the arch-Christian Antonio, who has given his heart away without reserve or security, whose self-sacrificing love is so great that he is willing to give his life away for his friend, Bassanio. His love is so great that he gives his word to repay Shylock without the certainty that he will be able to do so. He certifies to the duke that Jessica is not on Bassanio's ship (which he would be unable to do truthfully unless he were in the conspiracy to steal Shylock's daughter and property by some other means of transport). Finally, Antonio asserts that if Jessica will forgive Bassanio's breach of promise in parting with the wedding ring, he will give his word that his friend will never again violate his oath.

48 Shylock's Rights

> I once did lend my body for his wealth,
> Which but for him that had your husband's ring
> Had quite miscarried. I dare be bound again,
> My soul upon the forfeit, that your lord
> Will never more break faith advisedly.
>
> (v.i.249–53)

Thus, Antonio compares his great love with Bassanio's mercenary love of Portia; Bassanio's objective in sailing to Belmont was 'his wealth.' But if Antonio was unable to keep his word to Shylock when his body was 'upon the forfeit,' Portia surely has less security that Antonio can honour his word and ensure that Bassanio will remain faithful (now that the epic adventurer has Portia's 'golden fleece' in his possession). The soulful Antonio's pledge to 'be bound again' is not exactly valueless; it perhaps serves to inject the spirituality of Antonio into the carnal love of Belmont. Thus it would have the value to Portia of an iron cross on her husband's bosom, located between the hearts of herself and her husband, which might serve to cool the heat of their ardour.

The play ends with the uncircumcised and Jew-hating Gratiano vowing, 'I'll fear no other thing / So sore, as keeping safe Nerissa's ring.' Rings, which perhaps serve to seal financial bonds, symbolize the bonds of love and fidelity. The ring of flesh is Shylock's bond of fidelity to his God as rings of metal symbolize bonds of loving fidelity. Portia and Nerissa had given rings to Bassanio and Gratiano, extracting from them the promise that they will only part with the rings when their love has died. But the Christian lovers, in a prodigal and promiscuous manner, give the rings to Portia and Nerissa in the guise of Balthazar and a law clerk for liberating Antonio from Shylock's bond. When Nerissa asks Gratiano for the ring and pretends that she thinks her lover had given it to another woman, Gratiano swears he gave the ring to a law clerk and wishes the latter 'were gelt that had if for my part' (v.i.144). He had thought the gelded and 'paltry ring,' inscribed 'like cutler's poetry upon a knife,' to be insignificant (v.i.147–50). But Portia insists that fidelity should be 'riveted with faith unto your flesh' (v.i.169). After Portia and Nerissa pretend to threaten Bassanio and Gratiano with infidelity Gratiano vows, in the concluding lines quoted above, that he will take pains to ensure Nerissa's fidelity and will subject himself to the painful rite of fidelity.

We might now ask whether the marriage vows represent a synthesis of loveless Law and lawless Love. Is faithful and lawful love present at Belmont and does it represent a union of Christian and Jew, of antinomian and promiscuous Love and unprodigal and unforgiving Law? Is the spirit of Shylock partially present in Portia's and Nerissa's claims to fidelity, in their view that rings should be 'riveted with faith' into the flesh of their men?

We are compelled to answer all these questions negatively because the promiscuous passage of rings is comic, a matter of sexual foreplay rather than serious commitment. One feels that repeated breaches of faith would be a stimulus to consummate forgiveness or a consummation in forgiveness. Renouncing one's ring – even for a monkey – would be no tragedy for the Christian lovers. The erotic love of Belmont is prodigal, promiscuous, forgiving; more antinomian or Christian than rule-bound or Jewish, the marriage vows do not really blend the Old with the New.

The Christian merchants and their booties do not love as King Lear's Cordelia; only Shylock loves according to his bond. Cordelia's love unites the noblesse oblige of the graceful lord and the faithful service of the proud bondsmen, the sparkling charge of virgin youth and the pregnant bloom of mature experience. Only Cordelia's love is given shape or form by her bond; the cords of her heart (cor, cordis) measure and define her love. But since her bonds are her love, her love is unbounded or bound only by itself. This definite yet infinite love, bounded yet boundless, dutiful but free, is the marriage of Law and Love. Shylock and Antonio are alien to the erotic harmony of Belmont, and alien to one another. The dutiful love of Cordelia belongs to another play.

SHYLOCK'S RIGHTS

What we have attempted to establish in this chapter is that rights presuppose barriers to fraternity or solidarity, as in the opposition of Christian and Jew, and that respect for human rights presupposes a renunciation of the desire to convert others by force or fraud to one's way of life. Rights would be as alien to a universal fellowship of Love or Law as they are to Belmont's utopian harmony of erotic rhythm. Rights exist between aliens or strangers rather than between friends or lovers, between members of a religious or erotic communion.

We have presented the alien Shylock (in opposition to the charitable Antonio) as the archetypical rights-claimant who departs from type in so far as he wishes fondly to compel Antonio to become a Jew. If this interpretation is unpersuasive, what remains is Shylock as the prototype of a rights-claimant despoiled of his rights (unless, as we shall see in chapter 4, Antonio's life was not his own to dispose of in a contract). That is, if Shylock did not intend to circumcise Antonio, the compulsory conversion of Shylock is unjust. Compulsory communion, as in Jesus' parable of the Lord's feast, constitutes a violation of human rights. Shylock was dispossessed of his rights — either unjustly, by imperial Christianity, or justly, by forfeiture, by antecedent imperial Love. If conventional estimates of 'the Jewish character' bar acceptance of my interpretation of Shylock as a 'paternalist,' then Shylock must be understood as the prototype of a rights-claimant deprived of his rights.

Rights-discourse emerges at the same time as the public acceptance of the legitimacy of usury and flourishes with the emancipation of commerce from Christian Aristotelianism. Human rights, as we shall see in chapter two, develop in conceptual opposition to Christian charity. The bond of the rights-based society, chapter three will reveal, is based not on charitable duties, shared loves, or common attachments but on individuals' ability to keep promises or to honour their contractual obligations. The circumcision of Shylock's heart, according to Antonio, made the organ hard, but the hardness of the Jewish organ, to a sensitive soul, makes it less capable of love. But hardness of heart may be seen as strength of will, as the power to make good one's word. In the century following Shakespeare, the great jurisprudents and philosophers of rights did not celebrate bleeding hearts but hearts circumcised in accordance with law, hearts hard enough to father a new age.

Spinoza: the shrewdest of saints,
who blessed commerce as the engine conveying free thought

CHAPTER TWO

The Opposition of Rights-Based Justice and Christian Charity

We have interpreted *The Merchant of Venice* as portraying a genealogy of rights from the opposition of justice (Shylock) and charity (Antonio). The message that Shylock might have learned in the play is the message of the most saintly and shrewd of the rights-advocates, Baruch (or, after his excommunication from Amsterdam Jewry, Benedict) Spinoza. Spinoza's chief aim was religious toleration and freedom of thought. Because he thought the expansion of commerce fostered this end, he advocated commercial expansion, not because he loved the comforts and material security a commercial society provides but because he thought it brought in its train a civil society free of state enforcement of doctrine and punishment of doctrinal deviance. Spinoza thought he could find in Amsterdam what Shylock could not find in Venice (despite the wide tolerance associated with its commerce). Spinoza wrote: 'The city of Amsterdam reaps the fruit of this freedom in its own great prosperity and in the admiration of all other people. For in this most flourishing state, and most splendid city, men of every nation and religion live together in the greatest harmony, and ask no questions before trusting their goods to a fellow-citizen, save whether he be rich or poor, and whether he presently acts honestly, or the reverse.'[1] Spinoza thought that the state enforcement of doctrine is available only to those 'who desire to have no foreign relations, but to shut themselves up within their own frontiers ...'[2] International commerce is incompatible with civil religions. Spinoza thus thought it most important to separate ceremony and rite from faith and conscience, or the external aspect from the inner heart of religion. The ceremonial or ritual aspect of religion was useful to herding and agricultural peoples; it provided a social cement and a principle of obedience beyond force, a motive of devotion, and an incentive to military glory for people incapable of rational self-governance. But for a rational, commercial country, the ritual or ceremonial aspect of religion is unnecessary. Spinoza pointed out that 'in Japan, ... the Christian religion is forbidden, and the Dutch who live there are enjoined by their East Indian Company not to practise any outward rites of religion.'[3] Protestant interiority would seem to be the appropriate demeanour for profitable business rather than ritualist Judaism or ceremonial Catholicism. The Japanese, Spinoza implied, would have to drop their intolerance if they wish to profit from international commerce.

Thus Spinoza would counsel Shylock to forgo the external rite of circumcision for inner principal and external interest. Indeed, Shylock would have done well to take on all the outward appearance of a gentile – in short, to bend a little so that he not be broken or made broke. To be sure, to the extent that Shylock's pound of flesh represents the means to the compulsory conversion of Antonio, Shylock's objectives breach Spinoza's doctrine of rights. We are reluctant to believe that Shylock could be moved by the spirit of imperial Love, for it is well known, or commonly believed, that Jews lack the will or power to convert Christians. Indeed, as John Selden observed, conversion of Christians is so contrary to the nature of Jews that any attempt of a Jew to do so was punishable with the loss of life and property from the time of the adoption of Christianity as the official state religion of Rome until seventeenth-century England.⁴ Further, it is well known that Jesus' contemporary, Rabbi Hillel, presented a negative form of the golden rule. Hillel's injunction[5] – not to do to others what one does not want done to oneself – is the golden rule without the loving compulsion Jesus advocated (Luke 14: 21–4) to compel people into true religion. The negative or 'Jewish' form rather than the positive or 'Christian' form of the golden rule appears in the great founders of rights-discourse.

Thomas Hobbes, the most original and, with Spinoza, the most humane of rights-advocates, also condensed the laws of nature into a negative form of the golden rule.[6] Hobbes' doctrine, as he stated with precise wit, 'is almost in the self-same words delivered by our Savior.'[7] The minor addition of 'not' to Hobbes' saviour's rule is Jesus' commandment without the injunction to love your neighbour. The distinction between charity and justice, which emerged with rights doctrines, was brilliantly expressed by England's great exponent of justice. Hobbes' championship of justice over charity was not only an expression of possessive individualism but also an expression of his desire for security from the crime of heresy.[8] Hobbes' addition of 'not' to the golden rule suggests that rights-doctrines are defensive in relation to imperial love. One may fight for the right or merely for one's rights. To fight for one's rights is to adopt a defensive posture. Rights (as distinct from the right or righteousness) are what one defends.

Hugo Grotius, the learned and incisive jurisprudent, who began his career in his late teens as an advocate for the claims of the Dutch East India Company, defined rights as 'nothing more than what is just, and that, more in a negative than in a positive sense; so that *right* is that, which is not unjust.'[9] Grotius denied that it is ever right to compel another to abandon his faith, to use force to promote doctrine, or to persecute heretics.[10] Judaism, according to Grotius, inspires 'greater sanctity of manners, and the purest principles of obedience to lawful sovereigns'; it should not be suppressed even though it lacks the truth of Christianity.'[11] Grotius, as earlier noted, provided a liberal interpretation of Jesus' parable of compelling wayfarers to come to God's feast: 'for the term, *compel*, here signifies nothing more than an earnest entreaty.'[12] As Spinoza's compatriot,

Grotius was not blind to the advantages of religious toleration to trade and international relations. Grotius wrote that 'as the commerce and industry of the country greatly increased owing to strangers resorting to it, such great difference between natives and aliens was found inexpedient.'[13]

Grotius foreshadowed Locke's identification of rights and properties by comprehending liberty as a form of property. Grotius wrote that 'liberty in regard to actions is equivalent to *dominium* in material things.'[14] Property right enables the proprietor to do as he likes with his possessions. For example, Grotius put paid to the traditional notion that usury conflicts with the law of nature.

> It is quite true that apart from the rule of strict law and in accordance with the love which men should show one to another, particularly to acquaintances and fellow citizens, one who has superfluity should assist another in his deficiency. But in such case the assistance should be proportioned to the greatness of the need, not only without expectation of receiving anything beyond what is lent, but even if one knew that what is lent will not be returned. On the other hand, when the need is not pressing, but the borrower is able without inconvenience to return so much as he gets and something more, this reasoning does not apply; for the law of nature does not oblige us to seek another man's advantage at the expense of our own.[15]

In other words, charity is charity and business is business. Or, as Grotius' compatriot, Mandeville, put it a century later, 'Religion is one thing and trade is another.'[16] In a similar spirit, the charitable Hobbes rejected the medieval notions of the just price and the fair wage. Justice demands only what the market will bear; the just or the market price depends upon the demand for the good or service in relation to its supply.[17] Nevertheless, because neither Grotius nor Hobbes thought property right overrides the right of necessity, or the right of the starving to take what they need to subsist, they failed to sever entirely the relationship between rights-based justice and Christian charity.

However, in explicit refutation of Grotius' right of necessity, Samuel Pufendorf indicated how property right prevails over the right of the needy to the means of life. Pufendorf wrote: 'a Right seems to be given to idle Knaves, whose Vices have brought them into Want, to seize forcibly for their own Use the Fruits of other Men's honest Labours; and so continuing their Poverty and their Laziness together, to put a Necessity on Industrious Persons of feeding such useless Bellies for Nothing.'[18] The Grotian right of necessity conflicts with property right. If one has a right to take what one needs, then one is not obliged, as Grotius thought, to make restitution when one has the means. If the needy feel they have a right to subsist, they will not feel bound to acknowledge the charity of the bountiful wealthy. Access to the means of life is no longer to be considered a demand of justice but, for Pufendorf, becomes conditional upon the will and judgment of proprietors. Justice becomes the mutual respect for private property. The right to property separates the imperatives of justice and of charity. Pufendorf wrote:

he has such a Right over his own Goods, as shall in some measure prevail even against a Person in extreme Necessity: So far at least as that he shall have the Privilege of judging, whether the Man be an Object worthy of his Relief or not; that it may be in his Power to oblige and win a necessitous Person by his seasonable Succours: For nothing raises the Value of a Kindness so much as its being done for the Removal of an extreme Distress. But all this Merit and Obligation is cut off, when we give another, only what he might otherwise, as his own Right and Due, violently take from us.[19]

In this unctuous argument for the primacy of property right over Christian charity, Pufendorf succeeded in severing the links between justice and charity. Charitable duty no longer has a correlative right to charity. Rights-based justice consists in mutual respect for private property or in respect for persons as proprietors.

Following in Shylock's footsteps, Pufendorf preferred the 'mathematical strictness' of rights-based justice to the more indeterminate criterion of equity or fairness.[20] Respect for persons as proprietors is more precise and rigorous than respect for individual souls or human beings. With respect to Pufendorf's distinction between justice and equity, Jean Barbeyrac noted: 'Equity includes not only what is really and fully due to any one, although he cannot require it of us in strictness by any written Law, but all that is due to another upon a Principle of Humanity, or Charity, or any other Virtue, which is such, that if we do not our Duty, he to whom we ought to do it can't complain of any Wrong done him ...'[21]

Hobbes, who denied that proprietary claims are natural rights, championed equity – for what is not equity is *iniquity*, not merely inequity.[22] Pufendorf's depreciation of equity corresponds to his advocacy of a natural right to property. Anticipating Locke, Pufendorf argued that individuals acquire a right to property from their industrious appropriation from the common store of nature, although originally nature is owned equally by all.[23] Originally an inclusive right, property becomes an exclusive right, 'a *Right* in each particular Master of disposing how he pleas'd of his Own, and an *Obligation* in all other *Masters* to abstain from his Possessions.'[24] Pufendorf asserted that 'Property implies a Right of excluding others from your Possession' and of 'hindering others from sharing with you.'[25] If for Hobbes, 'justice and charity' are 'the twin sisters of peace,'[26] the kinship of justice and charity is not apparent in Pufendorf.

Locke thought Pufendorf's *De Jure Naturali et Gentium* to be 'the best book' written on the principles of politics.[27] Despite his affinity with Pufendorf on the principle of the primacy of property right, Locke seems to revert to pre-bourgeois ideas about the duty of charity. In *The First Treatise of Government*, Locke wrote:

God hath not left one Man so to the Mercy of another, that he may starve him if he so please: God ... has given his needy Brother a Right to the Surplusage of his Goods; so that it cannot justly be denied him, when his pressing Wants call for it ... '(T)would always be a Sin in any Man of Estate, to let his Brother perish for want of affording him Relief out of his Plenty. As *Justice* gives every Man a Title to the product of his honest Industry, and the fair Acquisitions of his Ancestors descended to him; so *Charity* gives every Man a Title to so much out of another's Plenty, as will keep him from extream want, where he has no means to subsist otherwise ...[28]

59 Justice and Charity

However, if one examines the passage in the context of Locke's argument, one will see that Locke was making a specific point against the extent of monarchical authority rather than advocating a general right to charitable relief. Locke was using the traditional argument for charity to advocate an unconditional title to property or a property right that is not conditional in the eminent domain of the monarch. Locke, in substance, argued for the emancipation of commercial and proprietary arrangements from the fetters of monarchical regulation. The Crown is to evince charity to its subjects (namely, proprietors whose title could be denied only by a 'Cruel and Uncharitable' Monarch). If one were to construe Locke's right to charity out of context as signifying more than the Crown's duty to recognize property rights – namely, as the right of the poor to the surplus of the proprietors – one's construction would be inconsistent with the rest of Locke's thought and practice. Locke championed Justice – providing everyone with 'a title to the product of his honest Industry' – rather than Charity or 'a Title to so much out of another's Plenty, as will keep him from extream want.'

Locke's laws of nature that limit the just acquisition of property are often thought to temper justice with charity. Locke stated that unquestionable and exclusive property right exists 'at least where there is enough, and as good left in common for others.'[29] However, this sufficiency clause, apparently limiting just appropriation, together with other natural law restrictions on capital accumulation is superseded, as C. B. Macpherson has shown, with the introduction of money into a 'natural' economy.[30] Moreover, Jeremy Waldron demonstrates that Locke's sufficiency principle would not necessarily limit appropriation in premonetary, as well as commercial, economies. Waldron's compelling interpretation is that, for Locke, one has a right to appropriate property *'certainly* in circumstances where there is enough and as good in common for others, and perhaps even if there is not enough and as good in common for others.'[31] Rights-claimants may be restricted by the necessity, or the right to life, of others, or, like Shylock, they might not be.

Chapter 5 of Locke's *Second Treatise*, which justified exclusive property right, completed the separation of charity and justice.

Pufendorf: Locke's mentor,
whose name has become synonymous with rights-activism

61 Justice and Charity

Locke's views on property were not uncontested in his lifetime. For example, Isaac Barrow wrote:

God, by the poor man's voice (or by his need and misery) demanding his own from us, we are very unjust if we presume to withhold it; doubtly unjust we are, both toward God and our neighbour; we are unfaithful stewards, misapplying the goods of our Master, and crossing his order: we are wrongful usurpers, detaining from our neighbour that which God has allotted him; we are in the court of conscience; we shall appear at the bar of God's judgment no better than robbers (under the vizard of legal right and possession) spoiling our poor brother of his good ...[32]

Also Knightly Chetwood, dean of Gloucester, defended the traditional view of property which barred the severance of justice and charity. Chetwood wrote: 'We are apt to take to for granted that our Estates ... are entirely at our own Disposal, legal Debts being discharged; but this is a great mistake, Charity is a principal Branch of Justice ... We are but Stewards, not Proprietors, even when Estates are gotten by the most justifiable Means.'[33] Thus while Locke's view that property right is not governed by the traditional restrictions of Christian natural law was contested in his day, Locke's arguments were more congenial to the large landed and commercial interests than those of Barrow or Chetwood. The latter do not belong in the pantheon of rights-advocates.

Locke's 'charitable' proposals when he was a commissioner for the Board of Trade would have struck Shylock (as understood by the most ardent anti-Semite) as uncharitable. Poverty, Locke thought, does not arise from scarcity of provisions or want of employment but from 'the relaxation of discipline,' from idleness and drunkenness made possible by begging and the 'places of ease and preferment' provided for the destitute.[34] The able-bodied are to be conscripted into the navy and those 'above fifty or maimed' are to be kept at hard labour in a house of correction for three years.[35] Since only licensed beggars are to be permitted, those who counterfeit a permit to beg are to have their ears cut off on the first offence and be transported to the colonies on the second conviction.[36] Young children are to be separated from their mothers so that the latter can find work. The children of mothers on parish relief are placed in working schools and are to be 'soundly whipt' if their dawn-to-dusk work does not earn a profit.[37] The children are to be fed on a 'bellyful of bread daily' and 'in cold weather, if it be thought needful, a little warm water-gruel.' If the proposals to cut off beggars' ears and to separate parents and children who cannot pay their way through life are considered severe by the soft-hearted and irresolute, we are to note that 'where universal degeneracy and corruption have taken place, gentle palliatives are ineffectual.'[38]

Locke is widely held, in the English-speaking world, to be the father of liberalism. In order to endow liberalism with a noble lineage not apparent in Locke, I have interpreted him as the illegitimate offspring of some real noblemen, such as Grotius, Hobbes, and Spinoza, rather than the bourgeois baron Pufendorf whom Locke acknowledged. If Locke is held to be the progenitor of liberalism, it is to be remembered that 'Our Father' profited from the slave trade, justified slavery in his writings, codified it in the constitutions he wrote for American colonies, advocated colonial conquest, and denied the right to rebel against the colonial power, lobbied for the destruction of Irish industry, and denied the utility of education for labourers. Martin Seliger thinks Locke's justification of slavery and colonial conquest is an integral part of his liberalism[39] while Peter Laslett thinks his position on slavery is inconsistent with his rights-advocacy.[40] The apparent inconsistency of slavery and liberal principle corresponds to the seeming inconsistency of my claim that Shylock is a prototypical advocate of human rights and that he aims to circumcise or kill Antonio. Whether these inconsistencies are real or apparent will be analysed in subsequent chapters. What we wish to establish here is that Locke championed justice or 'a Title to the product of his honest Industry' above charity or 'a Title to so much out of another's Plenty, as will keep him from extream want.'

Locke was fundamentally a proponent of 'the honest industry of mankind.' Since, according to Locke's labour theory of value, 99.9 per cent of value derives from labour,[41] the exploitation or 'right imploying' of labour becomes '*the* great art of government.'⁴² The mercantilist Locke was uncharacteristically poetic in a paean to a statesman who will promote justice or 'the right imploying' of labour in place of Machiavelli's martial prowess as the one great art of government. Locke declared: 'And that Prince who shall be so wise and godlike as by established laws of liberty to secure protection and encouragement to the honest industry of Mankind against the oppression of power and narrownesse of Party will quickly be too hard for his neighbours. But this bye the bye.' In this aside, Locke stated that economic science rather than martial art is the prime business of government. A strong state is a just state, that is, one that promotes 'honest industry' and respects proprietary title.

Christian charity does not so much complement, as run counter to, the imperatives of justice. Real charity, Locke seems to say in *An Essay Concerning Human Understanding*, consists in the English gift of marrying commerce and natural science. Scientific industry 'may be of greater benefit to mankind than the monuments of exemplary charity, that have at so great charge been raised by the founders of hospitals and alms-houses.' Inventors 'did more for the propagation of knowledge, for the supply and increase of useful commodities, and saved more from the grave, than those who built colleges, work-houses, and hospitals.'⁴³ Locke practised his philosophy; his will indicates that he did not wish to waste as much of his estate on the education, care, and relief of the needy poor as was customary at the time.⁴⁴

Bernard Mandeville's wholesale attack on charity and the charity schools in 1723 drew widespread notoriety to his *The Fable of the Bees*.⁴⁵ Although Mandeville was too clean-spirited to refer often to rights, he admirably captured and condensed the gist of Lockian liberalism. Mandeville wrote:

Trade is the Principal, but not the only Requisite to aggrandize a Nation; there are other Things to be taken Care of besides. The *Meum* and *Tuum* must be secur'd, Crimes punish'd, and all other Laws concerning the Administration of Justice, wisely contriv'd, and strictly executed. Foreign Affairs must be likewise prudently manag'd ... The multitude must be aw'd, no Man's Conscience forc'd, and the Clergy allow'd no greater Share in State Affairs than our Savior has bequeathed them in his Testament. These are the Arts that lead to worldly Greatness ...[46]

Mandeville, moreover, attributed his country's greatness to a single-minded devotion to commerce.

The *Dutch* may ascribe their present Grandeur to the Virtue and Frugality of their Ancestors as they please; but what made that contemptible spot of Ground so considerable among the principal Powers of *Europe*, has been their Political Wisdom in postponing every thing to Merchandize and Navigation, the unlimited Liberty of Conscience that is enjoy'd among them, and the unwearied Application with which they have always made use of the most effectual means to encourage and increase Trade in general.[47]

Mandeville's reduction of freedom of conscience to an expedient of trade appears cynical, an affront to the lofty principles of Lockian liberalism. Mandeville indeed does not enjoy an exalted position in the pantheon of liberalism. The Man-devil is recognized as the reincarnation of Shylock. But lest we dismiss Mandeville's equation of commercial expansion and free conscience as devilish cynicism, let us consult the undeniably noble apostle of Lockian liberalism. Charles de Montesquieu asserted: 'Other nations have made the interest of commerce yield to those of politics; the English, on the contrary, have ever made their political interests give way to those of commerce. They know better than any other people upon earth how to value three great advantages – religion, commerce, and liberty.'[48]

Montesquieu may have had a foreigner's bad taste in reducing all English political objectives to the interests of commerce, but he had the enlightened good taste to recognize Locke's theoretical condensation of English political experience as the consummation of all human strivings, and to recommend English commercialism to less-enlightened (priest-benighted) nations.[49]

Rights-doctrines, we have argued, arose from the separation of justice and Christian charity. Adam Smith followed a long tradition when he asserted that 'a beggar is an object of our charity and may be said to have a right to demand it – but when we use right in this way it is not in a proper but a metaphorical sense.'[50] The foundational thinkers of liberalism were not solely concerned to emancipate commercial practices from Christian teaching but were also concerned to liberalize Christian doctrine or to free conscience from imperial interpretations of the doctrine of love. Commercial expansion was a vehicle not just to wealth and power but also to the liberty and diversity of beliefs. The interests of commerce and the rights of conscience belong together. As interest is combined with principal in usury, interest combines with principle in rights. If the grasp of Shylock's principles is evident in Grotius, Hobbes, and Spinoza, the principles of Shylock's grasp are manifest in Pufendorf, Locke, and Mandeville.

A circumcision of the heart is the condition of rebirth into the rule of rights. The most humane of rights-advocates stated: 'Pity in a man who lives under the guidance of reason is in itself bad and useless.'[51] Spinoza's natural compassion is an obstacle to the reign of rights, for 'a man who lives according to the dictates of reason endeavors as far as possible not to be touched by pity.'[52] A sensitive heart must be overcome by a hard head. But to overcome something presupposes the existence of that which is to be overcome – namely, the compassionate heart of Spinoza. Neither Locke nor Lockians have to be told to overcome compassion. Perhaps the contemporary failure to see the necessity for overcoming compassion derives from the drying up of the natural wells, or lost access to the supernatural source, of charity. The separation of charity and justice is consecrated by means of a baptism in the font of rights.

Hobbes: the political philosopher
of the English-speaking world

CHAPTER THREE

Contractualism and Promise-Keeping: The Bond of Civil Society

In the previous chapter, we sketched the genesis of natural rights in the opposition of Shylock and Antonio, of natural justice and Christian charity. Liberal thinkers, following Shakespeare's linkage of commerce and toleration, have unambiguously rejected the poet's ambiguous judgment for Christian charity (Antonio) over Jewish justice (Shylock). Shylock's rights come to be recognized at the same time as, and corresponding to, the dissolution of the limitations to property right inherent in Christian Aristotelianism. Shylock represents not only property right and commercial tolerance but also keeping faith, honouring contractual obligations, being as good as one's word. The promises of the giving and forgiving Christians, especially those of the archetypical Christian Antonio, are utterly unreliable. Only Shylock's word is his bond. The relation between promise-keeping and contractual justice is the subject of this chapter.

Plato's *Republic* demonstrates that honouring one's word is the commercial man's conception of justice. At the outset of the

Republic, old Cephalus, the largest slave-owner and richest man in Athens but an unsuccessful aspirant to Athenian citizenship, defines justice as telling the truth and fulfilling one's contractual obligations. This position is easily dismissed because no sane person would tell the truth to a lunatic or return a borrowed weapon to a man deranged with anger. Modern ideologists have difficulty understanding the ancient philosopher's apparent irreverence for telling the truth. This chapter will attempt to explain the difficulty. Only Spinoza is free of the commercial 'mind-set' and only Hobbes is able to give it a philosophic justification.

Locke followed Grotius, Hobbes, and Spinoza in seeing the integral connection between trade and religious tolerance.[1] Holland, after all, had prospered with its tolerant practices. Locke made clear that 'neither Pagan nor Mohametan, nor Jew, ought to be excluded from the civil rights of the Commonwealth because of his religion.'[2] If we 'deal and trade' with them, we are obliged to tolerate their religious practices.[3] The exceptions to Locke's rule of religious freedom are the intolerant (such as Catholics who are not willing to make a rule of mutual religious toleration) and the faithless (those who are incapable of keeping promises).[4] Locke draws the obvious to our attention: one cannot do business with Antonio because of his intolerance and his incapacity for honouring his word. The circumcision of Antonio's heart would be a precondition of entering into the social contract of liberal doctrine.

Locke's excommunication of atheists from the benefits of commercial contractualism is interesting in so far as Locke has been charged with atheism in both his time and ours.[5] Both Hobbes and Spinoza were infamous for atheism. With judicious untruth, the shy Locke denied that he was 'so well read in Hobbes or Spinoza' and denounced 'those justly decried names.'[6] Given the climate of intolerance at the time, Locke should be forgiven for his injustice and untruth – or, even better, forgotten. However, whether or not Hobbes' and Spinoza's reputation as atheists was warranted, it is clear that both men did not worship a God which thwarts the natural desires of humanity. In marked contrast, Lockian Protestantism is of a markedly repressive character which seems to transcend the wordly asceticism of Shylock or the acquisitive capitalist. (One might compare Shylock's hatred of music and harmony (II.v.28–36) with Locke's view that music 'wastes so much of a young man's time' and that poetry is worse than a waste of time.[7] There can be no doubt that Shylock would espouse the entirety of Locke's *Some Thoughts Concerning Education*.) There is an other-worldly dimension to Locke's ascetic Protestantism. In *An Essay Concerning Human Understanding*, Locke asserted that morality is based upon a computation of 'our greatest interest, i.e., the condition of our eternal estate.'[8] In *The Reasonableness of Christianity*, Locke presented his view that morality cannot be grounded in this world, the world of facts, of natural desires and reason: 'The view of heaven and hell will cast a slight upon the short pleasures and pains of this present state, and give attractions and encouragements to virtue, which reason and interest, and the care of ourselves, cannot but allow and prefer. Upon this foundation, and upon this only, morality stands firm, and may defy all competition.'[9]

If Shylock might be uneasy with Locke's other-worldly asceticism, he would be relieved to learn that Locke's Christianity is not as suitable to the chosen as to the ill-chosen. '(T)he all-merciful God seems herein to have consulted the poor of this world, and the bulk of mankind: these are articles that the labouring and illiterate man may comprehend. This is a religion suited to vulgar capacities, and the state of mankind in this world, destined to labour and travail.'[10] With Locke as preceptor, Shylock would not have to be forced to convert; he would readily recognize the reasonableness of Christianity, the utility of other-worldly sanctions to those 'destined to labour and travail' for the men of commerce. After all, profession of belief in rewards and punishments in the afterlife is cheaper than paying taxes for the policing of property right. Our other-worldly interests (in entering heaven and evading hell) allow for the marriage of bourgeois interest and Christian virtue. Shylock could not deny the poetic power of Locke's advocacy of Christian duty – 'interest is come about to her; and virtue now is visibly the most enriching purchase, and by much the best bargain.'[11]

Neither Hobbes nor Spinoza introduced other-worldly sanctions to reinforce liberal virtues or contractual morality. For Locke, 'Faith and truth, especially in all occasions of attesting it, upon the solemn appeal to heaven by an oath, is the great bond of society.'[12] Since 'the great bond' of commercial society arises from honouring the terms of one's contracts and depends upon swearing divine oaths, Locke's excommunication of atheists from civil society is comprehensible. Hobbes' fool, who does not fear God and who does not honour his word, constitutes a problem. Hobbes' resolution of the problem, without Locke's aid of other-worldly sanctions, was a philosophic 'tour de force' because he was committed to a conception of justice that supersedes prudence. While eschewing what he so beautifully described as the 'dark doctrine of eternal torments,'[13] Hobbes insisted that 'there is no living in a commonwealth with men, to whose oaths we cannot reasonably give credit.'[14] Spinoza accepted the Lockian equation of the virtue of justice and the principle of self-interest without the balancing rod of heaven and hell. Contrary to Locke's view of 'the great bond' of commercial society, Spinoza asserted that there would be greater security against perjury and infidelity if oaths were sworn 'by the country's safety and liberty and by the supreme council, than if they are told to swear by God.'[15] Individuals are the judges of the value of the oaths sworn to God but the public is the judge of oaths sworn to the government or to the common good.

Spinoza was the only Machiavellian in the tradition of rights-discourse; that is, he was the only thinker to claim a natural right to break faith if keeping faith, in one's judgment, is contrary to one's interest.[16] To simplify, Spinoza's politics are those of Hobbes, stripped of the principle of contractual fidelity, or Hobbesian justice reduced to prudence. Spinoza's natural right of infidelity dramatized the tension between the Hobbesian subject's allegiance to the sovereign and to his own self-preservation; it rejected the Hobbesian repudiation of the right of rebellion and avoided the Lockian confusion concerning the individual right, and the majority's right, of rebellion. Spinoza then would not insist on the legitimacy of Shylock's bond or the shy Locke's 'great bond' of commercial society. Adverse consequences are always good reasons for repudiating one's bond.

Spinoza then might provide a warrant for the inquisitorial Lockian to excommunicate atheists from civil society. But if the alleged atheist Spinoza repudiated strict contractual fidelity, the alleged atheist Hobbes was as zealous as Locke in his adherence to the principle of pledging oneself in one's promising. Moreover, the bold Hobbes provided a philosophic foundation for 'the great bond' of modern society which the shy Locke prudently withheld. For the bold theorizing of the English philosopher – however staunch his opposition to the likes of Antonio – is uncongenial to practical men like Shylock.

Nevertheless, Hobbes enunciated philosophically Shylock's emphasis on contractual fidelity. The keeping of one's word is crucial to a society of strangers. Words represent the only commonality in a world of plurality, of particular experiences, of singular passions, and of solitary reason. To break one's word is, for Hobbes, to destroy all possibility of society. 'He therefore that breaketh his covenant, and consequently declareth that he thinks he may with reason do, cannot be received into any society, that unite themselves for peace and defence ...'[17] Hobbes repeatedly described injustice – the violation of faith, the failure to keep promises – as absurdity, logical contradiction, or insignificant speech. 'An injury therefore is a kind of absurdity in conversation, as an absurdity is a kind of injury in disputation.'[18]

Hobbes' philosophy is based upon a radical separation of a natural world of experience and an artificial world of words and contracts. The natural world is composed of particular particles in motion which combine to produce unique things and individual persons. The interaction of singular objects of sense and individual sensations generates a world of human plurality. In radical distinction from Marx's view of human experience as that of a species-being, Hobbes denied that there are any natural species or classes of beings. Hobbesian nominalism asserted that there is 'nothing in the world universal but names; for the things named are every one of them individual and singular.'[19] All physical objects, animals, and humans are unique, but are classified arbitrarily by human beings to create an artificial intersubjective world from naturally subjective worlds of experience.

The common world of speech is the product of art or artifice; the state is 'but an artificial man' in which 'the *sovereignty* is an artificial *soul*,' created, analogous to God's fiat in the creation, by human '*pacts and covenants*' or artificial chains to bind natural individuality.[20] Without speech, 'the most noble and profitable invention of all other,' 'there had been amongst men, neither commonwealth, nor society, nor contract, nor peace, no more than amongst lions, bears, and wolves.'[21] A Marxist or an Aristotelian may wonder how speech existed before society (unless one introduces a 'deus ex machina,' as Hobbes uncharacteristically did, to explain the origin of speech). However, Hobbes' point is that only words supersede the private worlds of individual experience. Breaking one's word is returning to the anarchic state of nature, to the raw competitive world of naked plurality or inhuman individuality. 'For as the objects of sense are all individual, that is, singular, so are all the fancies proceeding from their operations; and men reason not but in words of universal signification, uttered or tacitly thought on.'[22] For Hobbes, then, it is irrational to break one's word not because one can never profit from breach of promise (indeed all the Christians do in *The Merchant of Venice*) but because 'men reason not but in words of universal signification.' To break one's word is as irrational as to call the same object by different names (such as apple, angel, bomb, fried egg, courage).

Shylock foreshadows Hobbes' and Robert Nozick's emphasis on human plurality, and the impotence of reason to settle 'value' differences. Shylock says that there is no accounting for differences of affection or mood, of passionate loves and hatreds (IV.i.40–52). The pangs of scepticism about a common good are the birthpains of rights. 'As there is no firm reason to be rend'red' why some cannot abide 'a gaping pig' or 'a harmless necessary cat' or 'a woolen bagpipe,' Shylock says he cannot nor will not give a reason, nor feel bound to give a reason, for asserting his rights against Antonio (IV.i.53–65). The reason for rights, Shylock observes in anticipation of Nozick, is simply that they are ours; rights are properties. Just as the Christians have a right to their purchased slaves, 'The pound of flesh which I demand of him / Is dearly bought, 'tis mine and I will have it' (IV.i.99–100).

We will assess the legitimacy of Shylock's claims in the subsequent chapter when we explore the tension in Locke between the inalienable right to life and liberty and the right to alienate property (which may include life and liberty). What we are here concerned to do is to establish the connection between natural individuality and the importance of artificial bonds (maintaining one's word or covenant). Shylock holds to his bond because he recognizes that the sole bond and commonality of a commercial society are the contracts which bind strangers. Men do not share a common reason and nature. Reason is impotent to establish a common good or to settle the differences of particular wills. Humans are essentially will, not reason. The reign of rights is the rule of will – of Shylock's "tis mine and I will have it' established as a rule for all human beings.

A central paradox in Hobbesian doctrine (which is dramatically presented in Rousseau's account of the transformation of human nature in the social contract) is that the heteronomous wills of the individuals in the state of nature become the autonomous moral wills of civil society. The unreliable human animals of the Hobbesian state of nature become responsible agents capable of promising, giving their word, saying 'I will.' Hobbesian moral doctrine requires responsible agents but Hobbes repudiated freedom of the will. In combating the poison of Christian morality, in placing his body and soul against 'the dark doctrine of eternal torments,' Hobbes opposed the unscientific (moral) concept of free will. Humans are not distinguished from animals by free will or the capacity for moral choice, as Hobbes' Christian predecessors, and later Rousseau, Kant, and Hegel, asserted. The doctrine of free will 'maketh men, by imagining they can repent when they will, neglect their duties; and that maketh men unthankful for God's graces, by thinking them to proceed from the natural ability of their own will.'[23] The first half of this sentence is a swipe at the prodigal publican Antonio and the second half, at the righteous Pharisee Shylock. However much we might wish to commend Hobbes' attempt to lance the poison that nourishes and destroys monotheistic moralities, we are still left with the problem of how the animal man can become a responsible agent, of how the heteronomous creature of asocial nature can become the autonomous creator of social artifice.

The will, Hobbes said, is not free; it is determined by one's strongest passion. The permutations of the three basic passions (desire for power or the means to satisfy future desires, desire for glory or the imagination of one's power relative to others, and fear of powerlessness or the inability to avert violent death) vary from individual to individual. All persons, including the moral philosophers before Hobbes, consider those things to be good or to be objects of their will 'as their passions have dictated.'[24] Natural men are subject to the dictation of passion, not the freedom of will.

Yet the social and moral world is a construction of will, an artifice created by consent and guided by science or arbitrary speech. Scientific discourse is opposed to common usage. Scientific speech is arbitrary in that it is willed, consistent, and defined (as distinct from the inconsistent and indefinite meanings of common or customary usage). In his debate with Bishop Bramhall, Hobbes anticipated the 'moral constructivism' of Rousseau, Kant, Rawls, and Dworkin. Hobbes agreed with Bishop Bramhall's charge that Hobbesian doctrine amounts to the proposition 'that every man makes by his own consent the law which he is bound to keep.'[25] Bramhall believed this proposition to be erroneous because the 'positive law of God,' the law of nature, the law of conquerors, and the laws of ancestors are made without our consent. However, Hobbes asserted, biblical revelation is a law only to those who assent to its authority, as is custom, common law, and statutory law. 'And whereas he saith, the law of nature is a law without our assent, it is absurd; for the law of nature is the assent itself that all men give to the means of their preservation.'[26] The English-speaking world does not have to import from abroad, as John Rawls apparently thinks necessary, the principles of a morality which is not based on divine commands or natural facts. No deprecation of Kant is intended in an insistence that the English-speaking world has one thinker of his stature.

Yet why would the heteronomous creatures of nature assent to the autonomous creation of moral artifice? Or why would creatures of passion and fear stand by their contractual obligations? How is the empirical being, the puppet of that which manipulates his strings, capable of becoming the moral being, the lordly individual who is as good as his word? The usual answer is that the sovereign's sword will make individuals just. That is, a prudent fear of the sovereign's punishment, coupled to the fear of anarchy if 'law and order' is disregarded, is sufficient to hold individuals to their bond, their voluntary obligations. However, two points might be made against reducing Hobbesian justice to Spinozan prudential self-interest. First, Hobbes said that civil society cannot be maintained by 'terror of legal punishment'; men will obey only if their fear of disobedience is joined by a conviction that it is right to obey.[27] Secondly, there are, properly speaking, no selves (and thus no self-interest) in Hobbes' state of nature. Prior to self-interest is the interest in constituting a self, a continuous identity throughout time. One acquires a fixed identity (a self, a name, an address) only through pledging oneself, promising or giving one's word, just as things become identifiable only through naming. The act of promising creates an individual who will stand by his name in the future. The Christians in *The Merchant of Venice* are like Hobbesian natural individuals. They are not to be called liars but, because they are completely creatures of passion and hope, they are quite unreliable. Natural inclination is fickle or changeable. Those who live in the present are incapable of promising; they lack the power (or the means to some future good) of those who can fix their will for time to come. Promising creates the human self: breaking one's word is dehumanizing, regardless of the profit. The artificial chains which bind modern man, if broken, leave only amorphous, dissolute 'self-less' antagonists to Shylock.

The principle of contractual fidelity has never been as deeply or systematically presented as in the philosophy of Hobbes. Indeed David Hume insisted that no philosophical justification of promise-keeping is possible, except on the Spinozan basis of utility or social necessity.[28] Yet Hobbesian contractual fidelity became a staple feature of subsequent political theory. Adam Smith observed that 'when commerce is introduced into any country probity and punctuality always accompany it.' Smith noted: 'Of all the nations in Europe, the Dutch, the most commercial, are the most faithful to their word. The English are more so than the Scotch ...'[29] However, the honest Dutchman, Mandeville, averred that 'where Trade is considerable Fraud will intrude.'[30]

The apparent contradiction is that what the Dutchman called vice the Scots called virtue. However, closer analysis reveals that Mandeville was not criticizing the principle of contractual fidelity; he merely pointed out that merchants and manufacturers employ the arts of salesmanship and other business skills which appear to pre-commercial peoples as vice or fraudulence. The man-devil Shylock may be less than candid in setting the terms of his agreements, but he is as good as his word.

The Dutch man-devil would in no way disagree with the lofty sentiments of David Hume, who wrote: 'We blame all treachery and breach of faith; because we consider, that the freedom and extent of human commerce depend entirely on a fidelity with regard to promises.'[31] Adam Smith tarted up all-too-Humian utility in its Sunday best when he referred to 'that most sacred rule of justice, which commands the observance of all serious promises ...'[32] Man-devillian or all-too-Humian utility took on a postively angelic countenance in the writings of Immanuel Kant. The principle of contractual fidelity 'is beyond all refutation, and is the indispensable condition of all policy.'[33] Angelic duty and man-devillian interest are united in a commercial age. The breach of contractual fidelity rebounds on the debtor or borrower; it is both the interest and the duty of commercial men to honour their obligations.

David Hume asserted that there is no natural passion to counterbalance love of gain but 'by an alteration of its direction,' love of gain can be turned from theft to a passion for proprietary justice.[34] That is, if greed is a vice, then the virtue of justice is born of vice. The moral of *The Fable of the Bees* is:

> So Vice is beneficial found
> When it's by Justice lopt, and bound.

Are rights best understood as vices 'by Justice lopt, and bound'? Immanuel Kant asserted that 'a people composed of devils,' if they could understand their rational self-interest, could constitute a republic based on the rights of man.[35] Kant's doctrine of rights faithfully followed Hobbes' rejection of Aristotelian virtue in favour of justice as contractual fidelity. Indeed Kant represented the apotheosis of the scorn for Spinozan expediency, prudential self-interest, or utility. The icy beauty of Kantian morality could be compared with the crystalline purity of Shylock's 'Is that the Law?' (IV.i.309). When threatened with destruction for his intention to fulfil his bond, Shylock does not attempt to wiggle out from strict law in the name of equity or mercy but simply asks if the judgment against him has been made by right. For Kant and Shylock, equity ('Billigkeit') is cheap or not dear,[36] whereas for Hobbes and Spinoza fairness is dear; the antithesis of equity is iniquity. What is 'billig' differs in value from what is fair.

Kant made the curious assertion that Aristotle held that 'there is no such thing as a friend.'[37] Kant might have derived this proposition with somewhat greater validity from *The Merchant of Venice* than Aristotle's *Ethics* or *Politics*. To be sure, Kant's fervent prayer for friendship is below the dignity of Shylock. 'A friend in need – how must to be wished for (assuming that he is an active one, helpful at his own expense)!'[38] But Shylock would seize on Kant's view that no man is wronged by a failure of love or charity; a man is only injured by an omission of respect or a failure to heed the lawful claims of others.[39]

No person gave stronger support to Locke's 'great bond of society' than Kant. Truth and contractual fidelity are the fundamental obligations of a commercial society. Lying and breaking one's word dehumanize the liar and violate the rights of others as well as the natural purpose of communication and society.[40] Indeed, a lie 'always injures another; if not another individual, yet mankind generally, since it vitiates the source of justice.'[41] Truthfulness is not to be limited by any consideration of utility. Kant wrote: 'Truth in utterances that cannot be avoided is the formal duty of a man to everyone, however great the disadvantage that may arise from it to him or any other; and although by making a false statement I do no wrong to him who unjustly compels me to speak, yet I do wrong to men in general in the most essential point of duty ... and hence that all rights founded on contract should lose their force; and this is a wrong which is done to mankind.'[42]

Kant then gave evidence of the divine madness of philosophers of rights by asserting that we have a duty not to lie to a murderer who has asked us whether our friend, of whom he was in pursuit, had taken refuge in our house. Kant's duty to tell the truth and thus be the empirical, if not moral, cause of our friend's death might be related to Kant's inversion of the Aristotelian understanding of friendship. However, regardless of the consequences to our friend, how are we to assess the Kantian duty to tell the truth to one 'who unjustly compels me to speak'? Kant's duty is neither Spinozan prudence nor Hobbesian cowardice. However, to anyone not afflicted by right-blindness, truthfulness which assists a murderer is simply cowardice, just as a will to mutilate or kill, even when sanctioned by contract, is cruelty. However, Kant's 'cowardice' and Shylock's 'cruelty' must be understood within the context of their superstitious reverence for the bonds of a commercial society. The bonds of a rights-based society harbour Shylock's vices — his heartless greed, cruelty, and insensitivity, his scorn of charity, equity, and mercy — but combine them with his virtues — his fidelity, chastity, frugality, reliability, tolerance of diversity, respect for law and contractual justice, and above all probity, being as good as one's word. Perhaps Shylock's vices should, as Bernard Mandeville suggested, be considered to be the virtues of a commercial society. But whether vices or virtues, the characteristics of the rights-based society are those of the solitary individual, detribalized from community and bereft of friends. Shylock's attributes, in short, are those of one who confronts others as aliens or strangers.

Grotius: the creator of inalienable rights
who sold them out to the highest bidder

CHAPTER FOUR

Inalienable Right and Alienable Properties: Rights as Properties

The tradition of rights doctrines yields no easy answer to the questions of whether Shylock had the right to take Antonio's life and whether Shylock's adversaries had the right to purchase slaves. An emerging consensus in recent literature would seem to suggest that the usurer has the right to take Antonio's life (since any capitalist act between consenting adults is legitimate) but that the merchants do not have the right to own slaves (since the exploitation of slave labour is inconsistent with the free contractual character of wage labour). However, the issue is somewhat more complex than a clear-cut vindication of Shylock. While there is virtual unanimity in rights-professors that neither Shylock nor Antonio had the right to convert one another by fraud or force, no clear consensus exists within the tradition of rights-discourse with respect to the inalienable right to life and liberty. Can individuals forfeit the right to life and liberty? Do they have the right to alienate life and liberty, to part with them voluntarily, to make bargains with them or renounce them in commercial contracts?

Hugo Grotius seems to defend the inalienability of the right to life and liberty. 'Inalienable things are things which belong so essentially to one man that they could not belong to another, as a man's life, body, freedom, honour.'[1] However, there are various ambiguities in Grotius' formulation which reappear in subsequent rights-literature. First, the 'could' in the proposition that life and liberty 'could not belong to another' seems to conflate logical possibility or impossibility and moral permissibility or impermissibility. Second, the inalienability of life and liberty rests on the claim that they 'belong so essentially to one man' or that they are 'so far his own,' but one's belongings or one's property are normally alienable. Grotius seems to distinguish what is alienable (as contingent or accidental property) from what is inalienable (as essential property or the substance of one's being). But Locke, as we shall see, believes life and liberty to be inalienable precisely because they are not the property of the individual bearing the right to life and liberty.

An individual's life, body, freedom, and honour are inalienable in that he can defend them lawfully against any aggressor, but he may forfeit life, body, liberty, and honour for crime. A criminal is lawfully subject to capital or corporal punishment, loss of liberty and honour.

The inalienable right to life does not prohibit the forfeiture of life, nor does it prohibit the sacrifice of life 'in the service of his country.'[2] However, suicide, or the voluntary alienation of life without some redeeming social or spiritual significance, is rightly proscribed by law.[3] 'Likewise no one may pledge his life by contract.'[4] Thus Grotius seems to say that the bond between Shylock and Antonio is illegitimate, although the liability would be more Antonio's than Shylock's, unless the former could not be expected to know the consequences of a circumcision of the heart.

Grotius maintained in *The Jurisprudence of Holland* that one has an inalienable right to freedom, although one may forfeit it for crime. 'With us no one may entirely dispose of his freedom by contract, though a man may well bind himself to certain defined acts.'[5] That is, one may sell one's freedom retail but not wholesale. 'The contract of hire cannot be concluded except for a definite time ...'[6] However, in

The Rights of War and Peace, Grotius asserted that an individual may alienate his liberty to a master for protection and subsistence and, indeed, 'a whole people' may transfer its autonomy or self-governance to a sovereign representative for the security of life.[7] What appeared to Rousseau as collective slavery was justified by Grotius on the ground of the legitimacy of individual slaves. Grotius did not accept Shylock's equation of his right against Antonio and Antonio's right over purchased slaves. The right to life is inalienable but the right to liberty is alienable.

Hobbesian doctrine seems to be similar to that of Grotius. The right to life is inalienable in that a man may defend himself against anyone, even an officer of the sovereign, who threatens his life. A law-breaker, who has forfeited the right to live unpunished, still maintains the right of self-preservation, even though the sovereign has the right to kill him. The inalienable right to life includes the right to defend oneself against threatened death, chains, or imprisonment, the right to avoid testifying against oneself or one's kin in a court of law, and the right to evade 'any dangerous, or dishonourable office.'[8] Because the right to life is inalienable, for Hobbes as for Grotius, the contract between Shylock and Antonio would seem to be invalid.[9]

Yet Hobbes' attempt to decriminalize suicide poses problems for his philosophy of rights. Hobbes wrote: 'But I conceive not how any man can bear *animum felleum,* or so much malice towards himself, as to hurt himself voluntarily, much less to kill himself. For naturally and necessarily the intention of every man aimeth at somewhat which is good to himself, and tendeth to his preservation. And therefore, methinks, if he kill himself, it is to be presumed that he is not *compos mentis,* but by some inward torment or apprehension of somewhat worse than death, distracted.'[10] Hobbes' humanity has clouded the piercing rays of his intellect. In his judgment that suicide is madness rather than sin or crime, Hobbes presents individuals subject to a heteronomous law of nature (which commands self-preservation) rather than to self-legislated rules which arise from the right of self-preservation (which permits one, but does not oblige one, to preserve one's life). If natural law is dependent upon natural rights, as we have seen in our analysis of Hobbes in the previous chapter, then Hobbes was not in a position to deny the moral permissibility of suicide. For Hobbes made a radical distinction between the 'forbidding' language of law and the 'permissive' language of rights. 'For though they speak of this subject, use to confound *jus*, and *lex*, *right* and *law*: yet they ought to be distinguished; because RIGHT, consisteth in liberty to do, or to forbear: whereas LAW, determineth, and bindeth to one of them: so that law, and right, differ as much, as obligation, and liberty; which in one and the same matter are inconsistent.'[11]

The right of self-preservation is then a moral permit which secures its bearer the choice or option of continuing to live or terminating an unlivable existence. Hobbes' view that a man could not kill himself unless distracted by madness continued Grotius' confusion of logical, empirical, and moral possibility. Hobbes clearly recognized the logical and empirical possibility of alienating one's life. He cited the case of 'a fit of madness' which 'caused' many young maidens of a Grecian city to hang themselves. Rather than considering this case to be an instance of diabolic possession or to be inexplicable and uncontrollable, Hobbes commended the magistrate who ordered the maidens to be stripped naked and, by this means, cured the madness.[12] Although Hobbes' commendation of the magistrate is inconsistent with the liberalism of his rights-based doctrine and with his remarkably advanced views on sexual equality, it indicated that Hobbes thought that humans can love honour more than they fear death. Indeed, a central task of modern Leviathans is to decrease the strength of the motive of vainglory (or the desire for glory which is not based upon experience) and to enhance the power of prudence or the strength of the fear of violent death. The Hobbesian state with its monopoly of the means of legitimate violence must discourage heroic or holy warriors, revolutionaries, noble suicides, duellists, or in short, all those who do not fear death above dishonour. The samurai code of honour and the fanatical assassins' vision of heaven are incompatible with the mighty Leviathan whose blood is money.

No one, in the modern or post-feudal state, is to have an

independent sense of his or her own worth. No hereditary noble, sturdy yeoman, Joan of Arc, or Don Quixote can coexist with the pacific mission of commerce and Thomas Hobbes. Hobbes wrote: 'The *value*, or WORTH of a man, is as of all other things, his price; that is to say, so much as would be given for the use of his power: and therefore is not absolute; but a thing dependant on the need and judgement of another ... And as in other things, so in men, not the seller, but the buyer determines the price. For let a man, as most men do, rate themselves at the highest value they can; yet their true value is no more than it is esteemed by others.'[13] Thus, for Hobbes, the life and death struggle for recognition of one's power is pacified at the market-place. The competitive struggle for increased profits and wages lacks the violence of the state of nature, of holy wars, and of feudal battles for pre-eminence. One's private worth is determined at the market and one's public worth or dignity is conferred by the state. How much more civilized to have an honour's list to supplement the market than to have codes of honour which permit duels, hari kari, and revolutionaries! Could there be any doubt that Shylock would side with Hobbes against the crazy goyim?

The point is that Hobbes champions the inalienable right of self-preservation not because one cannot part with one's life but because, both logically and practically, one can. The inalienable right to life includes 'the security of a man's person, in his life, and in the means of so preserving life, as not to be weary of it.'[14] As Shylock says (IV.i.372–3), 'you take my life / when you do take the means whereby I live.' The fact that people, deprived of the means of enjoyment, can be weary of life is the ground of the Hobbesian moral claim to a commodious life for all individuals, or of the inalienable right of comfortable self-preservation.

The right of self-preservation thus does not depend on a natural fact (the alleged instinct to preserve oneself) or on divine decree but on 'the assent itself that all men give to the means of their own preservation.'[15] To have rights is conditional upon existence. Self-preservation is the logical and empirical condition of being a person or a bearer of rights. For Hobbes, self-preservation is not simply an innate drive.

Hobbes clarified some of the ambiguities in Grotius' account of freedom as both alienable and inalienable. Like Grotius, Hobbes thought one may sell oneself into slavery or may renounce one's freedom to a powerful protector in return for subsistence. But the relationship of master and slave is merely prudential, and not moral. The slave is not morally obliged to serve his master but may kill or enslave him as prudence dictates. Moral bonds or artificial chains begin precisely when physical bonds are removed, when one has freedom of movement.

However, Hobbes, like Grotius, does not enjoy a reputation for being a champion of liberty. Certainly neither thinker espoused Rousseau's doctrinaire attitude to popular sovereignty. Nevertheless, one would be quite mistaken to suppose Hobbesian theory to be essentially undemocratic or to assume that Hobbes' preference for monarchy is an integral part of his system of thought. In his preface to *De Cive*, Hobbes explicitly stated 'that monarchy is the most commodious government; which is the one thing alone in this whole book not to be demonstrated, but only probably stated.'[16] Hobbesian theory asserted that individuals must renounce the right of private judgment of right and wrong to a sovereign representative, authorized in the social contract, to make a public declaration of right and wrong in promulgated laws. Hobbes favoured representative over participatory government. The ancient republics of Greece and Rome were unstable, according to Hobbes, in large part because of the power of orators to inflame the passions without illuminating the intellect. But the tendency of republics to dissolve into civil war occurs 'only where the affairs of state are debated in great and numerous assemblies, as they were anciently in Athens, and in Rome; and not in such as do nothing else in great assemblies, but choose magistrates and counsellors, and commit the handling of state affairs to a few; such as is the aristocracy of Venice at this day.'[17] Hobbes was not a doctrinaire monarchist, aristocrat, or democrat, but rather a strong adherent to the principles of representative government. 'But if the *people* in a democracy would bestow the power of deliberating in matters of war and peace, either on one, or on some few, being content with the nomination of magistrates and public ministers, that is to say, with the authority without the ministration; then it must be confessed, that in this particular *democracy* and *monarchy* should be equal.'[18] In short, Hobbes had no substantive objection to parliamentary democracy or representative government. Most of the superficial objections to Hobbes' doctrine would be removed if one referred to the sovereign as *it* (indicating an artificial person, such as a people or a representative) rather than *he* (indicating a natural person, such as a monarch). A representative or a public authority is not a natural person who is the author of his own act, but an artificial person, like President Reagan, who is an actor but not the author of his own act.[19] Hobbes' authoritarianism consists solely in his insistence that there be some public authority, or some public authorization of one's right to perform a particular act. 'For such authority is to trump in card playing, save that in matters of government, where nothing else is turned up, clubs are trumps.'[20]

If one understands the Hobbesian sovereign as an artificial person, one is able not only to answer the superficial objections to Hobbes' doctrine but also to confront a profound difficulty in Hobbes' thought, namely, the relation of law to liberty. Hobbes made it clear that sujects may legitimately disobey the monarch as a natural person, but not as an artificial person. The commands of the natural person are not the laws of the public authority. 'For by disobeying Kings, we mean the disobeying of his laws, those his laws that were made before they were applied to any particular person; for the King, though as a father of children, and a master of domestic servants, yet commands the people in general never but by a precedent law, and as a politic, not a natural person.'[21] Justice, which is for Hobbes obedience to law, does not require that one obey dangerous, dishonourable, or unlawful commands of the sovereign. Prudence, not moral obligation, dictates that one obey a lawless ruler, just as the slave submits to the master only from fear of superior power.

The rule of law, as distinct from the reign of monarchical power and inclination, might be thought to be the prime condition of civil liberties. However, Hobbes consistently asserted that laws restrict rather than enlarge liberty. 'For law is a *fetter*, right is *freedom*; and they differ like contraries.'²² The Hobbesian principle of equal subjection to law is not seen by himself or by his readers to be a spirited defence of rights or liberties. By why does law restrict liberty, defined as the absence of external restraints to action? A grudging adherence to law might metaphorically be understood as 'external restraint' on individual actions. But if Hobbes were successful in indoctrinating individuals with respect for law (so that they obeyed law from conscience or from a sense of its rightness), then law would be internalized and would be no longer an external restraint to individual action. However, Hobbes is by no means alone in the English-speaking world in considering law to be restrictive of liberty or in rejecting the Rousseauan-Kantian principle that freedom is obedience to laws that we make (or could have made) for ourselves. Despite deference to the principle of the rule of law, the opposition of law and rights seems engrained in English-speaking countries (whereas the opposition is not so manifest in 'droit' or 'Recht' which, like 'ius,' means both law and right). That one could find one's freedom in obedience to law or that one could be forced to be free strikes most English-speaking persons as more than paradoxical or foreign. It is sinister – that is, leftish – or even totalitarian.

Against Rousseau's championship of political liberty or the liberty of the citizen, Hobbes championed civil liberty or what he calls 'the liberty of subjects' – 'such as is the liberty to buy, and sell, and otherwise contract with one another; to choose their own abode, their own diet, their own trade of life, and institute their children as they themselves think fit; and the like.'²³ Civil liberty, or the liberties of bourgeois subjects, will be increased to the extent that political liberty, or a citizen's right to direct participation in sovereignty, is renounced. Hobbes' judgment is restated in the third part of Robert Nozick's *Anarchy, State and Utopia.* Jan Narveson shares Nozick's view that the right of political participation includes the right to intervene in, and counteract, the workings of the free market. Thus Rousseau's political rights stand in opposition to the human rights guaranteed by the operation of the free market. 'But insofar as the right to a free market is established, the right to political processes cannot be. We must choose between them and ... it is clear that we must prefer the market to politics.'[24] While Hobbes was not as doctrinally opposed to popular sovereignty as contemporary libertarians, his system of thought differs from Rousseau's advocacy of citizens' direct participation in politics and from Rousseau's conception of freedom as collective self-legislation. Representative government, together with a primarily market economy, is the means to a tolerant, commodious, and rule-bound life. But the laws that restrain anarchy and facilitate commodious self-preservation are deemed to fetter liberty because the individuals bound by laws do not participate in their formulation.

Although Hobbes was more representative of Anglo-American liberalism than is commonly thought, he seems to conflict with liberal opinion in his view that the sovereign has the right to judge which doctrines promote civil peace and to promulgate orthodox doctrine. 'And though in matter of doctrine, nothing ought to be regarded but the truth; yet this is not repugnant to regulating the same by peace.'[25] But Hobbes did not wish to limit truth in the interests of peace, for all truth promotes peace and commodious living. Even 'the most sudden, and rough bustling in of a new truth, that can be, does never break the peace ...'[26] The sovereign's right to enforce doctrinal orthodoxy would not affect science, or matters whose truth and falsity can be demonstrated, as it would faith, or matters whose truth and falsity cannot be demonstrated. Indeed, Hobbes' desire to promote doctrinal orthodoxy arose from his concern to moderate the passion of religious fanaticism which he held to be largely responsible for the English civil war. An established church or state religion would not, as the civil religion of the Jews and heathens did not, divide subjects' allegiance to God and to the state, or foster conscientious dissent to the laws of the state. Above all, civil religions are concerned with the governing of actions and not of consciences; they do not attempt to subject the inner life of subjects to state prosecution. Christianity introduced the crime of heresy into the world. A fundamental aim of Hobbes' politics was the emancipation of humanity from the crime of heresy.[27] The persecution of heretics is unnecessary for moral conduct in this world or for our salvation in the next. Hobbes declared that the articles of Christian faith which are essential for salvation are simple and few. The state, in proclaiming what they are, is not attempting to instil true belief but merely attempting to keep the peace among warring interpretations of Christian faith. The state cannot interfere with the conscience or inner faith of Christians but merely with the actions 'either of the tongue, or other part of the body.'[28] Passionate preachers may be muzzled but their consciences remain free. Any attempt to enforce true belief by law, as Christian churches had often tried to do, is both ineffective and destructive of life. The laws of the civil authority do not govern conscience but only actions.

However, Hobbes is not recognized to champion the inalienable rights of conscience and free belief because, according to him, the state cannot interfere with the inner life of individuals. The inalienable right of free belief does not simply mean that individuals cannot in practice part with their beliefs, that they must believe what they believe. Yet Spinoza's defence of freedom of thought was similar to Hobbes' defence of the sovereign right to judge which doctrines are suitable for public profession. Spinoza wrote: 'Therefore, as the supreme right of free thinking, even on religion, is in every man's power, and as it is inconceivable that such power could be alienated, it is also in every man's power to wield the supreme right and authority of free judgement in this behalf, and to explain and interpret religion for himself. The only reason for vesting the supreme authority in the interpretation of the law, and judgement on public affairs in the hands of the magistrate, is that it concerns questions of public right.'[29] The sovereign controls the ceremonial or ritual aspect of religion but is impotent to regulate piety or the inner worship of God. Indeed, Spinoza's views on religious freedom seem to be an instance of his general principle that rights are coextensive with capacities or powers. 'Inward worship of God and piety in itself are within the sphere of everyone's private rights, and cannot be alienated ...'[30] Spinoza differed from Hobbes in that he thinks that governments cannot, without destructive consequences, attempt to regulate the actions of the tongue. Since 'ought' implies 'can,' and since 'even men of great experience cannot hold their tongues, far less the mass of the people,' governments ought not to repress free speech, because they can no more regulate speech effectively than they can regulate thought. Spinoza wrote: 'Since, therefore, no one can abdicate his freedom of judgement and feeling; since every man is by indefeasible natural right the master of his own thoughts, it follows that men thinking in diverse and contradictory fashions, cannot, without disastrous results, be compelled to speak only according to the dictates of the supreme power.'[31]

Spinoza thought, together with Hobbes, that the social bond depends upon each individual alienating the right to act according to his private judgment. However, Spinoza distinguished between the right to act as one pleases (which is alienated in the social contract) and the right to judge the sovereign and speak one's mind (which is not alienated). Spinoza anticipated Kant's and Bentham's dicta to obey punctually and to criticize freely. Individuals may speak against the public authority, as long as they do so in a rational or dispassionate manner. But they are guilty of sedition if they accuse the sovereign of injustice, if they incite mob hatred or violence, or if they attempt to change the law without the consent of the sovereign.[32]

That Spinoza may well be more liberal or progressive than Hobbes should not blind us to the problem he shared with Grotius and Hobbes. That is, does inalienable right mean simply the logical or practical impossibility of renouncing a right (for example, to the freedom of thought and speech)? Spinoza seems to argue for inalienable rights on precisely those grounds. However, if our rights are co-extensive with our powers, if we have a right to do what we can do and no right to do what we cannot do, then the notion of rights is fatuous. Perhaps we are indebted to Hobbes and Spinoza for exposing the fatuity of rights-discourse, or reducing it to a language of power. But Spinoza did not mean that one is completely powerless to alienate one's freedom in practice. Rather the renunciation of freedom is morally impermissible or impossible, possible in practice but 'with disastrous results.' But the grounds of the moral impossibility of alienating a right were insufficiently established in Spinoza's writings.

We might expect some light on the legitimacy of Shylock's bond from Locke's understanding of inalienable right and alienable property. Commentators on Locke have recently maintained that Locke held all rights to be alienable. B.A. Richards asserts that Locke anticipated the contemporary vogue in rights-literature by supporting prima facie rather than absolute rights. Richards says that 'no more will be done here to support' the position that Locke disavowed inalienable rights than to cite chapter IV of Locke's *Second Treatise of Government*.[33] In this chapter, Locke justified slavery on Grotius' grounds that criminals forfeit their right to life and liberty. But neither Grotius nor Locke thought forfeiture vitiated the inalienability of a right. To be sure, Locke's argument for inalienable right, in the context of justifying slavery, is difficult to stomach, even for someone raised on Lockian principles of consumption and evacuation. Locke wrote:

This *Freedom* from Absolute, Arbitrary Power, is so necessary to, and closely joyned with a Man's Preservation, that he cannot part with it, but by what forfeits his Preservation and Life together. For a Man, not having the Power of his own Life, *cannot*, by Compact, or his own Consent, *enslave himself* to anyone, nor put himself under the Absolute, Arbitrary Power of another, to take away his Life, when he pleases. No body can give away more Power than he has himself; and he that cannot take away his own Life, cannot give another power over it. Indeed having, by his fault, forfeited his own Life, by some Act that deserves Death; he, to whom he has forfeited it, may (when he has him in his Power) delay to take it, and make use of him to his own Service, and he does him no injury by it. For, whenever he finds the hardship of his Slavery out-weigh the value of his Life, 'tis in his Power, by resisting the Will of his Master to draw on himself the Death he desires.[34]

In this long and seminal passage, Locke boldly provided what Hobbes and Spinoza could not: a justification for Antonio to repudiate his bond with Shylock and to insist on his right to his purchased slaves. The uncharacteristically bold Locke, in this passage, distanced himself from Shylock. But let us examine the propositions of this passage closely. The right to life and the right to liberty are inextricably combined. An individual does not own his life and liberty, and hence cannot renounce life and liberty voluntarily. No man can legitimately commit suicide or sell himself into slavery. However, if one forfeits one's life by some act that deserves death, some individual acquires the right to appropriate the criminal as a slave. Locke, to be sure, failed to explain the specific nature of the crime of the west Africans justly enslaved by the Royal Africa Company or why Locke himself acquired the proprietary right over black slaves. But if his theory is incomplete in all respects, he did conclude with a charitable stipulation (quite alien to Shylockian Law) that the slave, although without the right to die at his own hand, may commit indirect suicide. By resisting the will of his master, the slave will be killed without the sin of the pagan stoic. By killing the slave, the master will be performing, not a sinful, but a merciful act. Antonio's charity is also evident in Locke's instructions that Governor Francis Nicholson of Virginia 'find out the best means to facilitate and encourage the conversion of Negroes and Indians to the Christian Religion.'[35] Locke's paternal concern for the human cargo in which he had invested differentiated him from the conventional image of Shylock.

Locke's general proposition, which seems a genuine advance from Grotius' understanding of inalienable rights, is that life and liberty are inalienable precisely because they are not our own to alienate. If something is our property, it is ours to alienate. Locke repeatedly stated that an individual cannot voluntarily renounce his right to life because his life is not his own property.[36] To be sure, one's lease on life may be forfeited when one violates the terms of the lease or the natural laws God lays down for the maintenance of His property. If our life were our property, then no one could take it without our consent but we could part with it voluntarily. For, as Locke said, 'the nature [of property] is, that *without a Man's own consent if cannot be taken from him.*'[37] But life and liberty are not an individual's property. Although individuals may forfeit their lease on life, they may not have their life and liberty taken from them, even with their consent.

However, Locke insisted that, although an individual has only a conditional title to life and liberty, he has an unconditional title to his own person or is an 'absolute Lord of his own Person.'[38] Locke asserted that 'every man has a *Property* in his own *Person*. This no Body has any Right to but himself. The *Labour* of his Body, and the *Work* of his Hands we may say, are properly his.'[39] Thus Locke seems to say that an individual possesses his life and liberty, but owns his person or has a property in his ability to labour. Because the ability to labour is 'the unquestionable Property of the Labourer,' it is alienable as is any other asset an individual owns. 'Thus the Grass my Horse has bit; the Turfs my Servant has cut; and the Ore I have digg'd in any place where I have a right to them in common with others, become my *Property*, without the assignation or consent of any body.'[40]

As C.B. Macpherson has pointed out, it is precisely because Locke postulates an absolute property in one's person to the labourer that the labourer is free to alienate his capacity to labour.[41] J.P. Day has thoughtfully indicated some linguistic confusions in Locke's concept of self-ownership.[42] However, the postulate that individuals own their ability to labour is a precondition for commercial expansion, capitalist appropriation, or the kind of contractual society which, as Locke put it, 'transfers that profit, that was the reward of one man's labour, into another man's pocket.'[43]

Ownership or property then entails the right to abuse as well as use what is owned 'so that he may even destroy the thing, that he has Property in by his use of it, where need requires ...'[44] Property entails the right to alienate what is owned, whether by gift, barter, or sale.[45] Peter Laslett writes:

For property to Locke seems to symbolize rights in their concrete form, or perhaps rather to provide the tangible subject of an individual's powers and attitudes. It is because they can be symbolized as property, something a man can conceive of as distinguishable from himself though a part of himself, that a man's attributes, such as his freedom, his equality, his power to execute the law of nature, can become the subject of his consent, the subject of any negotiation with his fellows. We cannot alienate any part of our personalities, but we can alienate that with which we have chosen to mix our personalities.[46]

Laslett concludes: 'The conventional judgement of Locke's view of property, that is described a natural, inalienable right, seems on this view to be exactly wrong. Property is precisely that part of our attributes ... which we can alienate, but only of course by our own consent.'[47]

If rights are individual properties, they are alienable or subject to bargains or trade-offs. Rights as properties are the negotiable items of commercial contractualism. Or if rights are inalienable they are not private property, or freely disposable at the will of the right holder. The failure to make this distinction leads contemporary exponents of Lockianism into confusion. For example, Raymond Polin says that because Locke conceived of rights as properties, rights are in essence alienable. Polin writes: 'Since, in fact, natural rights are applicable only to goods of which is the owner, it follows that some of them can be alienated; that is to say, that one can renounce the use of them or claims to them, wholly or in part ... Locke shows, in particular, that every property right can be restricted or even suppressed, provided that the interested party consents.'[48]

But if natural rights apply only to goods of which one is the owner, then it surely follows that not just some, but all rights are alienable. But Polin cannot ignore that, for Locke, 'the natural right to life and liberty is an inalienable right.'[49]

The confusion evident in Polin's view that Lockian rights are both alienable properties and inalienable possessions is perhaps warranted by the fact that Locke's concept of property encompasses both the inalienable rights to life and liberty as well as the alienable properties in one's person and estate. A.J. Simmons also fails to distinguish between inalienable right and alienable property. Simmons writes: 'According to all indications given by Locke, all of the rights that we have are in principle alienable. The only limitations Locke ever suggests on the transfer of rights are those set by the law of nature, and he appears to believe that that merely amounts to restating the claim that we cannot transfer rights we do not possess. No transfer of a right we do possess could violate a law of nature. Within the bounds of the law, we enjoy "perfect freedom" to dispose of our possessions, rights included.'[50]

If Simmons' point is intelligible, he is saying that we do not have a right to life and liberty because they are covered by the natural law prohibiting their alienation. Like Simmons, Robert Nozick understands rights to be individual properties. Moreover, he wishes to emancipate Lockian natural rights from the restrictions of natural law. Law limits the free choice of individuals to dispose of their rights, properties, or persons in any way they see fit. Nozick writes:

A person may choose to do himself ... the things that would impinge across his boundaries when done without his consent by another ... Voluntary consent opens the border for crossings. Locke, of course, would hold that there are things others may not do to you by your permission; namely, those things you have no right to do to yourself. Locke would hold that your giving your permission cannot make it morally permissible for another to kill you, because you have no right to commit suicide. My non-paternalistic position holds that someone may choose (or permit another) to do to himself *anything*, unless he has acquired an obligation to some third party not to do or allow it.[51]

Nozick's justification of any capitalist act between consenting adults fully validates Shylock's bond. However, the fundamental question is whether the alleged illegitimacy of Shylock's contract with Antonio depends, as Simmons and Nozick suggest, on the existence of a natural law which predates, and is inconsistent with, the empire of rights. In short, is Shylock more advanced than Locke who vacillated between the old dispensation of Antonio (natural law) and the new dispensation of Shylock (natural rights)?

To be sure, Lockian natural law does not restrict unlimited capitalist accumulation, as C.B. Macpherson, Leo Strauss, and others have shown. The natural law restrictions on property acquisition (regarding waste, appropriation by means of one's own labour, and leaving a sufficiency behind for others) all vanish in a commercial economy. Nozick's emancipation of human rights from natural law would enable people to sell themselves into slavery, or pledge their bodies and lives in a commercial contract. However, such liberties would not likely add much to the strength of a market economy. The prime condition of liberal capitalism is Locke's postulate that individuals are absolute proprietors of their persons, that they are perfectly free to sell their persons or alienate their labour without the restrictions of minimum wage laws, the regulations of professional associations, collective bargaining agreements, and equal rights legislation.

Clearly, if a woman is an absolute proprietor of her person, she is free to sell herself at the market price, free, for example, to take a job that pays men twice what she is offered. On the assumption of one's proprietorship of one's person, equal rights legislation violates a fundamental human right. Contemporary Lockians would do well to consider why Locke thinks one's person is an alienable property and why social-democratic or welfarist policies violate the fundamental human right to sell one's property as one wills.

Various thinkers have advocated, on Lockian grounds, common ownership of the non-human means of production in order to ensure that one obtain fair value for the property in one's labour.[52] But since one's person is considered a privately owned and alienable commodity, the socialist appearance of this proposal is deceptive. Measures inconsistent with Locke's understanding of private property would have to be taken to regulate the buying and selling of labour and to ensure that any profitable exchange of labour not be converted into material means of production. More genuinely socialist theories would have to confront, as social democratic practice in fact has attacked, the Lockian notion of absolute proprietorship of one's person.

In conclusion, both left- and right-wing Lockians would do well to appreciate the centrality of the idea of absolute proprietorship of one's person to Locke, 'the judicious Hooker' of contemporary rights-advocates. Indeed Nozick's revision of Locke, justifying the alienation of life and liberty, is injudicious, quite unnecessary to the legitimation of any commercial acts between consenting adults. Only a mythical Shylock would be liberated by Nozick's elimination of the natural law prohibitions on the alienation of life and liberty. Real Shylocks know that hookers have to be judicious.

Locke: the Whig rebel,
commonly taken for a revolutionary thinker

CHAPTER FIVE

Inalienable Right, Rebellion, and Revolution

NATURAL LAW AND THE RIGHT OF ARMED RESISTANCE

The previous chapter on inalienable right and alienable property seemed to present Locke in a one-sided manner, as a capitalist apologist, and to ignore the other side of Locke, as a champion of liberty, progressive reform, and even revolution. To be sure, these two sides are not incompatible.

In *The Communist Manifesto*, Marx and Engels made repeated reference to the heroic and revolutionary role of the bourgeoisie in combating feudalism and introducing a new order of things. Marx elaborated his view of the heroic role in historical drama of the capitalist class in *The Eighteenth Brumaire of Louis Bonaparte*. In this work Marx portrayed C.B. Macpherson's ignoble possessive individualist clothed and masked as J.G.A. Pocock's noble civic humanist.

But unheroic as bourgeois society is, it nevertheless took heroism, sacrifice, terror, civil war and battles of peoples to bring it into being. And in the classically austere traditions of the Roman Republic its gladiators found the ideals and the art forms, the self deceptions that they needed in order to conceal from themselves the bourgeois limitations of the content of their struggles and to maintain their passion on the high plane of great historical tragedy. Similarly, at another stage of development, a century earlier, Cromwell and the English people had borrowed speech, passions and illusions from the Old Testament for their bourgeois revolution. When the real aim had been achieved, when the bourgeois transformation of English society had been accomplished, Locke supplanted Habakkuk.[1]

While Marx's formulation is suggestive of the relationship between civic humanism (or republican idealism) and possessive individualism (or bourgeois materialism), Marx obscures both the 'revolutionary' side of Locke and the problem of materialists risking their lives for a cause. First, the suggestion that Locke was an exponent of post-revolutionary doctrine, of the unheroic possessive individualist, is misleading. Habakkuk's vision of divine justice and prayer for violent deliverance from tyranny was as present in Locke as in Marx or Shylock. And the solid faith of Habakkuk (1.ii.4) that 'the righteous man shall live by his faithfulness' combines the self-righteousness and self-assertiveness of the revolutionary rights-claimant. Second, Marx enormously oversimplified in presenting civic humanism to be a form of poetic self-deception necessary to cover the prosaic character of possessive individualism. Perhaps possessive individualism and civic humanism are not incompatible but were in fact combined in the person of Locke and others. More important, Marx failed to provide a materialist account of the heroism and sacrifice of the revolutionary epoch of the bourgeoisie. Revolutionary commitment and the desire for self-preservation are inconsistent, unless one makes the false hypothesis, which Marx did not, that revolutionary dedication arises from starvation or the awareness that revolution is the sole alternative to death. Perhaps the consistent materialist is the Hobbesian self-preservationist, the law and order advocate, the individual who sees revolution to be a threat to commodious self-preservation. Hobbes understood violent dreams of glory but 'vain-glory begetteth no attempt'; the reality principle prohibits heroic or revolutionary risk of life. However, Lockians have died fighting for their rights. Marx was surely wrong to see in civic humanism merely the Tartuffery of possessive individualism. That individuals risk their lives in revolution is surely evidence that they are moved by more than material interests.

If Marxian 'materialism' failed to provide an account of revolutionary spirit, Hegelian 'idealism' might make up the deficiency. What Marx saw as class struggle, Hegel understood as a struggle on the plane of ideals and self-images. The master-slave conflict is a struggle for rights, not material things, a struggle for the recognition of personality. In a Hobbesian state of nature, two equal individuals fight to the death for pre-eminence. Without the motive of vainglory or the desire for something immaterial, the naturally equal individuals would, as Pufendorf and Rousseau maintained, flee for their lives. If one vainglorious individual were to kill the other, the state of nature would remain. History or civilization begins when one Hobbesian individual, conscious of, and fearful for, his mortality, swallows his pride and offers to serve the other in return for sparing his life. The slave, unwilling to die for liberty, creates civilization through his labour. Moreover, in his forced deferral of immediate gratification, in the renunciation of consumption while producing, in the discipline of work and consciousness of death, the slave cultivates himself. The slave transforms his own nature as well as external nature, and thus confronts his master (whose nature is unchanged) under changed conditions with a new, historically acquired or second nature. History, for Hegel, is the history of the working slave. It is beyond our purpose to present Hegel's imaginative reconstruction of the forms of slave culture – Stoicism, Cynicism, and Christianity – which overturn the pagan culture of the masters. Suffice it to say that, for Hegel, the medieval Christian world is a form of impotence – an assertion of liberty, equality, and happiness which is not to be realized in the everyday world. In this world, the slave has no rights: he is not recognized as free and equal in terrestrial cities; the satisfaction of his personality is reserved for the Heavenly City. The other-wordly character of satisfaction is criticized in the Enlightenment and finally terminated in the bourgeois revolutions when the master and slave are dissolved in the bourgeois – the master without a slave and the slave without a master.

In the bourgeois epoch, the Platonic division between guardians and producers is overcome; all men work and all men fight. All men have rights: they are recognized as persons or proprietors; they are free and equal under the law. The bourgeois era is the end of history, a return to nature. The gains of the French revolution are to be extended spatially not temporally, geographically not historically. (The movements of national liberation, of blacks, and of women could be said to be spatial extensions of the empire of rights, of the Hegelian principles of universality and homogeneity. The Marxist view is that history is not over: the bourgeois produces the proletarian and thus the historical dialectic of master and slave only culminates in the era of the self-managing worker.)

What Marx called the heroic age of the bourgeoisie was for Hegel the point in history when the slave risks his life for liberty, when he scorns self-preservation for his rights. Lockian doctrine thus represents the consciousness of the slave asserting his mastery. Lockians fight for their rights under the banner of natural law.

In the preceding chapter, we stated that Hobbes' conception of the relation of law and liberty is inadequate. Locke disagreed with Hobbes' and Nozick's view that laws restrict liberty or abridge the freedom of choice. Locke wrote: 'For *Law*, in its true Notion, is not so much the limitation and *the direction of a free and intelligent Agent* to his proper Interest ... (T)*he end of Law* is not to abolish or restrain, but *to preserve and enlarge Freedom* ...'[2] The natural law prohibiting individuals from suicide or selling themselves into slavery does not restrict individual freedom for Locke as it does for Nozick. The logical and existential condition of free choice is that one be alive and free of bondage. Life and liberty are constitutive of human existence, not values to be conserved or alienated at will.

Nozick correctly states that Locke did not provide a philosophic foundation for natural law or for the view that one's life and liberty are not one's own property. The laws of nature are not the creation of an autonomous rights-bearing subject, as with Hobbes. The laws of nature are heteronomous in character, divine in origin; they are deductions from the proposition that life and liberty are God's property, not the property of any person. Just as Hobbes' individualism seems to bar the way to a naturalistic (Aristotelian or Marxian) account of language, Locke's individualism seems to preclude a naturalistic account of the proposition that our lives and liberties are not our own to alienate. God is the first mover of the market mechanism. Deprived of the communitarian premises of Aristotle or Marx, the enlightened Shylock relies on his God.

Let us turn to an examination of Lockian natural law and the inalienable rights Locke derived from it. The state of nature is, Locke claimed, 'a *State of Liberty*, yet it is *not a State of Licence*, though Man in that State have an uncontrolable Liberty, to dispose of his Person or Possessions, yet he has not Liberty to destroy himself, or so much as any Creature in his Possession, but where some nobler use, than its bare Preservation calls for it.'[3] There are a number of interesting aspects to this formulation. The first is that one has an absolute property or 'uncontrolable Liberty' over one's estate and ability to labour. Secondly, one does not have an absolute property or liberty over one's life. Thirdly and most interestingly, one does not have the right to destroy life except for some 'nobler' purpose than self-preservation. Locke seems to qualify here the 'Fundamental, Sacred, and unalterable Law of Self-Preservation.'[4] What is the 'nobler use' of humans than 'bare preservation'? Or what is the essential self which is nobler to preserve than bare life?

What is unusual in Locke's formulation is the apparent coexistence of the language of rights and the language of nobility. For the language of rights tends to drive from use the language of nobility (or of honour, or virtue, or decency, or courtesy) as competitive enterprises tend toward monopoly. Locke did not develop the idea of a 'nobler use' which might limit or balance the right to life, and thus we must infer its meaning from an examination of the purposes to which Locke applied the law of self-preservation.

To repeat, although man in the state of nature has 'an uncontrolable Liberty, to dispose of his Person or Possessions' because they are his property, 'he has not Liberty to destroy himself' because his life is not his own property. 'For Men being all the Workmanship of one Omnipotent, and infinitely wise Maker ..., they are his Property, whose Workmanship they are, made to last during his, not one anothers Pleasure.'[5] Because one's life is not one's property, one lacks the title to relinquish the power over one's life. That is, one cannot voluntarily sell oneself into slavery. As Rousseau was later to argue, Locke asserted that no man may legitimately consent to be a slave and no people can, by compact, subject themselves to a despot.[6]

Clearly, the proposition that one's life is not one's property is crucial to Locke's argument that despotism is never legitimate. Despotic power 'is a Power, which neither Nature gives, for it has made no such distinction between one Man and another; nor Compact can convey, for Man not having such an Arbitrary Power over his own Life, cannot give another Man such a Power over it ...'[7] For it is by no means foolish to consider that people might alienate their liberty for security and tranquillity or that a despotism, in so far as it is not overthrown in a rebellion, exists by virtue of the consent of his subjects (especially if one considers that Locke's conception of tacit consent confers legitimacy to government).[8]

Thus Locke thought one's life and liberty are inalienable rights precisely because they are not owned by the individual. Let us examine other rights that Locke held to be inalienable. Locke, unlike Hobbes, considered the freedom of conscience to be an essential and thus inalienable entitlement of human beings. The care of souls can never be 'visited in the magistrate by the consent of the people, because no man can so far abandon the care of his own salvation as blindly to leave it to the choice of any other ...'[9] The freedom of conscience is inalienable not because one's conscience is inherently private and, as such, cannot impinge upon others. Rather Locke understood conscience to pertain to the outer or public world of institutionalized worship and profession of belief rather than simply to an inner or private world of meditation and prayer that could never be restricted by public authority. Locke was concerned that the rights of conscience not be abandoned by the establishment of a state church or by the union of church and state.[10] When Locke stated that the boundaries between ecclesiastical and civil societies are 'fixed and unmoveable' regardless of the will of the people,[11] he was not saying that people in fact cannot create a church establishment or cannot relinquish to priests or ayatollahs the right to interpret what is needful for one's salvation. It is precisely because it is practically possible to renounce the freedom of worship that Locke insisted on the inalienable rights of conscience, just as the practical possibility of suicide is the basis of the inalienability of the right to life. Locke then was not putting forward the trivial argument that one cannot alienate one's conscience because it is inherently private. Rather, if one were to renounce the right to interpret what is needful for salvation to anyone with executive power or civil authority, one would lose one's essential humanity, one would have committed spiritual suicide.

In *A Letter Concerning Toleration*, Locke referred to natural right only with respect to the liberty of conscience. Although he presented a condensed account of the doctrine of his *Second Treatise* in *A Letter Concerning Toleration*,[12] he eschewed the vocabulary of 'right' for that of 'care,' and of 'natural rights' for 'civil interests' ('bona civilia'). One might speculate why Locke reserved the word 'right' for freedom of conscience. It is likely that he wished to indicate his orthodoxy in holding spiritual matters to be what is of greatest importance in life; worldly concerns, such as 'life, liberty, health, and indolency of body; and the possession of outward things, such as money, lands, houses, furniture, and the like,'[13] are not really a matter of right when one is concerned with one's eternal well-being. Only from a secular perspective do 'interests' and 'cares' become 'rights.' Or perhaps 'rights' are what are really worth fighting for; one looks out for one's interests, attends to one's cares, but fights for one's rights. One may make negotiations and compromises respecting one's interests but one battles for one's rights. That is, perhaps the vocabulary of rights is a combatant's language. One who would employ the language of rights must present oneself as judge and executioner of the law of nature. One whose interests are ignored or whose cares do not receive attention may quietly nurse a grievance, but one whose rights are violated must go down swinging or be convicted of empty rhetoric.

What Locke called civil interests in *A Letter Concerning Toleration* became natural rights in his *Second Treatise*, and the rights of conscience became the inalienable right to judge and execute the law of nature. When individuals consent to form a civil society, they entrust the right to judge to an elected legislative power and the right to execute to the executive power. But this trust does not involve a renunciation of right any more than entrusting one's money to a bank transfers one's money to the banker. Anyone is free, as it were, to start a run on the bank if he thinks the bankers have mismanaged his deposit. 'And where the Body of the People, or any single Man, is deprived of their Right, or is under the Exercise of a power without right, and have no Appeal on Earth, there they have a liberty to appeal to Heaven, whenever they judge the Cause of sufficient moment.'[14] The people are always free to take up arms whenever they judge the legislative or the executive has acted contrary to their trust.[15] 'And this Judgement they cannot part with, it being out of a Man's power so to submit himself to another, as to give him a liberty to destroy him; God and Nature never allowing a Man so to abandon himself, as to neglect his own preservation: And since he cannot take away his own Life, neither can he give another power to take it.'[16] Indeed, Locke believed that the popular right of armed resistance would be exercised less frequently when the legislative power is in the hands of elected representatives. However, the point here is that Locke justified the right of resistance in terms of the inalienable right to interpret the laws of nature, which cannot be transferred to a sovereign legislative but only entrusted to a legislative subordinate to the sovereign people. The legislative power is never sovereign, Locke asserted, because individuals do not own their lives and thus 'no Body can transfer to another more power than he has in himself ...'[17]

What Lockians have fought for, Nozick takes for granted. Nozick takes for granted the separation of church and state, the emancipation from traditional and ecclesiastical authority, the abolition of slavery, the overthrow of despotisms, the institution of elected legislatures, the prevalence of contractual or market relations between individuals recognized as proprietors. Lockian natural law serves as a norm of conduct for which Lockians have done battle. Lockian natural rights, which Nozick assumes, conserve or secure the fruits of the revolutionary struggles engaged under the banner of Lockian natural law. In short, Nozick takes for granted what Lockians have fought for but dismisses the basis of the call to battle – namely, that one's life is not one's property and thus one is not free to do whatever one likes with it.

For Locke then, one is not free to relinquish one's life unless some 'nobler use, than its bare Preservation calls for it.' Bare preservation, we may infer, refers to the servile existence of those unwilling to risk their lives for liberty. One might say that Hobbes consistently developed the laws of self-preservation not qualified by Locke's 'nobler use.' Rebellion is never legitimate in so far as it puts at risk commodious self-preservation. Further, Hobbes' consistent elaboration of the inalienable right of self-preservation renders the duty to fight for one's country questionable.[18] The materialist right of cowardice replaces the idealist right of conscientious objection. Locke's 'nobler use' obviates the difficulties in Hobbes' account of the duty of self-preserving individuals to risk their lives in war; it allows Locke to justify armed resistance to government when the alternative is, or is suspected to become in the future,[19] servile existence or 'bare preservation.' The noble or liberal use of life is to fight for the right, or more precisely, for one's rights. The laws of nature are determined by soldiers' right, not scholars' writ. Rights are forcefully claimed, and are not simply cleverly discovered or skilfully negotiated.[20] The 'nobler use' of life is to take up arms or, as Locke put it, to make Jephthah's appeal to Heaven,[21] and in that appeal do God's work in arbitrating conflicting interpretations of the laws of nature. That Jephthah had to kill his daughter to fulfil God's will is not noted by Locke. Hobbes is more attentive to the casualties of war and civil war. The rebel's vocation is heroic. It is a calling for which 'bare preservationists' are not equipped. To call a civil interest a natural right is, for Locke, to sound the call for battle.

REBELLION AGAINST GOVERNMENT AND
REVOLUTION AGAINST PROPERTY

Most contemporary Locke scholars assert that Locke's justification of armed resistance against untrusted governments amounts to a right of revolution.[22] Locke did not refer to a right of revolution, and rarely to revolution. In an early tract on government, Locke referred to revolution as a cataclysm; he bemoaned the religious pretensions which have moved 'almost all those tragical revolutions' suffered by the fairest of islands.[23] In the *Second Treatise*, Locke referred to revolution as a tragic rupture in the form of government, but qualified this assessment in noting that, despite 'the many revolutions,' the British have always restored the ancient constitutional balance of Crown, Lords, and Commons. Locke wrote: 'This slowness and aversion in the People to quit their old Constitutions, has, in the many Revolutions which have been seen in this Kingdom, in this and former Ages, still kept us to, or, after some interval of fruitless attempts, still brought us back gain to our old Legislative of King, Lords and Commons: And whatever provocations have made the Crown be taken from some of our Princes Heads, they never carried the People so far, as to place it in another Line.'[24]

We note in this passage that Locke's teaching on revolution is not very 'revolutionary.' It is commonly thought, by those who see in the *Second Treatise* a justification of a right of revolution, that Locke meant something conservative by revolution, a bringing back of order. Indeed, we shall show that if Locke advocated a right of revolution, he justified political, not social, revolution. John Dunn writes: 'Revolution for Locke ... is an act of restoration, of the re-creation of a violated political order.'[25] Yet the passage cited above does not state that revolution restores a violated order but that, despite the apparent disorder of revolutions, the English have cautiously held on to the old ways.

The word that Locke used more often than 'revolution' was 'rebellion.' While Locke appeared to use the words as synonyms, scholars have attributed to Locke a right of revolution, not of rebellion. The reason for this would seem to be twofold: first, that the *Two Treatises of Government*, as Locke's 1690 preface suggests, was written to justify 'the Revolution,' 'the English Revolution,' 'the Whig Revolution,' or 'the Glorious Revolution'; second, that Locke thought an untrustworthy government, rather than an untrusting people, re-bels or re-institutes a state of war. Thus, according to the common view, the government rebels against the people in violating individual rights and a popular revolution, such as the English Revolution, restores the right order of liberty and property within a state.

What is objectionable in attributing a right to revolution in Locke is that the idea of revolution as a total transformation of government and society, as the creation of something novel and unprecedented, is both anachronistic and incompatible with the framework of natural rights. We shall examine in chapter seven the revision of Locke's ideas in the eighteenth century, when the idea of revolution as the creation of a brave new world became common currency, and shall demonstrate then the unsuitability to revolutionary projects of a doctrine that rights can neither be created nor destroyed. What we wish to establish here is that, although 'the name Revolution, in the sense in which we use it, was born in England in 1688–9,'[26] the baby was sickly – that is, the word 'revolution' was so covered with the afterbirth of the older connotation of restoration that the new sense of creation and transformation was present only in a confused and ambiguous manner.[27]

The attribution to Locke of a right to revolution seems to derive from associating Locke's *Two Treatises* with the Glorious or Whig Revolution. However, as Peter Laslett has shown, 'John Locke's *Two Treatises of Government* is an Exclusion Tract, not a Revolution Pamphlet.'[28] That is, the *Two Treatises* were written in 1679–81, at the time of Locke's participation in the gutter anti-Catholicism of the Papist plot, when Whigs agitated to exclude the Catholic James II from the Crown. 'It is certain that Locke knew all about what was going on, and that he took no opportunity to disapprove the forced confessions, the judicial murders, mob oratory and agitation.'[29] Locke's hagiographers appear more embarrassed about the great philosopher's participation in the fabricated papist plot to assassinate Charles II than about his investments in the slave trade.[30] Whether or not Locke descended to the moral level of Titus Oates, the probability that Locke wrote the *Two Treatises* at the time of his anti-Catholic agitation throws light on his justification of armed resistance to government, despite the fact that Locke's theory of armed resistance in *The Second Treatise* is not coloured by his Orange antipopery.

Rights-advocates typically adopt a defensive posture. But Locke's right of armed resistance seems to assert that the best defence is a good offence. Locke's *Second Treatise* did not assert that the government is dissolved only when the government has already violated people's rights but also 'when they endeavour to invade the Property of the Subject' (sec. 221) or *'endeavour to take away, and destroy the Property of the People'* (sec. 222) or *'endeavour to grasp themselves, or put into the hands of any other an Absolute Power* over the Lives, Liberties, and Estates of the People' (sec. 222) or 'when he goes about to set up his own Arbitrary Will, as the Law of the Society' (sec. 222) or 'endeavour to set up the declared Abettors of his own Will, for the true *Representatives* of the People' (sec. 222). By 'attempting by force on the Properties of any People' (sec. 231), that is, in making the 'indeavour to take' away the people's rights (sec. 227), the government introduces a state of war, or rebels against the people. Armed resistance is justified if the people 'universally have a persuasion, grounded upon manifest evidence, that designs are carrying on against their Liberties' (sec. 230). The government rebels against the people in their 'Endeavours to get, and exercise an Arbitrary power over their People' (sec. 230) or when it 'by force goes about to invade the Rights' of the people (sec. 230). Locke's argument that the government not the people initiates rebellion seems questionable when Locke insisted that public trust dissolves not only when the government has violated rights, but also when the people think the government is endeavouring, attempting, designing, or going about to do so.

Locke's political practice conformed to this construction that pre-emptive strikes against potentially tyrannical governments are justifiable. Prior to the revocation of the Edict of Nantes in 1685, an event which proved to all right-thinking Englishmen that intolerant

Catholicism was a threat to liberty and property, Locke, with his fellow Whigs, had failed to persuade his compatriots that diabolical papists were plotting to assassinate Charles II. When the Whig fabrications failed to exclude the Catholic James, then Duke of York, from the succession, some Whigs, with Locke's connivance, actually plotted to assassinate Charles and James. Peter Laslett, Richard Ashcraft, and J.G.A. Pocock implicate Locke in the Monmouth rebellion of 1685, as well as the Rye House plot.[31] In short, Locke anticipated that James II's Catholicism would be a threat to human rights, prior to actual encroachments on the liberties and properties of James' subjects.

If we strip Locke's argument of the Tartuffery that only governments initiate rebellion, we will restore the word 'rebellion' to its common signification. Locke asserted that 'it is plain, that shaking off a Power, which Force, and not Right hath set over any one, though it hath the Name of *Rebellion*, yet is no Offence before God ...'[32] Our concern here is not to question Locke's certainty about what is offensive to God, but to establish that what Locke justified 'hath the Name of *Rebellion*.' In short, contrary to the conventional view that Locke justified a right of revolution, and not of rebellion, the Lockian right of armed resistance against government is a right of rebellion, not revolution. Peter Laslett correctly declares: 'Locke was no revolutionary in any case, in the conventional sense. How can we go on associating him with "The English Revolution," whatever that may mean, now that we know that he wrote in anticipation of events? Perhaps it is time we abandoned the phrase itself and the system of muddled and superficial generalization which goes with it.'[33] A natural right to revolution is 'insignificant speech.' Rebellion, because it preserves the proprietary framework of legitimacy, is consistent with Lockian natural rights.

SHYLOCKIAN SELF-INTEREST, LOCKIAN REBELLION, AND SOCIAL REVOLUTION

In the previous chapter, we suggested that Shylock would unquestionably side with the bourgeois self-preservation of Hobbes rather than the heroic noble creed of suicidal revolutionaries. But perhaps an ethic of self-preservation and Locke's doctrine on rebellion are not necessarily opposed. If Shylock's immediate affinity would be with Hobbes, he would be open to the wisdom of Locke's judicious doctrine on rebellion. For Locke's right of rebellion, however heroic or noble, does not entail the abandonment of Hobbesian self-preservation for a lofty ideal of justice.

Locke stated that any single individual, who is deprived of his rights by government, has a right to rebel. However, he assured his readers: 'Nor let anyone think, this lays a perpetual foundation for Disorder: for this operates not, till the Inconvenience is so great, that the Majority feel it, and are weary of it, and find a necessity to have it amended.'[34] Thus, while individuals have a right to rebel, prudence dictates that they exercise their rights only when they have power on their side. The right of rebellion imposes no duty to aid the victims of governmental oppression. Locke wrote:

> For if it reach no farther than some private Mens Cases, though they have a right to defend themselves, and to recover by force, what by unlawful force is taken from them; yet the Right to do so, will not easily engage them in a Contest, wherein they are sure to perish; it being as impossible for one or a few oppressed Men to *disturb the Government*, where the Body of the People do not think themselves concerned in it, as for a raving mad Man, or heady Male content to overturn a well-settled State; the People being as little apt to follow the one, as the other.'[35]

The individual right of rebellion does not lead to sedition or anarchy, Locke felt, precisely because individuals are self-seeking, because they could not care less at injustices suffered by others. Removing the padded gloves of moralism and writing with the breath-taking impact of Machiavelli, Locke described his fellow men: 'The examples of particular Injustice, or Oppression of here and there an unfortunate Man, moves them not.'[36] Only when a majority of the society is personally harmed is the individual right of rebellion likely to be exercised. Prudence dictates that one waive one's right to rebel until one has power on one's side.

However, the power of the majority is also the right of the

majority. Locke's principles of individual rights and of majority rule, potentially in conflict with one another, come together when the rebellious individual is in harmony with the will of the majority. Two questions arise. How is a majority will to express itself in such tyrannical conditions as justify a rebellion? (For it is not to be supposed that the tyrant allows a referendum regarding his overthrow.) Second, who constitutes the majority? Did Locke allow the poor as well as the rich a right of rebellion?

All individuals, in Locke's understanding, are propertied in some sense. Even if they have no estate, they have a property in their person or productive abilities, as well as in their life and liberty. Since the government has the duty of protecting property right, the right to rebel (which has its source in the failure to protect property right) belongs, it might be thought, to all individuals. However, Locke made clear that if there is to be no taxation without representation, there is to be no parliamentary representation without taxable estate. Locke stated that 'no part of the People however incorporated can pretend to [a right to be distinctly represented], but in proportion to the assistance, which it affords to the public ...'[37] For if the people, as individuals and as a collectivity, do not tax themselves, then the government 'invades the *Fundamental Law of Property*, and subverts the end of Government.'[38] Locke avoided the tension between the principle of individual right and of majority rule in asserting that taxes 'must be given with his own Consent, i.e., the Consent of the Majority, giving it either by themselves or their Representatives chosen by them.'[39]

How are we to interpret the equation of an individual's consent with that of a majority of parliamentary representatives? Perhaps Locke thought the corporate interest of the landed proprietors who elect the representatives and the parliamentarians who raise taxes and pass laws regulating property is more than enough to offset the differences of interest and opinion among the class of landed proprietors. In short, there may be a general will respecting property among 'the Industrious and Rational' class, in opposition 'to the Fancy or Covetousness of the Quarrelsom and Contentious.'[40] Indeed, in the state of nature, 'there could be then little room for Quarrels or Contentions about Property,'[41] on condition that men followed the laws of nature or of reason. However, the state of nature is warlike because most individuals disregard the laws of nature. Since 'the greater part [of humanity are] no strict Observers of Equity and Justice, the enjoyment of the property he has in this state is very unsafe, very unsecure.'[42] The Lockian state of nature is not a Hobbesian war of all against all, because there is a condition of concord among 'the Industrious and Rational.' Rather it is a Marxian class war of 'the Industrious and Rational' class against the idle and prodigal classes above and below it in the social hierarchy. To be sure, Locke thought that labourers rarely unite in a common front, as do merchants and landowners. Locke explained:

for the labourer's share, being seldom more than a bare subsistence, never allows that body of men time or opportunity to raise their thoughts above that, or struggle with the richer for theirs, (as one common interest) unless when some common and great distress, uniting them in one universal ferment, makes them forget respect, and emboldens them to carve to their wants with armed force; and then break in upon the rich, and sweep all like a deluge. But this rarely happens but in the male-administration of neglected, or mismanaged government.[43]

Locke then was no stranger to the politics of class warfare. The question is whether Locke's right of rebellion justifies the poor taking a carving knife to the rich (when the former constitutes a majority). Locke never denied explicitly a right of rebellion to those lacking material property (the sign of industry and rationality). We cannot say that because Locke wished to restrict the franchise to those with taxable estate, the right of rebellion is necessarily limited in a similar fashion. Nor can we argue from the fact that Locke thought armed rebellion by the irrational poor would be catastrophic to the position that Locke thought the irrational poor do not have a right of rebellion. For rights imply the right to do wrong, and perhaps Locke supported the right of the poor to a catastrophic rebellion. In short, we cannot argue from the desirability or undesirability of a policy to the right or lack of right to an act. If rights imply the right to do wrong (in this case, to exercise the right to rebel when the consequences would be catastrophic), they also imply that one may have no right to do what is right. Kant was certain that the ancien régime was unjust, that its overthrow was desirable, and that individuals had no right to rebel against unjust governments. How then can we determine whether Locke would justify a rebellion of an irrational (or propertyless, in the usual sense) majority? How are contemporary Lockians to take their stand on illiberal but democratic movements in central America?

The concluding chapter of Locke's *Second Treatise* is predicated on a distinction (which Hobbes and Kant fail to make) between a dissolution of government and a dissolution of society. Rebellion against government does not necessarily produce Hobbesian anarchic civil war or the dissolution of society. Thus, when the executive or legislative branch of government acts contrary to the trust vested in them, that is, 'when they endeavour to invade the Property of the Subject,'[44] sovereignty reverts to the people. The people, contrary to Hobbes, remain a collectivity or a society in the absence of government. 'The usual, and almost only way' a society is dissolved, Locke stated, is from the sword of foreign conquest.[45]

A revolution of a propertyless majority is like a foreign conquest in that it overturns property rights. Rebellion and the dissolution of government do not violate property right; revolution and the dissolution of society do. The primary condition of rebellion is, according to Locke, the dissolution of government in the form of an alteration of the legislative branch, a legislative elected by men of taxable estate. Locke writes: 'The Reason why Men enter into Society, is the preservation of their Property; and the end why they choose and authorize a Legislative, is, that there may be Laws made, and Rules set as Guards and Fences to the Properties of all the Members of the Society, to limit the Power, and Moderate the Dominion of every Part and Member of the Society.'[46] A revolution of those without material estate, of fence-breakers, would alter the legislative and would undermine the proprietary reason for the existence of society. A movement of the poor is more than a rebellion. In that it overturns existing society, and the holdings or entitlements on which it rests, a movement of a propertyless majority is a revolution. Edmund Burke, in other words, was faithful to Lockian doctrine when he justified the American rebellion and castigated the French revolution. The American rebellion, initiated by a substantial minority, changed the government without changing society. Respecting Lockian proprietary claims, the American rebels preserved what Burke considered the material basis of tradition. American society and way of life were conserved in contrast to the French, whose revolution, in violating property right, uprooted French society from its past. The un-Lockian loyalists who were faithful to Britain and subsequently came to Canada were riff-raff or 'losers' – Amerindians, Blacks, French Catholics, Highland Catholics, Dutch- and German-speaking Protestants – in short, un-American, fearful of Lockian Whiggery, no part of what Locke and Burke considered 'society.'[47]

When Locke and Burke referred to the people entitled to rebel, they meant the class of proprietors. The people with a right to rebel are those who preserve society amidst the dissolution of government, those who do so because they have a stake in preserving the sacred boundary marks. Those without material property will not only topple illegitimate governments but also overturn society, propriety, and tradition in a violent revolution. The Lockian right of rebellion pertains to those who are not suffering from grievous want or oppression and who have a reasonable chance of success. Marxists could learn from Lockian realism. The past century has shown that the revolutionary ranks of the people derive more from the 'kulaks' and 'mid-peasantry' than the 'rural proletariat,' and more from the 'labour aristocrats' than 'unskilled proletarians.'[48]

Locke's right of rebellion is a mean limited by two extremes: the anti-rebellious doctrine of Hobbes (who did not distinguish between rebellion and revolution and who did not think taxation of the wealthy to be a fundamental injustice) and the revolutionary doctrine of Marx (who aimed at the revolutionary overthrow of society, and not just government, and who thought the unpropertied are the revolutionary agents to overturn a society based on private property). In that the right of rebellion does not require extreme heroism or nobility or subvert property right, Shylock would give respectful attention to Locke's arguments. If the right of rebellion entails the option of exercising or waiving one's right, and if the right is to be exercised only when the balance of power favours the successful prosecution of one's rights, only an improvident fool, one who is loyal to something beyond one's interests, would fail to attend to Locke's theory.

Nevertheless, Locke's right of rebellion is subject to natural law. While rights secure options (such as, whether or not to rebel against the government), laws prescribe or proscribe conduct. The natural law prohibiting the alienation of one's life and liberty prescribes, as we have seen, the separation of church and state, the institution of elected legislatures to safeguard property right, the prevalence of market relations or relationships between persons (individuals recognized as proprietors), and the overthrow of despotisms or regimes where persons or the rights of property are not legally protected. Nevertheless, the duty of rebelling against illiberal regimes is always qualified by the right of self-preservation, the right to exercise one's entitlement to rebel only when it is prudent to do so.

Robert Nozick takes for granted all that Lockians have demanded under the aegis of natural law. If Lockian natural law is unfounded as Nozick asserts,[49] the edifice of human rights is constructed without a foundation. Whether or not human rights can be constructed from a notion of human personality, rather than built on Locke's natural or divine law, is the subject of the next chapter.

Hegel: the most muscular of thinkers,
who pressed historical content into the form of natural rights

CHAPTER SIX

Rights as the Personalization of Right

According to our moral intuitions, Shylock's attempt to acquire the foreskin of Antonio's heart was wrong but, according to the argument of this book, he may have had a right to do so. For rights, as we have seen, imply the right to do wrong. Locke's right of rebellion provides the option of resisting or not resisting injustice, and of exercising or of waiving the right, depending on the circumstances and prospects of success. Similarly J.S. Mill's right of self-determination does not mean that the secession of nationalities who feel themselves to be oppressed is always right (either correct policy or morally desirable).[1] Rather the right of national self-determination, for Mill, aims to secure the option of consenting to remain within existing political arrangements or of embarking on a course of national independence, however ill-advised that course of action might be. Thus the wrongness of rebellion or secession is not an argument against an individual, class, or people having a right to rebel or secede. A majority of North American women think abortion is morally wrong but a much larger majority think women have a right to an abortion.² The wrongness of Shylock's intention does not vitiate his right over the person of Antonio.

According to Locke's argument, Antonio could alienate his person to Shylock but could not alienate his life and liberty. The personal, for Locke, is the alienable. One has a free title or an absolute property in one's person. Perhaps the notion of the person is crucial to the separation of rights from the right in liberal doctrine.

The right to do wrong is the moral core of liberalism. The liberal's proudest claim is to defend the right of another to say or do what he holds to be morally reprehensible because he respects the moral autonomy of the other. Mill's championship of 'permissiveness' in *On Liberty* does not constitute a declaration that bigamy, divorce, pornography, or drug use is morally desirable, for the liberal defence of the sanctity of choice or personal autonomy entails that various choices will be morally repugnant to the liberal. Mill has no doubt that polygamy is a repressive and regressive insitution but defends the Mormons' right to contract polygamous marriages.

The question we are investigating is how rights come to be so separated from morality that one can refer, without absurdity, to a right to do wrong. The hypothesis we are entertaining is that when rights are conceived as the properties of persons, they take on the characteristics of property defined by the 'jus utendi et abutendi.' Thus the personalization of impersonal justice (which prescribes conduct unconditionally) and of impersonal law (which proscribes conduct unconditionally) into the moral properties of individuals entails the abuse of rights, the divorce of rights from the right, or the moral permit to speak foolishly as well as wisely, to 'sell out' or to 'keep the faith,' to spend one's money wastefully or to relieve suffering, to rebel against or acquiesce in injustice, to abort a foetus or carry it to term. Locke's conception of the person as absolute property or his view of the personal as that which is free from the regulation of natural law is suggestive of this hypothesis.

However, the proprietary conception of the personal (the realm of what is most one's own) is not apparent in common usage or in moral theories grounded in a respect for the person. In order to establish the Lockian conception of the person as the foundation of our understanding of the moral-legal person, we must first explore the history of rights-literature to assess whether a richer or fuller account of human personality is present in philosophic or common usage than that which appears in Locke. In doing so, we shall maintain that the spare frame of Locke's conception contains the inner structure of the richer and more variegated conceptions of the person in philosophic and common usage.

The meaning of 'person' is as often taken for granted and used uncritically as is the related notion of rights. If we were to use a dictionary, we should find as subcategories under the primary meaning of 'person' as an individual human being both the meanings of 'personage' (or an individual of rank, note, and distinction) and of 'an inferior human being.' We might protest that what we mean by a person refers neither to outstanding personalities or notable personages, nor to social inferiors. But an instinctive protest, without reflection, would be a mistake. For the notion of a person, both in philosophic literature and in common usage, combines the antithetical significations of 'personage' and 'inferior human being.' As Hegel declared: 'Man's chief glory is to be a person, and yet in spite of that the bare abstraction, "person," is somewhat contemptuous in its very expression.'[3]

Hegel thoughtfully pointed out the important truth that persons are abstractions, not concrete individuals. The abstraction 'person' is both glorious and contemptible in that it neutralizes or neuters concrete differences between individuals. Common speech is quite familiar with the idea of a person as an abstraction from gender. A chairperson is either male or female and neither male nor female. The status of being a person may seem glorious to some and contemptible to others. The same individual may wish to be considered a person in some contexts, and as more or less than a person in more intimate contexts. Persons are abstractions from differences of sex, race, age, religion, class, or nationality. Respect for persons corresponds to an injunction not to discriminate on the basis of race, religion, and creed. Yet, for Hobbes and Spinoza, respect of persons is iniquity or the breach of equity.[4] The rights-advocate is than a respecter of persons (in the sense of abstractions from all differences of power and position) but is no respecter of persons (in the sense of personages or personalities, powerful individuals, those occupying a high social station).

Our notion of persons contains richly contradictory significations, as Hegel points out. Let us consider a conversation from *Silence Observed* between Michael Innis' super-sleuth Sir John Appleby and a young man enamoured of a female thief. 'Now let us suppose that the Rembrandt was not, in fact, the legal property of this young person –' 'I consider that to be a derogatory and offensive expression ... She was a lady, and she had better be referred to with proper respect ...' Sir John uses 'person' in Grotius' sense, namely, in the manner in which individuals are apprehended by law.[5] But the young man is fearful of his beloved and himself being apprehended by the law. Also as a lover he does not wish his beloved to lose her particularity in Appleby's reduction of her to a mere person, and, as an aristocrat, he does not wish his beloved to be reduced to the status of a commoner and treated as merely equal before the law.

However, for Grotius, the law does not necessarily apprehend individuals as equal; that is, persons are not necessarily equal. Grotius wrote that '*Right* is a moral quality annexed to the person, justly entitling him to possess some particular privilege, or to perform some particular act.'[6] Grotius then asserted that rights are to be understood as privileges and persons are to be understood as the privileged. Pufendorf elaborated this understanding of the moral-legal person: '*Men* are conceived as different *Persons*, upon Account of their different State or Office ...'[7] It is precisely in this sense of person that Hobbes and Spinoza find respect of persons to be iniquitous. One's person is one's social role, standing, or status.

Persons are then legal-moral abstractions which both refer to and abstract from determinate socio-political hierarchies. One's person is, in the juridical sense, what is least personal, least one's 'ownmost' or 'innermost.' One's person exists for others, not for oneself. Hobbes characteristically provided the greatest insight into the notion of a person furnished by the history of political thinking. Hobbes constructed moral personality from the etymology of person:

123 The Personalization of Right

The Greeks have *prósōpon*, which signifies the *face*, as *persona* in Latin signifies the *disguise*, or *outward appearance* of a man, counterfeited on the stage; and sometimes more particularly that part of it, which disguiseth the face, as a mask or a vizard: and from the stage, hath been translated to any representer of speech and action, as well as tribunals, as theatres. So that a *person*, is the same that an *actor* is; both on stage and in common conversation; and to *personate*, is to *act*, or *represent* himself, or another; and he that acteth another, is said to bear his person, or act in his own name ...'

Thus Hobbes anticipated the existentialist doctrine that all humans are actors. Humans take on a role or assume a person; human being or existence is the manner in which individuals present themselves to, and mask themselves from, others. Natural persons represent themselves or are the authors of their own act. Public representatives or authorities are artificial persons – that is, actors who are not the author of their own act. Hobbes then generalized the legal notion of a person to all aspects of human experience and demonstrated brilliantly how the legal abstraction of a person is experienced by individuals and lived in everyday life. One's person bears the same relation to natural individuality as what one sells is related to what one owns. One's person is what one 'sells' to others. It is both one's own and not one's own.

Thus Hobbes demonstrated how the abstract generality of legal personality is particularized into our notion of the person. One's person or personality has come to mean one's singularity, idiosyncrasy, or difference from others. Personality refers to one's individuality which may be composed, as Hegel says, of both universality and particularity but which is understood, in common usage, to refer to the particular qualities that distinguish one from another, rather than to one's common humanity or the qualities one shares with others. For Grotius and Pufendorf, those differences which constituted one's person are class differences. For Hobbes and most modern thinkers, one's person does not refer to class 'privi-leges' and differential rights but to those differences which are the product of one's actions. Whatever privileged position one acquires is the result of talented effort not the accident of birth. The inequalities which constitute individual personality and social persona are modified by the formal equality of legal personality or the absence of legal barriers to the acquisition of property. Class structure is no longer legally recognized, as it was by Grotius and Pufendorf. All meet as equal proprietors or as persons at the market-place. The universality of money (or the recognition that anyone's money is as good as anyone else's) becomes the basis of moral principle; the universalizability of an aspiration become the measure of its rightness. Thus persons are not only distinct individuals, with different amounts of power, prestige, and property, but also equal human beings, sharing a common humanity as individual proprietors, recognized as equal before the law.

By the time of Hegel, Grotius' and Pufendorf's view that the law could encompass differences of social status was unacceptable; such legacies of Roman law, Hegel declared, are simply irrational.[9] After the French revolution, the claims to personhood by members of the lower classes are less easily ignored and hereditary personages have sunk to the level of being mere persons. Can we now declare obsolete the earlier view that rights are privileges and persons are the privileged? Surely we can definitively say that rights are not privileges and persons are not privileged. But although rights are often understood, in common usage and in philosophic literature, in opposition to privileges, the conjunction of 'equal' and 'rights' in 'equal rights' is not normally taken to be a redundancy. Does 'equal' add something to the idea of a right or merely unfold what is contained in the notion of a right? Thoughtful individuals such as Herbert Hart, John Rawls, or Ronald Dworkin yield no clear counsel as to whether the relationship of 'rights' and 'equality' is analytic or synthetic. Thus we might conclude that Grotius' and Pufendorf's concept of rights and persons is not dead, but alive in a state of unconsciousness. We have to argue for equal rights; we cannot assume that rights entail equality. Since we cannot assume that equality inheres in the concept of rights, we may be forced to conclude that rights are, and are not, privileges just as persons are, and are not, privileged.

However, let us return to Hegel's statement that persons are abstractions rather than concrete individuals. The question is: from what are persons abstracted? We might answer: from social differences (of class, race, sex, and so forth). The key question (which may help us understand how rights could both be and not be privileges) is whether what is abstracted is preserved in the abstraction. Are class, race, and sex differences preserved in the concept of the person which abstracts from these differences? In *The Yuppie Handbook*, we read that all yuppies (young urban professionals) have cleaning persons. They do not have charwomen or cleaning ladies. Just as ladies became women and women became ladies, while the class distinction between ladies and women remained intact, so cleaning ladies have become cleaning persons, while the gender division of cleaning remains largely unshaken. Doubtless there are no fewer black cleaning persons than there were black charwomen or black cleaning ladies.

The moral-legal person does not normally abstract from hair colour, right- or left-handedness, tallness, fatness, health, or beauty. These differences are deemed trivial or insignificant in relation to the concepts of rights and persons. Indeed contemporary moral philosphers tend to deprecate the Greeks who held stature, health, and beauty to be excellences, akin to moral or intellectual virtues. But moral and intellectual virtues are not normally abstracted from the notion of a person, unless the differences in native ability and acquired discipline appear so marked as to engender debate whether some (idiots, lunatics, criminals, and the like) are so incapacitated as to lack rights or legal personality. Thus the moral-legal person does not abstract from differences, such as physical or moral stature, that are considered either trivial or difficult to discern. If manifestly handicapped individuals are considered persons, they are held to be persons despite, or regardless of, their handicap. Persons then abstract from or bracket this 'despite' or 'regardless.' (Despite their lack of character or intelligence and regardless of their race, sex, and social background) all persons have a right to run for public office. What is bracketed or abstracted from personality is tacitly contained in that abstraction.

We abstract from racial and sexual differences, or say that all persons have a right to a job regardless of race or sex, precisely because racial and sexual discrimination exists, and is, for the proponents of equal rights, to be combated. If racial and sexual discrimination did not exist, we would not have to abstract race and sex from the concept of a person, any more than hair colour or stature. Because hair colour and stature are not a significant part of our social hierarchy, the moral-legal person does not abstract from them. If we were to encounter a constitution that guaranteed an equal right to a job or public office regardless of hair colour or stature, we would expect that society to have a tradition of respect for those of a particular hair colour, girth, and height as well as an attempt to overcome discrimination against those less fortunately endowed. In short, the abstraction 'person,' or subject of rights, is conceptually tied to the hierarchical forms from which it abstracts its egalitarian person.

We abstract race, sex, and social background from our concept of a person and assert that all persons have a right to run for public office precisely because we recognize that race, sex, and class are barriers to running, and winning the race, for public office. Our glorious respect for persons is, as Hegel noted, connected with a contempt for persons. Further, our lack of respect of persons, in Hobbes' and Spinoza's sense, maintains a respect of persons, in the sense of personalities and personages. In Marxian categories, the moral-legal person is an egalitarian superstructure built upon an inegalitarian socio-economic foundation. The formal equality contained in our idea of rights and persons corresponds to the fundamental inequality of life chances for individuals in different social classes.

This tension between equality and inequality at the heart of the notion of rights and persons is related to the Lockian or proprietary conception of rights and persons. All individuals have an absolute property in their persons, unless their person is forfeit from crime. They all have rights, that is, they are all recognized as proprietors, even if they have no property except in their person. All persons are equally proprietors while large inequalities of property emerge precisely from the postulate of absolute proprietorship of one's person (which allows the purchase of labour and hence the expansion of holdings). Proprietorship of one's person produces both equality and inequality, or formal equality and substantial inequality.

If the personalization of right into rights tends to produce both equality and inequality, the emergence of personal rights engenders other contradictory qualities. The personalization of right into rights may well have accentuated both sensitivity and insensitivity to the concerns of others. Simone Weil, the most original of twentieth-century philosophers of rights, thought the personalization of justice into rights gives birth to a hardness of heart. 'If you say to someone who has ears to hear: "What you are doing to me is not just," you may touch and awaken at its source the spirit of attention and love. But it is not the same with words like "I have the right ..." or "you have no right to ..." They evoke a latent war and awaken the spirit of contention. To place the notion of rights at the centre of social conflicts is to inhibit any possible impulse of charity on both sides.'[10] For Weil, the assertion of personal rights rather than impersonal right is likely to produce contention and intransigence, culminating in the rule of force or injustice. 'Rights are always asserted in a tone of contention; and where this tone is adopted, it must rely upon force in the background, or else it will be laughed at.'[11] Rights are allied to power, as obligations are linked to love. We make claims *against* others; we have obligations *to* others.

In contrast to Weil, John Finnis thinks that the personalization of rights engenders sensitivity or imaginative sympathy with respect to the life-situation of others. Finnis says that the language of rights is used to express 'a relationship of justice from the point of view of the person(s) who benefit(s) from that relationship.'[12] The proliferation of rights-discourse invites individuals to see the world from the perspective of the persons claiming their rights, while at the same time hardening the heart of those who refuse to consider the well-being of others. Perhaps the personalization of right into rights engenders both the individual who looks first to 'number one' regardless of everyone else as well as the individual who cares for the underdog, tolerates those who think and live differently from oneself, and respects the legitimacy of interests antithetical to one's own. Finnis is surely correct that the great strength of rights-discourse is the encouragement it gives (relative to pre-modern notions of impersonal justice) to considering the viewpoints of others, the different situations of persons, and the perspectives of justice born from the various lots in life.

However, Finnis want to eat his cake and have it too; Thomistic justice is subjected to the perspectivalism of rights-discourse without the relativism of most modern rights-advocates. He insists that the personalization of *the* right (into *my* rights, *your* rights, *her* rights, *our* rights, *their* rights) is not the relativization of right. Finnis argues for absolute rights, not subject to trade, bargaining, or compromise, against the contemporary tendency to understand rights as alienable properties, or the stuff of trade-offs and bargains.[13] However, in asserting that rights are absolute, unconditioned, and unconditional, Finnis uproots *rights* from the entire context of significations the word has had in the last four hundred years. The language of rights for Finnis is a manner of describing a Thomistic 'common good.'[14] Finnis knows that most rights-advocates are sceptical about a common good binding rights-bearing persons within a moral community, and that most rights-advocates conceive rights and goods (or 'values') as conceptually distinct, and potentially in conflict with one another ('the right versus the good'). Finnis' view that individual rights and 'the common good' cannot conflict with one another is aberrant to say the least. What gives Finnis' *Natural Law and Human Rights* greater stature than most books on rights is that he recognizes the enormous gulf between the Thomism he espouses and modern rights-discourse, while ignoring it at the same time.

Finnis asserts that the shift in perspective from Thomistic natural law to Suarez' and Grotius' conception of a right as a possession 'could be so drastic as to carry the right-holder, and his right, altogether outside the juridical relationship which is fixed by law ...'[15] Finnis observes that Hobbes drew the logical conclusion from developing Suarez' and Grotius' concept of a right: 'Pushed as far as Hobbes's purposes, this contrast between law and rights deprives the notion of rights of virually all normative significance.'[16] Rather than accepting the argument advanced in *Shylock's Rights*, Finnis is compelled to deny the distinction between law and rights, a distinction that is not unique to Hobbesian theory but is embedded in common English usage.

If Hobbes' distinction between law and rights is unacceptable, Finnis also objects to Locke's and Pufendorf's understanding of a right as 'paradigmatically a liberty' and to 'their successors ... who today defend the "choice" theory of rights ... And even those who defend the "benefit" theory of rights are far from using the idiom of Aquinas, since (in common with ordinary language-speakers and lawyers in all modern languages) they speak of a "right" as something beneficial which a person *has* ..., rather than "that which is just in a given situation" ...'[17] In short, Finnis admits that everyone other than himself understands rights to be distinct from classical natural law. Only by using a private language can Finnis exclude the right to do wrong, inherent in the understanding of rights as possessions or options. Finnis asserts that rights-discourse is more 'supple' and perspectival than natural law but denies that rights are relative to the bargains that rights-bearing persons make in particular situations with one another.

The absolute rights Finnis defends exclude private property, and if one takes Finnis' argument rigorously, exclude capitalism as well. Since property must be used for the common benefit, 'the owner has, in justice, duties not altogether unlike those of a trustee in English law.'[18] If the owner does not use his property for the common wealth, the state may rightly redistribute property by means of taxation or expropriation. 'The private owner of a natural resource or capital good has a duty in justice to put it to productive use or, if he lacks the further resources required to do so, to dispose of it to someone willing and able to do so.'[19] Land which is not used for housing or agriculture, the holding or exchange of property 'for the purposes of merely financial gain uncorrelated with any economically productive development or use,' the hoarding of wealth 'and in general the withholding of liquid assets from capital markets in which they might be mobilized for productive use' are subjected to Thomistic prohibitions.[20] We might well ponder how investment decisions necessary to capitalist expansion could be made, compatible with Finnis' rules that limit the rights of proprietors.

Thus Finnis' advocacy of absolute rights, which do not include private property, appears inconsistent with the use others make of the language of rights. Indeed, Finnis makes an interesting observation that makes one wonder if the language of rights is compatible with absolute right. Of 'the equal and inalienable rights of all members of the human family' listed in the Universal Declaration of Human Rights, the rights either take the form 'everyone has the right to ...' or 'no one shall be ...' Finnis asserts that while these formulations are grammatically identical, the 'everyone has the right to' formulation is subject to article 29 (which limits these rights in terms of 'the just requirements of morality, public order and the general welfare in a democratic society'), whereas the 'no one shall be ...' formulation is not so limited. Taboos or prohibitions against torture, slavery, arbitrary imprisonment, and so forth seem more absolute than the permissive 'everyone has the right to' form. In sum, Finnis' absolutism seems to accord more with the forbidding language of law rather than the permissive language of rights. Finnis' most interesting observations run counter to his thesis that absolute justice can be expressed by means of rights-discourse.

Further, although 'everyone has the right to' may be grammatically the same as 'no one shall be,' we tend not to think that prohibitions confer rights. Taboos against incest, for example, are not normally thought to be the source of a child's right not to be sexually assaulted. Such prohibitions or laws seem to be embedded in an absolutist superego. No rights-advocate, however egalitarian, marches under the banner of Equal Repression. Rights seem to be most at home in a flexible ego in the service of the libido. Finnis' use of the language of rights to defend a position of absolute justice uproots that language from its history or context of significations. Only the popularity of the language of rights from the Kremlin to the Vatican can account for the inappropriate employment of personal rights in the service of absolute justice. The perspectival character of rights-discourse entails the relativization of absolute justice. The personalization of right into rights transforms absolute and impersonal justice into a form of justice dependent on the will and viewpoint of persons, on the specific compromises, bargains, and contracts that persons make, based upon their specific situation, the power they have at their disposal, and their needs and aspirations. My argument is not against Finnis' absolutism, but against the appropriateness of rights to express it. Indeed, Finnis virtually admits as much: 'But when we come to explain the requirements of justice ..., then we find that there is a reason for treating the concept of duty, obligation, or requirement as having a more strategic explanatory role than the concept of rights.'[21] Thus Finnis' doctrine tails off in the direction of Weil's teaching that rights are secondary or derivative concepts, inherently incapable of expressing the unconditional requirements of justice.[22] Finnis' attempt to articulate a Thomistic conception of the common good in the language of Lockian rights contradicts the absolutism he professes.

The personalization, privatization, and relativization of right or justice as individual rights derives from Locke's view that rights are personal properties, and persons are themselves properties. Raymond Polin, as we have seen, commends Locke for understanding all natural rights as alienable properties (ignoring, as we have seen, life, liberty, and conscience). Rights are to be understood, according to Richard Wasserstrom, as 'valuable commodities.'[23] Rights as properties have the merit of flexibility; they can be limited in part or entirely suspended, provided that the owner of the right consents to their renunciation. We might compare the flexibility of personal rights with the radical inflexibility of impersonal rights. Note the odd use of the impersonal pronoun in Adam Ferguson's statement that 'men are conscious of their equality, and are tenacious of its rights.'[24] To substitute the personal for the impersonal pronoun would destroy the uncompromising power and Rousseauan savagery of the statement. If Ferguson had stated 'men are conscious of their equality, and are tenacious of their rights,' we might think 'What do they want?' or 'How much to buy them off?'

To understand rights as the properties of persons is to account for the seemingly paradoxical right to do wrong. If one owns something, one may use it as one likes, short of using it to inflict violence on someone else. A right as a personal property does not have to be put to a humane, honourable, noble, charitable, decent, gentle, or liberal use. Since rights are dissociated from morality or *the* right (the natural or moral law), the time has perhaps come to cease using the word 'rights' in unconscious association with 'rightness.'

Hobbes joined Locke in conceiving of rights as personal properties. Hobbes stated that to determine to each 'his proper rights' is to set 'forth rules for all things, whereby we may know what is properly our's, what another man's.'[25] But Hobbes insisted that 'there be no propriety, no dominion, no *mine* and *thine* distinct' in the state of nature.[26] Each has an equal and unlimited claim on the common store nature provides for humanity. 'But that right of all man to all things, is in effect no better than if no men had right to anything. For there is little use and benefit of the right a man hath, when another as strong, or stronger than himself, hath right to the same.'[27] Thus, according to Hobbes, there are, in effect, no natural rights because there are no natural properties.

In Locke's state of nature, an individual's right to acquire property, unlike Hobbes, is not unlimited (at least until the introduction of money). Initially, the accumulation of property is limited by the amount of labouring acquisition an individual can provide himself, by the provision that one must not let property waste or rot, and by the stipulation that 'enough, and as good' be left for others (or else one's right will be questioned by others). Locke painted the charming portrait of rational and industrious proprietors, eschewing waste and unjust greed, cutting down the primal forest and creating, from the God-forsaken wild and waste, cultivated and smiling fields of golden wheat. All individuals benefit from progress, from the enlargement of holdings and the rational exploitation of natural and human resources.

In marked contrast to Locke's account of the genesis of property rights in England, Hobbes stated that virtually all property in land in England derived from Crown grants, conditional on military service, given to the king's favourites, after the Norman conquest. In contrast to Locke's rational and industrious proprietors who cleared and cultivated the land, Hobbes' proprietors of land 'afforested it for their recreation.'[28]

Locke was clear that conquest yields no right over the land of the conquered, and thus any land grants given by the conqueror to his military commanders are illegitimate. But if the government subsequently desires to 'take away all, or part of the land from the Heirs of one' who had received a crown grant, 'then all free and voluntary *Contracts* cease, and are void, in the World.'[29] The point is not that Locke thought that the receiver of stolen property, who knows its source in conquest, has a legitimate title to the property which Locke denied to the thief or conqueror. Rather the significant point is that Locke tacitly admitted all proprietary claims, or 'all free and voluntary Contracts' based upon property titles, have their origin in conquest. Such a view would seem to undercut the peaceful and law-abiding state of nature where Locke found his natural rights or properties. Subsequent political thinkers, not wishing to abandon rights as properties, or the right personalized into properties, looked to history rather than nature as the source of rights.

Hume: the philosopher who put Tory fat on Lockian bones

CHAPTER SEVEN

The Historicization of Right as Civil Rights: Old Property, New Money, and Potential Wealth in One's Person

CLASS PERSPECTIVES ON HISTORY

Eighteenth-century Britain experienced a flourishing of the commercial revolution and the emergence of a historical consciousness. From the 1690s, and the birth of the Bank of England, national debt, public credit, joint stock companies such as the East India and South Sea companies, government contracts in munitions and supplies, new opportunities for profitable investments arose to compete with the customary practice of reinvesting one's surplus in land. 'All this was a far cry from the days, still within the memories of those living in 1700, when land had been virtually the sole, and certainly the best, investment for a man with surplus income.'[1]

The historical consciousness in this century of triumphant Whiggery arose, it shall be argued in this chapter, from the opposition between old and new wealth, between the landed and the moneyed interest, flourished in an uneasy alliance between the landed and moneyed interests, and culminated, following the French revolution, in the awareness of the dominance of new wealth over old property, and in the emergence of labour as a new historical force. Locke, Mandeville, and Hume did not think labour had a significant political effect, except on the occasion of a temporary disturbance occasioned by extreme dearth, but, by the 1760s and 1770s, Ferguson and Smith recognized that labourers were significant participants not only in the national economy but also in the national polity. By the 1790s, in the aftermath of the American rebellion, the Gordon riots, and the French revolution, the debates between Burke and Paine (and other 'friends of labour') manifested not only the recognition of labour's interest but also the possibility of labour effectively pursuing that interest.

The following interpretation of eighteenth-century British political thought will seem overly schematic, a Procrustean attempt to impose the categories of Lockian doctrine on subsequent thought. This chapter is *an* interpretation of eighteenth-century rights-doctrine, not *the* interpretation of all social, political, and historical analysis in the century. The argument advanced is that the emerging historical consciousness is experienced in three ways, corresponding to Smith's three classes, landowners, capitalists, and workers, but is contained within essentially ahistorical Lockian categories of natural rights.

The landed perspective experiences history as heritage, including Bolingbroke's and Swift's nostalgia for the good old (pre-commercial) days, the popular Whig view of an ancient constitution (a hypothetical history from which partisans laid claim to purported evidence for 'historical' rather than natural rights against the government), and, in conceptual form, in Hume's and Burke's awareness of the present as rooted in, and deriving nourishment from, the past. Hume, Ferguson, Smith, and Burke all accepted, despite their reservations about the idea of a social contract founded on consent, Locke's doctrine that the inheritance of property constitutes tacit consent to the social and political arrangements of one's forbears. One generation is thus bound to another within a historical tradition, understood as a transmission of inheritances.

Money, however, acts as a solvent of tradition. Capital experiences

137 The Historicization of Right

history not as the preservation of custom but as the expansion of customers, not as a heritage from the past but as an awareness of progression or temporal accumulation. The perspective of capital is manifest in Mandeville's tongue-in-cheek lament for the decline of Christian or pre-commercial virtues,[2] and Hume's championship of contemporary manners over ancient virtues, a position later espoused by Smith and Ferguson, despite their concern about the diminution of men by the division of labour and the decline of military virtues in a commercial age. From Hume to Burke, a Whiggish tinge coloured the most sceptical of the 'new' Whiggery; no trace of Swift's account of the decline from ancient Brobdignagians to modern Lilliputians can be found in Hume, and in Burke only at his most rhetorical. Thus, from the time of Walpole's ascendancy, even those most favourable to the landed interest and most alert to the lack of historical credentials of the contractualism of new money were friendly to commercial expansion and to the notion of historical progress. Locke's fantastic notion that the use of money depends upon universal agreement[3] and thus that a commercial society is founded upon consent or a social compact was not denounced as non-empirical speculation in the 'sceptical' age of empiricism, enlightenment, and historical sociology. Locke's view that consent to the use of money facilitated vast inequalities in possessions was accepted[4] but also, and more enthusiastically, his view that no one is harmed by increasing inequality because the poorest labourer in a commercial society is materially better off than the richest potentate in a primitive society.[5] Based on credit or belief in the future, the perspective of capital is forward-looking, looking backward only to reassure itself of the distance it has travelled. This schema of the landed perspective of history as heritage and the capitalist perspective of history as accumulation only loosely conforms to the Country-Court, and even more faintly to the Tory-Whig dichotomy of the eighteenth century. These ideal-typical perspectives of land and capital were mixed in various degrees in actual individuals, parties, and thinkers of the eighteenth century.

The perspective of labour does not recognize history as the bearer of heritage or progress but as something to be created. History, as the future to be created, does not arise from the heritage of past achievements or the experience of present progress. Unlike the landed perspective, labour does not look to the past as a repository of experience, of precedents, of the tried and true. The empiricism of the landed perspective contrasts with the experimentalism of labour's perspective. Like capital, labour looks to the past for negative, rather than positive, standards. The past, for Thomas Paine and Mary Wollstonecraft, constitutes a legacy of force and superstition, something to be overcome in the new world to be created. The basis of labour's perspective is the Lockian view that one has a property in one's person, coupled to the un-Lockian view that hitherto labourers have not received full value for their property.

Adam Smith, in the course of an argument against apprenticeships for young labourers, wrote: 'The property which every man has in his own labour, as it is the most original foundation of all other property, so it is the most sacred and inviolable.'[6] Smith's radical followers, such as Paine, Thomas Cooper, and John Thelwall, developed the Lockian doctrine that all individuals have a property in their person, together with the Lockian views that government exists to protect (internal as well as external) property and that taxation without representation is theft.[7] They concluded that all individuals have a right to elect parliamentary representatives and suggested that democratic suffrage will enable those with property only in their person to get full value for their property. Following the curious application of the adjective 'sacred' to rights by the celebrated free-thinkers David Hume and Adam Smith, Thomas Paine asserted: 'Personal rights, of which the right of voting for representatives is one, are a species of property of the most sacred kind ...'[8] Paine developed this conceptual linkage between property, sanctity, and rights as follows: 'The protection of a man's person is more sacred than the protection of property; and besides this, the faculty of performing any kind of work or services by which he acquires a livelihood, or maintaining his family, is of the nature of property. It is property to him; he has acquired it; and it is as much the object of his protection as exterior property, possessed without that faculty, can be the object of protection in another person.'⁹ While Paine's *The Rights of Man* envisioned a welfare state which secures or protects the inner property of one's person, Paine was more a rebel than a revolutionary. That is, in Lockian categories, Paine advocated the dissolution (and overthrow) of government, not of society. Similar to Locke, Paine thought society was based on property right, and rebellion is to restore the lost rights upon which social cohesion is based. Paine, no more than Locke, aimed for a revolutionary overthrow of society, that is, of property right.

Paine followed Locke in deriving rights from nature rather than history. Paine was emphatic that rights can neither be created nor destroyed. 'Time with respect to principles is an eternal *Now*: it has no operation upon them: it changes nothing of their nature and qualities.'¹⁰ Rights do not emerge or evolve in time. 'If it had not a right to begin, it has not the right to continue.'¹¹ Thus, the perspective of labour in the eighteenth century lacked the revolutionary historicism of Marxism. While looking to the future and scorning past experience (except perhaps some hypothetical distant past, comparable to the old Whigs 'ancient constitution'), labour rebels did not wish to cut the links to the present in revolutionary experimentation. They did not see themselves as creating a new and higher order of rights but as restoring natural rights which had been lost or stolen in the course of history.

Marxian history as world creation entails the historicizing of natural rights. Paradoxically, the reactionary Burke came closer to a Marxian position on rights than any of the eighteenth-century labour radicals. Reacting against the democratic perspective of labour, Burke advanced a more thoroughly historicist position on rights than his predecessors in the Scottish enlightenment and his leading antagonist, Thomas Paine. Burke wrote: 'All titles terminate in prescription; in which (differently from time in the fabulous instances) the son eats the father, and the last prescription eats up the former.'¹² Chronos devours Lockian natural rights which re-emerge historicized in Burke as civil rights. The historical dimension of Burke's thought arose both from class conflict or social turbulence as well as from inner turbulence or 'personal' conflict.

Burke's persona was that of the noble Christian Antonio fulminating against 'the Jew brokers,' the agents behind the scene of the French revolution.[13] But, as Hobbes pointed out, one's person is a façade, a mask or a disguise. Under the mask was the character of Shylock. All of Shylock's principles were maintained despite Burke's lofty anti-Semitism. The historicist Burke was Shylock acting as Antonio.

LOCKE'S ASPIRATION TO WED LAND AND MONEY

Our account of eighteenth-century rights-discourse begins with the commercial revolution of the 1690s. John Locke was one of the first shareholders of the Bank of England, founded in 1694, to facilitate loans to the government for its increased military expenditures in European warfare. Parliament, rather than the Crown, stood security for the national debt. The Bank of England and the new government annuities represented profitable investment alternatives to land (in addition to the new joint stock companies). While the Bank of England paid 8 per cent interest to investors, a levy of 20 per cent of rents was levied on land to pay for the debts arising from the War of the Spanish Succession. That is, investors were betting that parliament could ensure the collection of taxes (primarily from land) to pay the interest on their investment.

Tories, such as Jonathan Swift and Lord Bolingbroke, thought the Glorious Revolution had 'mingled us too much in the affairs of the Continent,' had despoiled the landed interest by war debts that did not even serve the purpose of increasing trade, and had made parliament into a vassal of the new moneyed interest.[14] Lord Bolingbroke wrote to Lord Orrery in 1709: 'A new interest has been created out of their fortunes, and a sort of property which was not known twenty years ago is now increased to be almost equal to the terra firma of our island.'[15] Country Whigs, such as Robert Molesworth, thought that 'every merchant, banker, or other monied man, who is ambitious of serving his country as a senator, should have also a competent, visible land estate, as a pledge to his electors that he intends to abide with them, and has the same interest with theirs in the public taxes, gains and losses.'[16] Under the Tory government of Robert Harley, Molesworth's desire became law. Potential conflict (and ultimate reconciliation) between the landed and moneyed interest could be understood in terms of the Lockian principle that property title includes a right to consent to the payment of taxes, if not of each individual, at least of parliamentary representatives whose interest is similar to the proprietor's. As Locke said, with respect to the burden of taxation, 'The Merchant (do what you can), will not bear it, the labourer cannot, and therefore the landholder must. ...'[17] Lockian justice seems to demand that the landed gentry should have a monopoly in parliament. 'Struggle and contrive as you will, lay your taxes as you please, the traders will shift it off from their gain; the merchants will bear the least of it, and grow poor last.'[18]

After Locke's lifetime, when the excise (or tax on items of popular consumption) replaced the land tax as the chief source of government revenues, the Lockian view that landowners were the ultimate source of government revenues was still prevalent at mid-century.[19] The potential conflict between the landed and moneyed interest was attenuated by barring the non-landed classes from parliament. This conciliation of conflicting proprietary claimants was a condition of property right being accepted as natural and universal, rather than historically specific.

Besides his participation in the main engine of the commercial revolution, Locke, two years after the founding of the Bank of England, assisted Isaac Newton in the Great Recoinage. Coins in England had circulated with roughly 20 per cent of the silver clipped off. Locke's view, which prevailed in the recoinage, was that coins should be restored to the nominal weights fixed in Elizabeth's reign. Locke's chief opponent, William Lowndes, wished to fix the shilling at 80 per cent of the value of silver (to take into account the 20 per cent clipped off and to maintain the amount of coin in circulation). Locke refused to recognize that silver could have a different value as coin and as bullion. Joyce Appelby writes: 'Locke's errors were obvious to the dozen or more writers who rushed into print to challenge the great philosopher.'[20] The effect of the recoinage was, as Locke's critics anticipated, a marked reduction of the coin in circulation, with much of the newly minted silver melted and exported as bullion, and thus a drastic deflation. The immediate victims of the recoinage were the banks, all of which, except the Bank of England and the Bank of Scotland, collapsed.[21] The shortage of coin enabled the Bank of England to introduce paper notes as a circulating medium. Having survived the recoinage, the Bank of England's stock doubled in 1697.[22] If the errors of 'the great philosopher' were obvious, the errors of the stockholder of the Bank of England were less palpable.

The drastic deflation, and depression of trade, consequent upon the recoinage, 'pressed particularly hard on the poor' and rewarded only 'the payers of direct taxes and the king's creditors.'[23] Thus, not only the landlords, who received their rents in the recoined money and who bore much of the tax burden, prospered but also the financiers who received, beyond the stipulated interest, a repayment of recoined money for the old money they had loaned. Locke's *Some Considerations of the Lowering of Interest and Raising the Value of Money* suggests that he was not altogether blind to the consequences of the recoinage, and may even have anticipated them within a grand design of harmonizing the conflicting landed and moneyed interests. Locke asserted that the landholder's interest is the chief care and the 'settled, unmoveable concernment in the commonwealth.'[24] If, as Locke thought, the interest of the nation is identical with the interest of the landowning class, then the recoinage was a boon to the nation. 'An infallible sign of your decay of wealth is the falling of rents, and the raising of them would be worth the nation's care: for in that, and not in the falling of interest, lies the true advantage of the landed man, and with him of the public.'[25] Endebted landowners might profit by a legislated maximum interest rate of 4 per cent. 'But I hope we may yet think that men in England, who have land, have money too; and that landed men, as well as others, by their providence and good husbandry, accommodating their expenses to their income, keep themselves from going backwards in the world.'[26]

Thus Locke provided the theoretical basis for the fusion of the landed and moneyed interests which constituted the Whig hegemony. During the eighteenth century, land required increasing capital to make it competitively productive. Locke's pious wish that those 'who have land, have money too' overlooked the small landowners (without Locke's aristocratic connections and sources of income). But the landowners who were not beggared by taxes and capital expenditures increasingly had 'money too' to invest in government annuities and stock companies. The surplus reaped in the cities could be ploughed back into a more capital-intensive countryside. Locke's recoinage, and advocacy of non-legislated rates of interest, enabled men to profit by the commercial revolution and 'keep themselves from going backwards in the world.' The Tory jeremiads of Swift and Bolingbroke might represent the unsuccessful landowners at the beginning of the eighteenth century, but Lockian vistas of a golden capitalist agriculture blocked a wholesale revolt of old land against new money. The natural right of property (as distinct from specific historical claims of specific classes) is predicated on a natural harmony of interests between the classes of civil society.

Class conflict, for Locke, is destructive; it places property right in jeopardy and is both cause and effect of the deterioration of national wealth. While Locke recognized conflict between the landed and moneyed classes,[27] he endeavoured to show that conflict was based upon apparent, rather than real, differences of interest. Locke's economic proposals can be understood as an effort to harmonize old property and new wealth.

Locke's economic arguments are to be assessed within the context of his broader policies about government and society. For example, Joyce Appelby wonders why Locke's argument for the immutability of silver as a commercial measure and medium satisfied his contemporaries when his economic reasoning was widely seen to be clearly wrong. Appelby suggests that 'Locke's denial of the intrinsic value of coin carried with it a limitation of government in economic affairs.'[28] That is, Locke's views on money satisfied his contemporaries in that they accord with the natural rights to property. Property right is not, as with Hobbes, in the hands of the mighty Leviathan. Locke's argument implies that 'the command over the goods, labor, and land of the nation had passed into private hands at the same time that money transformed into entrepreneurial capital provided the direction and scope for social change.'[29]

Locke's mercantilist principles were midway between the Hobbesian view of the sovereign, as the source of property and of the principles of just distribution, and Adam Smith's laissez-faire principles. While 'the system of natural liberty' or laissez-faire seems to flow from Lockian principles, Smith's principles of free competition were only practised (in part) in the nineteenth century, when Britain had a clear competitive edge, even virtual monopoly position, in relation to her competitors. Appelby notes that Locke 'replaced the invisible hand of the market with the official hand of mercantile regulation.'[30] In short, the visible hands of the stockholder of the Bank of England and the commissioner of the Board of Trade helped to shape the market in favour of rural and urban employers of labour.

PHILOSOPHY AS BIPARTISAN IDEOLOGY

Hume carried on Locke's grand aim of uniting landed and commercial interests, although by the 1740s little effort was necessary to consolidate these interests. Scholars have remarked on the gulf separating seventeenth-century rationalism from eighteenth-century empiricism (as if Locke's political economy were not a thoughtful abridgment of British experience and as if Hume, and his followers in the Scottish enlightenment, had emancipated themselves from speculative principles, and had comprehended the modes of social organization in completely empirical terms). The historical dimension of Scottish thought, I shall argue, arises not so much from a rejection of Hobbesian and Lockian rationalism but from a vacillation between Hobbesian and Lockian principles on property, consent, contract, liberty, and rights. That is, Hume, Ferguson, and Smith accepted the Hobbesian view that property right could not be prior to, but must be a consequence of, civil government. However, they fiercely rejected Hobbes' corollary that proprietary entitlements derive from the sovereign. Hume, Ferguson, and Smith accepted Locke's basic teaching on property but with the proviso that property right is not natural but historical in origin. Hume writes that 'all questions of property are subordinate to authority of civil laws, which extend, restrain, modify, and alter the rules of natural justice, according to the particular *convenience* of each community.'[31] Ferguson and Smith distinguished the 'natural' or 'original' right to life and liberty from the 'artificial,' 'adventitious,' or 'acquired' right of property and command.[32]

We might note the tension between nature and history with respect to rights. The tension might have been eased had the enlightened Scots assimilated natural rights to historical properties, but they did not do so. To be sure, for Hume, 'all right is derived from the convention to establish property,'[33] but the changing rules or conventions defining property are not recognized to constitute the substance of rights. Duncan Forbes refers to Hume's 'economic orientation' where 'property and rights are thought of solely in economic terms.'[34] While this economic reductionism may be deprecated, we may note that rights are not reduced to properties. That the Scottish historical school did not historicize right stems from the non-assimilation of right to property. Rights remain natural while properties are historical.

John Dunn asserts that there is a fundamental break between Locke's 'theocentricism' and the 'practical atheism' of the Scottish enlightenment, between the applied theology of the English rationalist and the social analysis of the Scottish empiricists.[35] Dunn is right to assert that, for the North Britons as for Locke, 'Obligation, property and right in human society all depend upon the stability of possessions. All of them are natural in the sense that they are made necessary by the intrinsic characteristics of human beings.'[36] But the 'practical atheism' of the proponents of 'the Invisible Hand' did not impede them from referring to natural rights not only as 'absolute'[37] and 'inalienable'[38] but also as 'sacred.'[39] If the gulf between Locke and Hume were as large as Dunn pretends, the atheist Hume could not have called the 'theocentrist' Locke 'really a great Philosopher, and a just and modest Reasoner.'[40]

In the writings of David Hume, we encounter a philosopher,

namely, someone of the 'skepsis' or penetration of Hobbes, someone who illuminates a world (not just a region) of experience. But we do not encounter political philosophy in Hume as in Hobbes. As with Locke, Hume's politics have no demonstrable relationship to his philosophy. The possibility of developing a philosophy of rights beyond Hobbes (as Hegel did by synthesizing historical content – what Hegel calls 'Sittlichkeit' and which appears in Hume and Burke as manners – and the ahistorical form of Hobbesian rights and duties) was not actualized.

The central propositions of Hume's philosophy were not applied to his political doctrine, and specifically his teaching on rights. Hume's scepticism about personal identity, or about a subject subsisting throughout changing experiences, is nowhere evident in his account of rights. The subject of rights, namely, the person, is not subjected to critical scrutiny in Hume's political doctrine as in Hobbes' political philosophy. Hume's seminal philosophy about the difference between facts and values, or 'is' statements and 'ought' statements,[41] is conspicuously absent in his rights-doctrine. One cannot be sure whether rights are, for Hume, matters of right or of fact. Although his political teaching seems to be positivistic, emphasizing that rights refer to an empirical world of precedent, tradition, custom, and legal convention, Hume never reduced rights to rites. Rights have only one foot in the realm of fact, or what is, but have the other in the realm of right, or what ought to be. Hume writes that, whether necessary or not, the Glorious Revolution confirmed 'all the rights and privileges, which ought to be sacred to a free nation ...'[42] Or Magna Carta provides 'for the equal distribution of justice and the free enjoyment of property; the great objects for which political society was first founded by men, which men have a perpetual and unalienable right to recall, and which not time, nor precedent, nor statute, nor positive institution, ought to deter them from keeping ever uppermost in their thoughts and attentions.'[43] Doubtless the rights-moralism was designed to appeal to Lockian prejudices of the day, but there is not indication that Hume did not share them. However, not even the most charitable interpreter could assert that Hume's mixture of 'is' propostions and 'ought' propositions in his rights-discourse constitutes a bridge between the 'is' and the 'ought.' Rather, what Hume, as a philosopher, found problematic, Hume, as a professor of doctrine, found self-evident.

Further, Hume's philosophic inquiry into causality did not impede him from identifying property as 'a species of *causation*' in that it 'has the greatest influence' on the passions of pride and humility and has the power to procure men benefits.[44] Hume's scepticism about natural laws centred on the proposition that apparently necessary connections between phenomena are no more than the effects of custom. 'All our reasonings concerning causes and effects are deriv'd from nothing but custom; and that belief is more properly an act of the sensitive, than of the cognitive part of our natures.'[45] Yet Hume could not replace Lockian natural (or rational) rights with customary rights or historically changing assessments of utility because property right is, Hume repeatedly assured us, 'absolutely necessary to human society.'[46]

Although the influence of custom is present in Hume's political doctrine, Hume presented custom in less than the radical manner suggested by his philosophy. Custom, which can 'convert pleasure into pain, and pain into pleasure,'[47] lacks the potency to transform human nature (which in Humian doctrine is invariant). Hume's radical denial of 'eternal rational measures of right and wrong'[48] is muted by his insistence that 'the mind of man is so formed by nature, that, upon the appearance of certain characters, dispositions, and actions, it immediately feels the sentiment of approbation or blame ...'[49] My purpose here is not to write a list of the contradictions between Hume's philosophy and his politics but to justify my interpretation of the philosopher Hume as a Lockian Tory, a professor of commercial doctrine from the perspective of the landed interest. That is, Hume's reflections on custom, habit, and tradition, as they relate to rights, will not be considered as philosophy but as the viewpoint of a spokesman for landed gentry who have overcome Swift's and Bolingbroke's abhorrence for commerce.

Hume's acceptance of Lockian doctrine was tempered by a Hobbesian fear of civil war. Civil war is, for Hume and later for Smith, the 'summum malum.'[50] Hume's reservations about Lockian contractual doctrine appear to arise from a Hobbesian apprehension about civil war. Hume wrote: 'We find, that magistrates are so far from deriving their authority, and the obligation to obedience in their subjects, from the foundation of a promise or original contract, that they conceal, as far as possible, from their people, especially from the vulgar, that they have their origin from thence.'[51]

Curiously enough, Hume accepted virtually all the principles of the contractual theorists he criticized. Hume asserted that 'it cannot be denied, that government is, at first, founded on a contract ...'[52] Because of natural equality amongst men, 'nothing but their own consent could, at first, associate them together, and subject them to any authority.'[53] Hume thought Locke went too far in thinking 'that, even at present, when it has reached its full maturity,' authority 'rests on no other foundation' than consent.[54] If only consensual governments are legitimate, 'this supposes the consent of the fathers to bind the children, even to the most remote generations ...'[55] Indeed a tacit promise 'is the most that can be pretended' as a basis for legitimate government.[56] Indeed, for Locke, the enjoyment of inherited property constitutes tacit consent of the son to the form of government to which the father was obliged. Property right is the basis of tradition, of continuity between generations, of the legitimate transmission of one form of government to the subsequent generation. Like Locke, Hume thought inheritance a natural right.[57]

However, Hume thought that tacit consent is appropriate only when 'a man imagines, that the matter depends on his choice.'[58] Immigrants may choose allegiance to a new country, but most cling to old habits and habitats. The poor, especially, lack the money, language, or skills to emigrate. Thus, merely to inhabit a territory cannot properly be said to constitute tacit consent to obey the government. The poor in particular, lacking the utilitarian motives for law and order of the wealthy, need another principle of obedience than the Whig principles of consent and utility.[59] The Tory principle is authority or reverence for antiquity. 'Antiquity always begets the opinion of right.'[60] Legitimacy, for Hume, derives either from consent or from 'long possession.' 'Time and custom

149 The Historicization of Right

give authority to all forms of government, and all successions of princes; and that power, which at first was founded only on injustice and violence, becomes in time legal and obligatory.'[61] Governments in the long run depend upon opinion and not force, upon authority not power. Initially all governments were 'founded on usurpation and rebellion, and whose title is not at first worse than doubtful and uncertain. Time alone gives solidity to their right; and operating gradually on the minds of men, reconciles them to any authority, and makes it seem just and reasonable.'[62]

Hume's doctrine is that men obey governments more from habit and interest than from a duty born of a promise or an act of consent. But does habit or interest generate right? Is Hume not merging empirical description – that men defer most often and most easily to an old title – with moral prescription? Hume never said that habits, customs, and ancestral titles are always right. He would probably agree with Adam Ferguson that long-standing, habitual, and repeated governmental oppression produces no legitimacy, authority, or right to govern. Indeed, Hume seems to fall back on consent as *the* principle of legitimation. 'My intention here is not to exclude the consent of the people from being one just foundation of government where it has place. It is surely the best and most sacred of any.'[63] Even when men habitually obey without any thought that they have promised to obey, 'they willingly consent, because they think, that, from long possession, he has acquired a title, independently of their choice or inclination.'[64] Thus the claim, initially usurped by violence and fraud, becomes a right, in the course of time, only when people authorize it, recognize it, or 'willingly consent' to it.

Hume took issue with Locke's views that absolute government is necessarily illegitimate in so far as it does not depend on the consent of the governed and that taxation requires the consent of elected representatives. Hume conceded that rebellion against absolute government 'is just, tho' the principles be erroneous.'[65] Although rebellion is usually disastrous, the people retain an inalienable right of resistance to injustice.[66] The popular right of rebellion, for Hume, is not based on a breach of contract, but in situations of extreme insecurity, on a utilitarian calculation of the prospects of success.[67] Hume's position, seemingly midway between Hobbes and Locke, is to 'draw the bond of allegiance very close, and consider an infringement of it, as the last refuge in desperate cases, where the public is in the highest danger, from violence and tyranny.'[68]

Hume disagreed with Locke that taxation requires the consent of taxpayers' elected representatives because, unlike Locke, Hume recognized that taxes do not fall solely on land. Since Locke's death, the chief source of government revenues derived from the excise rather than the land tax. Nevertheless, since excises on manufactured goods, such as beer and candles, were passed on to consumers, rather than being borne by the manufacturers, many persons continued to think that taxation indirectly fell on landowners. Hume thought that the opinion that all taxes fall on land is false, but would be a useful fiction 'by checking the landed gentlemen, in whose hands our legislature is chiefly lodged, and making them preserve great regard for trade and industry.'[69] But Hume certainly did not want to limit the monopoly of landed gentlemen in parliament, as it was the only way to offset court corruption, Whig placement, government contracts, speculative stock-jobbing, and financial profiteering on the national debt. The growth of public debt to finance foreign wars corresponded to the growth of a large standing army (that is, a potential danger to citizens' liberties). Moreover, public debt benefited London financiers at the expense of the rest of the nation.[70] Public debt, and the consequent high level of taxation, forced landowners to oppress tenants and labourers, and made a country militia impotent to stand up to a despotic and corrupt court party, living off the fat of government annuities and contracts, and policed by a standing army. In an uncharacteristically immoderate manner, Hume asserted that 'either the nation must destroy public credit, or public credit will destroy the nation.'[71] Even with the control of both houses of parliament by the landed interest, the connection of government members with the commercial corporations was, for Hume, a serious source of concern.[72] Thus, although a warm friend to commercial interests and an advocate of a taxation policy favourable to commerce and industry, Hume recognized that landowners do not bear the sole tax burden but should be the only class represented in parliament. If Locke's principle of no taxation without representation were admitted, then the franchise would have to be extended. However, Hume's description of the English electors – less than 10 per cent of the population – as 'an undistinguishing rabble' and his suggestion that the franchise should be restricted to those with an estate worth 200 pounds per annum militate against the notion that taxation is legitimate only with consent.[73]

Hume's doctrine of stability of possession links his principles of property and government. 'Right is of two kinds, right to **POWER** and right to **PROPERTY**.'[74] It is long possession which validates claims to power and to property. Indeed, the temporal dimension might have allowed Hume to reduce all right to property in so far as over time men 'bring the balance of power to coincide with that of property.'[75] In the short run, however, there may be temporary imbalances between political power and proprietary title. Thus rights as powers are conceptually distinct from rights as properties.

For Hume, the laws of nature are man-made, artifice born of natural necessity. Hume elaborated: 'the three fundamental laws of nature, *that of the stability of possession, of its transference by consent*, and *of the performances of promises*. 'Tis on the strict observance of those three laws, that the peace and security of human society entirely depend; nor is there any possibility of establishing a good correspondence among men, where these are neglected. Society is absolutely necessary for the well-being of men; and these are as necessary to the support of society.'[76]

Shylock would doubtless be somewhat bemused by the distinction between Locke and Hume as to the source of natural laws and rights but would doubtless be sustained by the reflection that, whatever their differing premises, he has all party agreement to his commercial principles. Whether they are based on natural necessity or historical custom, individual reason or collective experience, present consent or precedent authority, Shylock's rights, affirmed by the English Whig, are reconfirmed a half-century later by the Scots Tory.

Smith: the source of 'das Adam Smith-Problem':
the moral sentiment of sympathy
versus the economic motive of self-interest

153 The Historicization of Right

COMMERCIAL LIBERTY VERSUS HUMAN EQUALITY

Hume's friend and compatriot Adam Smith, while renowned as a champion of the principles of commercial liberty and the natural harmony of class interests, was, at times, a sharp critic of commercial civilization. With the Scottish highlands, as it were, at his back door and the highlander Ferguson as a colleague, Smith could experience the differences between the commercial lowlands and the pre-commercial highlands. While favouring commercial over pre-commercial principles and practices more consistently than Ferguson, Smith recognized, much more emphatically than Hume, that commercial civilization exacts a price, that the balance sheet drawn up in favour of capitalism has entries in the debit side. On the credit side is increased individual liberty and security and decreased personal dependence and servility. On the debit side is increased material inequality and constricted life skills, born of the very division of labour which generates the wealth and liberty Smith championed.

Smith wrote: 'commerce and manufacturers gradually introduced order and good government, and with them the liberty and security of individuals among the inhabitants of the country, who had before lived almost in a continual state of war with their neighbours, and of servile dependency upon their superiors.'[77] The commercial development of the Scottish lowlands had emancipated Scots commoners from the feuding, feudal, and futile clan systems of the Highlands. Smith generalized this vision of commercial progress into a theory of civilization. But the rosy dawn of commercial development does not enlighten a cloudless sky.

Smith followed Locke in asserting that labour is the source of all exchangeable value. In a rude society, one in which the division of labour is not advanced, 'the whole produce of labour belongs to the labourer ...'[78] However, in a civilized society, one with an extensive division of labour, 'the whole produce of labour does not always belong to the labourer.'[79] In a civilized society, labourers not only support themselves by also the landowners and capitalists. 'As soon as the land of any country has become private property, the landlords, like all other men, love to reap where they never sowed, and demand a rent even for its natural produce.'[80] However, Smith reserved his fire for the large entailed estates of the landed aristocracy rather than attacking private property in land generally.[81] The land of an idle and ignorant aristocracy is not productively employed but wastefully maintains a host of feudal retainers and unproductive servants. With land in the hands of capitalist farmers, skilled in what John Stuart Mill was to call 'the labour of abstinence,' land will be rationally employed, stock accumulated for profitable reinvestment, and general living standards will rise. The profits of capitalist owners of land and factories might be called, Smith says, 'the labour of inspection and direction.'[82] Thus, the appearance of injustice in commercial society – that the labourer does not receive the whole produce of his labour in commercial societies, as he did in primitive societies – was solved by Smith in Lockian fashion; the labour of the body is exchanged for the owners' mental labour at fair market value.

However, workers will only receive fair value for their productive contribution if governments act to block the natural capitalist inclination to engross markets, limit competition, and enact legislation restricting the mobility of labour or the combination of labourers. (Smith favoured the unionization or combination of labourers in so far as capitalists have a combined interest or have favourable access to government.) 'The property which every man has in his own labour, as it is the original foundation of all other property, so it is the most sacred and inviolable.'[83] By 'sacred and inviolable,' the Scotsman meant that labour should be freely vendible; no legislation should impede the labourer from selling himself at the best market price. However, the labourer's interest is 'little heard, and less regarded' while the capitalists 'by their wealth draw to themselves the greatest share of the public consideration.'[84] For Smith, class harmony is an ideal, not an actuality. 'Laws and government may be considered ... in every case, as a combination of the rich to oppress the poor, and preserve to themselves the inequality of goods, which would otherwise be soon destroyed by the attacks of the poor ...'[85]

155 The Historicization of Right

Nevertheless, Smith was far from consistently maintaining a Rousseauan position on the increasing inequality and injustice of a commercial society. In *The Wealth of Nations* and his *Lectures on Justice*, Smith justified the increasing inequalities of commercial civilization in a thoroughly Lockian manner. Despite gross disparity of income in commercial nations, 'a workman, even of the lowest and poorest order, if he is frugal and industrious, may enjoy a greater share of the necessities and conveniences of life than it is possible for any savage to acquire,'[86] even 'an African King, the absolute masters of the lives and liberties of ten thousand naked savages.'[87]

In *The Theory of Moral Sentiments*, Smith outdid Locke by denying that commercial civilization creates any substantial inequalities. The apparent rapacity of the rich is 'led by an invisible hand to make nearly the same distribution of the necessities of life, which would have been made, had the earth been divided into equal portions among all its inhabitants ...'[88] Indeed, in this work famous for the sublimity of its principle of altruistic sympathy in contrast to the Shylockian self-interest of *The Wealth of Nations*, Smith declared that the lower orders have a better go of life than their social betters. 'In ease of body and peace of mind, all the different ranks of life are nearly upon a level, and the beggar, who suns himself by the side of the highway, possesses that security which kings are fighting for.'[89] Beggars, as Smith says, have no right to charity.[90] Even if we have no duty to provide beggars with either sympathy or the means of subsistence, our duty to truth entails that we leave *The Theory of Moral Sentiments* to fertilize lowland cornfields.

An abrupt return to the cleanliness of Shylockian principle is in order. The aim of *The Wealth of Nations* – to emancipate rational self-interest through a competitive market – runs counter to the unenlightened prejudice, which Smith understood to be comparable to religious intolerance,[91] that government should police or regulate a market for subsistence requirements. Laws prohibiting corn dealers from hoarding, raising prices, or exporting grain in a period of scarcity 'were evident violations of natural liberty, and therefore unjust; and they were both, too, as impolitic as they were unjust.'[92] Thus, what Edward Thompson calls moral economy, Smith called impolitic economy. But Smith would not accept the opposition of moral and political economy. For the system of natural liberty is concerned with rights, not simply with utility or wealth. Indeed Smith had a haughty scorn for mere utility. Smith wrote, with respect to the export of grain during a period of scarcity, that 'to hinder ... the farmer from sending his goods at all times to the best market, is evidently to sacrifice the ordinary laws of justice to an idea of public utility, to a sort of reasons of state ...'[93] The rise in the price of grain, consequent upon a free market during a time of scarcity, puts everyone but especially 'the inferior ranks of people, upon thrift and good management.'[94]

Smith's principles of political economy led to diametrically opposed political positions. Edmund Burke developed Smith's principles of natural liberty, while dissociating himself from Smith's view of the natural equality of men. Burke's opponents championed Smith's view of the natural equality of mankind or his theory that human differences are the effect, not the cause, of the division of labour. The radical Smithians did not repudiate the 'system of natural liberty' but elaborated Smith's labour theory of value, his conception of an individual's sacred property in one's person, and his view that taxation entails representation,[95] into a more democratic or egalitarian liberal doctrine. As is evident from the fact that a number of radicals espoused his ideas, Smith cannot be described as an uncritical apologist for capitalism. Smith recognized, as did Ferguson, that a powerful productive collectivity is not composed of capable self-reliant individuals. The division of labour which produces collective power (the wealth of nations) also produces constriction of individuals' capacity and intelligence. The level of skill, intelligence, imagination, judgment, and initiative required of jobs subjected to a capitalist division of labour is less than that required of pre-commercial, even savage, occupations.[96] The mighty Leviathan, composed of a divided labour force united by self-interest and the natural 'propensity to truck, barter and exchange,' dwarfs individuals.[97] The celebrated champion of competitive capitalism anticipated the core of the Marxian critique of that system.

157 The Historicization of Right

FROM NATURAL TO CIVIL RIGHTS

If the historization of right is a radical departure from seventeenth-century rationalism, credit for the advance does not fall to the radical Smithians, such as Thomas Paine, Richard Price, Joseph Priestley, Mary Wollstonecraft, John Thelwall, or Thomas Cooper, but to the conservative Whig Edmund Burke. Burke reacted to the radical interpretatons of natural rights with the assertion that 'men cannot enjoy the rights of an uncivil and of a civil state together.'[98] Adam Smith's distinction between natural rights (to life and liberty, which are prior to government) and property rights (which are acquired with civil government) disappeared and was replaced in Burke's vocabulary by inherited rights, rights which are historically specific, which vary in time and in place, which differ according to class, nationality, and religion.

If eighteenth-century thought began with Shylock's commercial principles enunciated by Locke and Mandeville, it concluded with Burke as Shylock personating Antonio. By presenting Burke as Shylock in the guise of Antonio, I intend to convey what Isaac Kramnick sees to be the tension between aristocratic and bourgeois ideology in Burke's writings,[99] what Leo Strauss and Burleigh Wilkins see as Burke's integration of modern natural rights within a classical or Thomistic framework of natural law,[100] and what Alfred Cobban calls Burke's simultaneous 'culmination of' and 'revolt against' Lockian political doctrine.[101] I also wish to draw attention to the centrality of anti-Judaism to Burke's thought.

Neither Burke's critics nor his champions in the scholarly literature have noted the many anti-Semitic references central to his analysis of the French revolution.[102] Burke's anti-Semitism might be understood as an expression of his defence of the politics of old prejudices against enlightenment principles. However, Burleigh Wilkins claims that Burke was not prejudiced against Jews.[103] The only evidence I can see for Wilkins' claim is Burke's statement contrasting the Jews in France who 'have assignats on ecclesiastical plunder' with the 'very respectable persons of the Jewish nation' resident in London. Burke's uncharacteristic tolerance of some respectable Jews is contained within the following passage:

Burke: the personator of Antonio,
who provided Shylockian principle with a noble lineage

I am told, that the very sons of such Jew-jobbers have been made bishops; persons not to be suspected of any sort of *Christian* superstition, fit colleagues to the holy prelate of Autun, and bred at the feet of that Gamaliel. We know who it was that drove the money-changers out of the temple. We see, too, who it is that brings them in again. We have in London very respectable persons of the Jewish nation, whom we will keep; but we have of the same tribe others of a different description, – house-breakers, and receivers of stolen goods, and forgers of paper currency, more than we can conveniently hang. These we can spare to France, to fill the new episcopal thrones: men well versed in swearing; and who will scruple no oath which the fertile genius of any of your reformers can devise.[104]

We see that Jews are a symbol of both the anticlericalism and the new money ascendant in the French revolution. Even Burke was not so unbalanced as to claim that actual Jews were in reality the historical agents of the French revolution. Burke wrote: 'The monied men, merchants, principal tradesmen, and men of letters ... are the chief actors in the French revolution.'[105] But, as symbols, they condensed the legalism and anticlericalism of enlightenment ideology and the rootless cosmopolitanism of the moneyed interests and professors of natural rights. Curiously enough, Burke's leading opponent, Thomas Paine, characterized Burke's aristocratic biases as Jewish, expressing the degenerate exclusivity of a self-styled nobility.[106] Paine contrasts his principles of 'universal peace, civilization, and commerce' with Burke's Jewish championship of militaristic monarchism.[107] Whether from cosmopolitanism or lack of it, Jews are alien to the world of Christian commerce – that is, to a commercial world that is claimed to be compatible with Christian principles. Burke, disguised as anti-Shylock or as the spiritual Antonio, gives Shylockian principle a lofty foundation. In calling Burke Shylock impersonating Antonio or professing 'the healing voice of Christian charity,'[108] I am crediting Burke with intelligence, in contrast with the thoughtless and painful Jew-hatred of Gratiano.

Burke's *Thoughts and Details on Scarcity* repeats Adam Smith's laissez-faire principles, his detestation of a regulated market in grain and subsidized wages in a period of dearth. There is no need for justices of the peace to oversee commercial contracts in so far as all contracts are based on compromises and common interest. Labour is a commodity the value of which, like any other good, is determined by market demand. There must be no public support for labourers 'in calamitous seasons, under accidental illness, in declining life, and with the pressure of a numerous offspring' because it is 'not the necessity of the vendor, but the necessity of the purchaser that raises the price.'[109] The low price of labour is attributable to a superabundance of labourers. Although the class of rich proprietors 'are the pensioners of the poor,' in 'absolute, hereditary, and indefeasible dependence on those who labour,' governments lack the power to assist the poor in periods of dearth. The rich are so few in number that channelling their consumption to the poor would not alleviate want or misery. The public granaries in Geneva and the papal states ruin agriculture by forcing farmers to sell at fixed prices.[110] Burke called the tendency to tamper with trade in a time of famine an 'ill-founded popular prejudice.'[111] While one might think this popular prejudice has something to do with Christianity (in so far as both the centres of Calvinism and Catholicism maintain an illiberal policing of the grain trade), the arch-Christian Burke assured us that 'the laws of commerce ... are the laws of nature, and consequently the laws of God ...'[112]

Burke did not adopt Mandeville's view that Christian vices become commercial virtues, and vice versa. Rather his piety reflected that of David Hume and Adam Smith. Burke wrote of 'the benign and wise Disposer of all things, who obliges men, whether they will or not, in pursuing their own selfish interests, to connect the general good with their own individual success.'[113] As well as adhering to the principle of natural liberty and self-interest, Burke was a strong adherent of the Christian duty of charity. Nevertheless he belongs in the tradition of rights-discourse because he draws a sharp distinction between justice and charity. Burke wrote:

Whenever it happens that a man can claim nothing according to the rules of commerce, and the principle of justice, he passes out of that department, and comes within the jurisdiction of mercy. In that province the magistrate

161 The Historicization of Right

has nothing at all to do: his interference is a violation of the property which it is his office to protect. Without all doubt, charity to the poor is a direct and obligatory duty upon all Christians ... But the manner, mode, time, choice of objects, and proportion, are left to private discretion ...[114]

That is, the rights of property override the duties of charity. Nevertheless 'the healing voice of Christian charity' presents itself throughout Burke's writing. Burke insisted: 'The body of the people must not find the principles of natural subordination by art rooted out of their minds. They must respect that property of which they cannot partake. They must labour to obtain what by labour can be obtained; and when they find, as they commonly do, the success disproportioned to the endeavour, they must be taught their consolations in the final proportions of eternal justice.'[115] (Shylock's eyes widen. 'So that is what the sanctimonious gentiles go on about. And I thought their other-worldliness naive.') But Burke did not merely offer the labouring poor the consolation of heaven. Spirits, like opium and tobacco, are 'a medicine of the mind.'[116] Those who wish to prohibit distilling grain into spirits during a famine lack Burke's charitable liberality. 'But, if not food, it greatly alleviates the want of it. It invigorates the stomach for the digestion of poor meagre diet, not easily alliable to the human condition.'[117] (Shylock's eyes close again. 'I could not say that. Not even the most fanatical Jew-hater could think I could say that.')

Burke then espoused the principles of Smithian political economy. However, Burke did not follow Smith's attack on the entailed estates of the nobility. Smith dismissed the system of entailed land as follows: 'They are founded upon the most absurd of all suppositions, the supposition that every successive generation of men have not an equal right to the earth, and to all that it possesses; but that the property of the present generation should be restrained and regulated according to the fancy of those who died, perhaps, five hundred years ago.'[118] What Burke saw more clearly than Smith is that a 'moral' stand against entailed land – an argument in terms of right rather than utility – entails the undermining of property title, the right of bequest and of inheritance. If each generation has an equal right to the earth, and is free to make whatever proprietary arrangements it chooses, intergenerational titles to property cannot be permitted. If property right is secure, each generation is 'entailed'; that is, both free to enjoy the rights it inherits from the previous generation and constrained to accept whatever patrimony it receives. In Lockian terms, each generation, in confirming property rights, tacitly consents to the entire system of political and civil rights handed on to it.

Burke asserted that, from Magna Carta to the Declaration of Right (on which the constitutional monarchy of William and Mary was founded), 'it has been the uniform policy of our constitution to claim and assert our liberties, as an *entailed inheritance* derived to us from our forefathers, and to be transmitted to our posterity; as an estate specially belonging to the people of this kingdom, without any reference whatever to any other more general or prior right.'[119] Englishmen, at the time of the Glorious Revolution, wished 'and do now wish, to derive all we possess as *an inheritance from our forefathers*.'[120] Entailed rights include those who inherit, and exclude those who do not. Unequal rights and properties derive from the principle of inheritance. 'The characteristic essence of property, formed out of the combined principles of its acquisition and conservation, is to be *unequal*.'[121] Burke's grand principle of the hierarchy of property is not extended to one's property in one's person; in Burke's view, any five workmen (one good, one bad, and three middling) are worth the same as any other group of five working men.[122]

Old property is the ballast of the ship of state which is staffed by 'its ability, as well as its property.'[123] Burke's writings lack the Lockian tacit identification of property and ability, of justice and equality of opportunity. Indeed Burke stated that 'Jacobinism is the revolt of the enterprising talents of a country against its property.'[124] Burke was clear-sighted enough to distinguish the property from the ability of the nation, when he advocates that both active, forward-looking ability and the cautious experience of property be represented in a state. The state should be understood as a joint stock company. 'In this partnership all men have equal rights, but not to equal things. He that has but five shillings in the partnership, has as good a right to it, as he that has five hundred pound has to his larger proportion. But he has not a right to an equal dividend in the product of the joint stock; and as to the share of power, authority, and direction which each individual ought to have in the management of the state, that I must deny to be amongst the direct original rights of man in civil society.'[125]

Burke later abandoned the analogy of the state to a joint stock company because partnerships 'of mere occasional interest may be dissolved at pleasure' whereas civil society is not based on a contract dissolvable at will. Nor is it 'a partnership in things subservient only to the gross animal existence of a temporary and perishable nature' but a partnership in all excellence. 'As the ends of such a partnership cannot be obtained in many generations, it becomes a partnership not only between those who are living, but between those who are living, those who are dead, and those who are to be born.'[126]

Without representing property as well as ability in a state, society would dissolve into egoistic atomism, 'into an unsocial, uncivil, unconnected chaos of elementary principles.'[127] Property is not just the condition of civility and culture but is the material basis of tradition, of the transmission of the cultural treasures of the past into the present and the future. Those without reverence for the past are uprooted from the source of spiritual nourishment and lack direction for a confident future. Landed property, well rooted in the traditions of a nation, is the repository of a national heritage. 'This nobility forms the chain that connects the ages of a nation, which otherwise (with Mr. Paine) would soon be taught that no one generation can bind another.'[128] The creditors of the Crown, the moneyed interest which grew with the debt of France, despoiled the ancient landed interest of their property. The proprietary claim of the latter 'is prior in time, paramount in title, superior in equity' to the claims of the Crown's creditors.[129] New money is rootless, not conscious of tradition, generational interconnection, stripped naked of all civility, aware only of its egoistic needs and its power.

But one of the first and most leading principles on which the commonwealth and the laws are consecrated, is lest the temporary possessors and life-renters in it, unmindful of what they have received from their ancestors, or of what is due to their posterity, should act as if they were the entire masters; that they should not think it amongst their rights to cut off the entail, or commit waste on the inheritance, by destroying at their pleasure the whole original fabric of their society; hazarding to leave to those who come after them, a ruin instead of a habitation – and teaching these successors as little to respect their contrivances, as they had themselves respected the institutions of their forefathers.[130]

Inherited civil rights are known and determinate, in contrast to indeterminate natural rights. Englishmen 'preferred this positive, recorded *hereditary* title to all which can be dear to the man and citizen, to that vague speculative right, which exposed their sure inheritance to be scrambled for and torn to pieces by every wild litigious spirit.'[131] The British propensity to prescriptive rights, rights born of long historical possession and respected on account of their antiquity, is a preference for experience, the tried and true, over experiment, the novel and unprecedented. This dispostion is prudent, cautious, and conservative but not opposed to reform or renovation. The ancestral mansion of the British constitution is not to be destroyed and rebuilt according to the whim of some jumped-up enlightenment architect, but is to be repaired and renovated upon the foundations and style of the ancient edifice. New rooms can be built upon it, to accommodate different persons and different interests, new porches and shutters to screen the sun and the wind may be added to it, with new pathways and gardens. Indeed, the old building may have become more attractive and livable in the course of ages.

Our properties and liberties are an inheritance which 'furnishes a sure principle of conservation, and a sure principle of transmission; without at all excluding a principle of improvement. It leaves acquisition free; but secures what it acquires.'[132] English conservatism, the preference for solid experience over untried reason, is not merely a cultural peculiarity of country gentlemen but is grounded upon the precepts of nature. The English tradition, based on the inheritance of property, corresponds to the genetic transmission of family and species characteristics. Inheritance not only ensures continuity but also allows change. 'By a constitutional policy, working after the pattern of nature, we receive, we hold, we transmit our government and our privileges, in the same manner in which we enjoy and transmit our property and our lives.'[133] While natural rights are not certified by history, historical rights are certified by nature.

Burke's opponents were mistaken in thinking that Burke was a principled monarchist, aristocrat, or adherent to the British constitutional settlement of powers between Crown, Lords, and Commons. Burke's opponents failed to realize that only one thing was sacred to Burke, because they shared his reverence for property right. Burke insisted that he was indifferent to any specific form of government.[134] This insistence is elaborated in the following passage: 'for the protection of property, all governments were instituted. First, therefore, restore property, and afterwards let that property find a government for itself. The number of its inhabitants constituted the strength of a nation, but it was property alone on which government was formed. If the formation of government was committed to the no-property people, the first thing they would do, obviously would be to plunder those who had property, and the next thing would be to plunder and massacre each other.'[135]

Thus, the monarchist loyal to old world inequality was a great friend of republican and 'egalitarian' rebels in the New World precisely because the American revolution, like the Glorious Revolution, was not in fact a revolution.[136] Honouring property titles with Burkian reverence, American rebels did not make a revolutionary break with the old world of British traditions.[137] In Lockian fashion, Burke supported the right to rebel against governments which fail to respect inherited liberties and properties, and opposed a right to overturn society and disrupt tradition in a revolutionary disregard for inherited title.

What is revolutionary about Burke is his advocacy of violent counter-revolution and military intervention in France.[138] The natural order of things, hierarchy based on property, apparently cannot be trusted to right itself. The French ship of state has to be purged of its crew and its ballast restored by means of foreign intervention. The revolutionary regime was not, to Burke, an illustrative example of the pernicious results of tampering with the course of nature, useful to maintain in existence for the edifying instruction of the class of resentful labourers. Doubtless Burke wished to crush the revolution by force because the lower orders are incapable of apprehending the great chain of being or the natural order of ranks. In addition, however, Burke's principles prevented him from maintaining that the injustice of the French revolution, if long continued, would remain injustice. Burke's rejection of ahistorical rights entails that rights begin in time, and indeed can be the product of a violent creation.

For Burke as for Hume, prescription or long possession 'through long usage, mellows into legality governments that were violent in their commencement.'[139] Burke referred to 'the solid rock of prescription' as 'the original ground of all known property' and 'the soundest, the most general, and the most recognized title between man and man ...'[140] Since 'all titles terminate in prescription,' 'the last prescription eats up all the former.'[141] Thomas Paine's view that the old oaks of the British constitution 'were the Robespierres and the Jacobins of that day'[142] denies historical rights equally to the landed aristocracy and to the Jacobins. Burke's justification of prescriptive rights paradoxically could be taken to be more revolutionary than the natural rights of Paine. The solid rock of reaction is of the same stuff as the axe of revolution. Burke cannot be as unmoved as Paine by the Hegelian dictum that world history is the world's court of judgment,[143] or the Marxian dictum that rights are nothing but the official recognition of fact.[144]

Paine attacked the Burkian principles of prescription and heritable rights but did not criticize the inviolability of property right, including the inheritance of property. Moreover, he agreed with Burke that property entails inequality. 'That property will ever be unequal is certain'[145] He was in accord with Burke's view that the purpose of government is to safeguard property right[146] but included in the category of property what Locke called one's property in one's person. Government is to secure the rights of proprietors, especially if 'personal labour is all the property they have.'[147] Paine differed from Burke in thinking that labourers have a right to enjoy the full fruit of their labours.

However, it is highly questionable whether a Lockian or Smithian labour theory of value can serve as a guide to the just allocation of resources. As Burke said with respect to Rousseau, those who see society as a nexus of unsocial independent individuals refuse 'the just price of common labour.'[148] In reality, society is not composed of self-made men who can command at the market the precise value of their individual productive contribution. Even if we were able to calculate precisely the value of one's property in one's person and even if we were to disregard Burke's touching concern for the leisured or cultivated classes, each individual labourer would not only have to work for himself or herself but for those too young, too old, or too ill to labour. Further, if we are to have an expanding rather than a stationary economy, part of the value of an individual's produce must be taken from individual consumption for collective investment. Alexander Lindsay correctly observes that the labour theory of value is incompatible with the doctrine that value is a social product and thus 'there cannot be justice for individuals unless their claim to be regarded as separate individuals, each with an absolute right to a definite reward, is given up.'[149]

Paine's individualist commitment to property right thus conflicted with his aspirations for social justice. The Lockian framework precluded the actualization of a radical interpretation of the labour theory of value. Paine is caught between Burke's and Marx's insistence that individual rights and revolutionary purposes are incompatible. Natural rights are inappropriate vehicles for epochal change.

Mill: the old liberal reconsidering
whether unnatural acts are truly self-regarding

CHAPTER EIGHT

The Right to Be Offensive: Rights and Manners in Liberal Doctrine

SHYLOCK'S RIGHTS VERSUS ANTONIO'S MANNERS

Hegel might well have been summarizing the moral of *The Merchant of Venice* in the following statements: 'To have no interest except in one's formal right may be pure obstinacy, often a fitting accompaniment of a cold heart and restricted sympathies. It is uncultured people who insist most on their rights, while noble minds look on other aspects of the thing ... [T]o have a right gives one a warrant, but it is not absolutely necessary that one should insist on one's rights ...'[1] For Hegel, Shylock's rights (Hobbesian-Kantian claims validated by universalization or the form of law) must be supplemented by Antonio's manners, the dimension Hegel called 'Sittlichkeit.' The form of universal or natural right takes on specific historical content as 'Sitten,' customs, mores, manners, a set of acquired, cultivated, or cultural characteristics. The dimension of 'Sittlichkeit' supplies what is lacking in Shylock or the pure rights-claimant depicted above, namely, heart, sympathy, cultivation, and nobility. The sense of community, of belonging to, and identifying with, something beyond the self, is alien to a social contract of rights-claimants. Without such a sense of belonging to a community, all forms of public service must appear as individual self-sacrifice, even as a violation of rights in the case of compulsory military service.

Shylock lacks Antonio's manners, the graceful and attractive qualities which identify him as belonging to a specific community. Shylock's lack is not just a matter of religion or class; it is also a matter of age. As Hobbes acutely pointed out, youth are 'lovers of honour more than of profit, because they live more by custom than by reason; and by reason we acquire profit, but virtue by custom.'[2] By contrast, the old 'live more by reason than custom; because reason leads to profit, as custom to that which is honourable.'[3] The young are more other-oriented than their elders; their aims are both more generous and vain since they have not profited from the experience of age. Their youthful enthusiasms and attachments have not shattered on the rocks of age, and their dreams are more for glory than for money. As lovers of honour, youth fashionably rebel against convention, or passively do what is done. The old are less held by custom; they love their creature comforts more than the good opinion of others, money more than honour. The old Shylock is the rationalist; the young Antonio, the traditionalist. Historians assert that the Roundheads (parliamentary partisans) tended to be older than the cavaliers or royalists. To draw a transhistorical lesson from the English civil war, old Shylock is less cavalier than young Antonio. Hobbes had greater penetration than Kant or Mill in seeing that the liberal deprecation of custom in favour of reason is an old man's philosophy. That youngest of old men dedicated his masterpiece to Sidney Godolphin who, from any rational calculation of profit and loss, was a loser. Hobbes, while bringing Shylock's outlook to consummate philosophic expression, acknowledged the worth of the reckless and prodigal Antonio.

However, Antonio's manners are not incorporated in Hobbes' *Leviathan* as they are in Hegel's *Philosophy of Right*. Hegelian *Sitten*

171 The Right to Be Offensive

appear in Burke's writings as manners. Burke wrote: 'Manners are of more importance than laws. Upon them, in a great measure, the laws depend. The law touches us but here and there, and now and then. Manners are what vex or soothe, corrupt or purify, exalt or debase, barbarize or refine us, by a constant, steady, uniform, insensible operation, like that of the air we breathe in. They give their whole form and colour to our lives. According to their quality, they aid morals, they supply them, or they totally destroy them.'[4] Burke distinguished manners, morals, and laws. His emphasis on manners relative to moral or legal rights may be thought to be characteristic of conservative, as distinct from liberal, thought. Although Hegel emphatically repudiated Burkian anti-Semitism, and the defence of prejudice, prescription, and privilege, the Hegelian element of 'Sittlichkeit' might be thought to represent a conservative dimension in Hegelian political philosophy. To be sure, Hegel's thought is not characterized by a Burkian priority of manners to rights. Hegel repudiated any tradition or heritage which is not in accord with the Hobbesian-Kantian framework of rights. Hegel's repudiation of irrational 'Sitten' might be thought to constitute a liberal element within his political philosophy. That is, the relationship between manners and rights might be characterized as a relationship between conservative and liberal elements within a political philosopher who is not readily characterized as a professor of a determinate doctrine.

No liberal could exalt manners over rights. Indeed, in my view, no decent human being could champion manners uncritically – for 'good manners' is but a species of the genus manners (which include the manners of snobs, xenophobes, racists, sexists, or the community standards that prevail in illiberal as well as liberal circles). Even if the manners are everything one might expect from an Anglican gentleman, his morals matter more to his Maker, and to those who know him well, than his impeccable manners. However, manners cannot be ignored, even by the most rugged individualist or the most doctrinaire rights-advocate.

What I wish to demonstrate in this chapter is that a tension, or a relation of attraction and repulsion, between rights and manners pervades liberal doctrine. For example, while the contributors to *The Federalist* are renowned for their thoughtful proposals about constitutional arrangements to safeguard property right, religious liberty, and freedom of expression from fractious minorities, and envious majorities, Alexander Hamilton wrote, in *Federalist* 84, that 'the only solid basis of all our rights' is 'public opinion, and ... the general spirit of the people and of the government.'[5] The Burkian position that rights are derivative rather than primary, that they are constituted by, and do not constitute, civil society is evident in *Federalist* 84. What Burke called manners Hamilton called 'public opinion' and 'the general spirit of the people.'

The tension between individualist morality and social manners is even more evident in the writings of Immanuel Kant. Kant deprecated manners as 'small change indeed (zwar nur Scheidemuenze).'[6] Manners, namely, propriety, 'the practice of accessibility, affability, courtesy, hospitality, mildness,' and so forth, 'are only externals or accessories.'[7] Manners arise from external constraint or compliance; morals, from an inner imperative. Respectability or decency is 'honestas externa.'[8] Manners are also distinct from morals, as description is distinct from prescription, or as an observable world of actual conduct is distinguished from an invisible world of moral imperatives. Kant wrote that the laws of morality do not derive 'from the perception of the course of the world – how things happen and how men in fact do act (although the German word 'Sitten,' like the Latin word 'mores,' designates only manners and way of life). But reason commands how one ought to act, even though no instance of such action might be found ...'[9] The Kantian rights-based morality thus seems to separate radically manners and morals, outward observance and inward motivation, social facts and individual values.

If Kant appeared to subordinate manners to rights in his moral theory, he thought scandalous or indecent conduct to be properly a legal offence, if the indecent conduct manifests a disrespect for his fellow citizens rather than a bold challenge to custom.[10] Unfortunately, Kant failed to provide guide-lines as to the difference between worthy and reprehensible contraventions of social norms or manners. Kant said that individuals have a right to respect, which imposes upon others the duty of 'respectability and decency' in 'outward behavior.' To flout community standards of decency 'might encourage imitations' and is 'extremely contrary to duty.' However, 'respect for others, which is owed them and which sets an example for men, cannot degenerate into a blind imitation (whereby custom, *mos*, is elevated to the dignity of a law), because such a tyranny of popular manners would be contrary to the duty of man to himself.'[11]

John Stuart Mill's *On Liberty* championed an individual's right to speak or act in a heterodox or eccentric manner, in a manner which is offensive to most, indeed all, other members of the society of which he is a member. Yet, like Hamilton and Kant, this individualistic morality is bound to, and limited by, a code of social manners that Mill alluded to but generally took for granted. Like Kant, Mill apparently disdained 'the despotism of custom' or the 'tyranny of public opinion' but also, like Kant, Mill argued that 'a violation of good manners' or 'offences against decency' may be rightly prohibited by law.[12] Contemporary liberal thinkers, such as Herbert Hart, Joseph Tussman, Maurice Cranston, Ronald Dworkin, and Joel Feinberg, follow the framework of Mill's *On Liberty* and exhibit a systematic tension between individualist morality and social manners or between individual rights and public offensiveness. It will be argued, in examining these thinkers, that the polar opposites of rights and manners are bound together in forces of attraction and repulsion, that 'libertarian' liberalism which aims to cast off enforceable standards of public decency is untenable, that a 'paternalist' code of social mores cannot curtail individual liberties without ceasing to be liberal, and hence that an uneasy tension between individual rights and community standards is inherent in liberalism. Failure to comprehend this dialectic of rights and manners not only limits the comprehensiveness of liberal theory but also leads to illiberal practice or to the state enforcement of liberal doctrine. This chapter will elaborate the relationship of manners and rights within liberal doctrine and will conclude with a stirring defence of political rights or public offensiveness.

FIVE PROPOSITIONS CONCERNING THE RELATION OF MANNERS AND RIGHTS

Our examination of the dialectic of individual rights and social manners aims to establish the following propositions:

1 That claiming rights tends to be inherently offensive, that making claims, or imposing one's person, on others is often antithetical to social mores or 'good manners.' Rights affirm or assert the self or person; manners exalt the disappearance of self or person.

2 That nevertheless individualist self-expression is justifiably limited by 'manners' or community standards of conduct.

3 That violations of rights are subject to legal punishment while breaches of manners may be subject to social stigma or loss of status rather than state enforcement. If loss of status is a sufficient inducement to socially acceptable conduct, then manners are self-policing (as distinct from the state enforcement of rights).

4 That standards of public indecency tend to obliterate the difference between publicly offensive actions that are political in character and those that are apolitical, and thus are used (wrongly, in my view) to limit politically offensive conduct.

5 That liberal doctrine on rights in relation to public offensiveness tends to favour the toleration of those offensive activities which are apolitical over those which are political in character (in contrast with my illiberal position that political liberties deserve greater immunity from state intervention than apolitical liberties). That is, a view that the state has no business in the bedrooms of the nation coexists with an advocacy of ubiquitous surveillance agencies to monitor 'subversive' activities (or the kind of activities that keep the spirit of Rousseauan republicanism alive).

1 Hobbes, as we have seen, derived the meaning of person (rights-claimants) from the Greek 'prósōpon' and the Latin 'persona.' Persons are actors, role-players. One's persona is one's mask, disguise, or façade – the part, role, or status one assumes. The etymology of 'persona' (through sound) reveals that, in classical drama, the actor not only had a mask but also a megaphone to carry

his voice to the most distant members of the audience. In short, persons are noisy.

Although the sonic qualities inherent in the word 'person' are not usually noted, philosophers have pointed out that rights-claimants are characteristically loud and assertive. David Lyons writes that 'people are entitled to act in ways connected with having rights: to demand respect for them, to challenge those who threaten to infringe them, to be indignant and perhaps noisy and uncooperative when their rights are violated, and so on.'[13] Joel Feinberg asserts that '*having a claim consists in being in a position to claim, that is, to make claim to* or *claim that*. If this suggestion is correct it shows the primacy of the verbal over the nominative forms.'[14] That is, claiming, demanding, and insisting are prior, in rights-based justice, to the unclaimed claims of the victims of injustice. Jan Narveson states that rights-claimants are composed of the 'pushy ... crabby, thin-skinned, cantankerous, touchy, and quite possibly bitchy.'[15] The squeaky wheel draws attention to its rights. Narveson's portrait of rights-claimants may be a caricature but it suggests the serious question of how to weigh the clamour of claims against the unvoiced cry of 'the silent majority.' Rights are asserted with the clever articulation of lawyers, and not with the 'dumbness' of the downtrodden, with the confidence of the self-assertive, and not with the diffidence of the self-effacing.

2 Mill's *On Liberty* defends the individual right of self-expression, limited only when one's liberty harms another. Mill's notion of harm is widely considered to be vague.[16] Does harm include what conservatives and socialists call psychological damage, moral corruption, or economic exploitation? Perhaps the fundamental question pertains to the maxim 'volenti non fit injuria.' That is, can one harm another with his own consent? The theme of *The Merchant of Venice* re-emerges. Does a class of consensual but harmful activities exist or not? Can there be any harm in any agreement between consenting adults, whether a commercial contract, a non-commercial exchange of goods and services, or a sexual encounter?

Robert Nozick's 'libertarian' liberalism justifies any capitalist acts between consenting adults. Nozick writes: 'my non-paternalist position holds that someone may choose (or permit another) to do to himself *anything*, unless he has acquired an obligation to some third party not to allow it.'[17] Laws regarding health and safety at work, regulating interest rates, licensing professionals, are unwarranted 'paternalist' interventions in the free market economy just as laws governing sexual behavior or drug use are paternalist restrictions on personal freedom. Mill's position was different from Nozick's in that commercial transactions are not self-regarding and hence immune from state intervention.[18]

On Nozick's principles, a man may voluntarily pledge his life or his religion, or may sell himself into slavery. If the class of harmful but consensual activities is indeed void, then the state is not justified in prohibiting incest, bigamy, sodomy, duelling, suicide pacts, euthanasia, or voluntary submission to maiming, torture, or killing. Liberal opinion is divided on the question of the limits of appropriate legal prohibition of consensual relationships between adults. Herbert Hart, for example, champions the decriminalization of homosexuality, prostitution, and pornography but disagrees with Mill's advocacy of the toleration of polygamy and trade in harmful drugs.[19] Hart, while following in Mill's footsteps, acknowledges that Mill's libertarian principles reflect 'too much of the psychology of a middle-aged man whose desires are relatively fixed, not liable to be artificially stimulated by external influences; who knows what he wants and what gives him satisfaction or happiness; and who pursues those things when he can.'[20]

Despite the legacy of Mill, no liberal, to my knowledge, has advocated the wholesale decriminalization of all consensual acts that are deemed harmful. Nozickian principles lack specific examples of legal reform which accompany the less 'libertarian' principles of Mill and Hart. I suspect that current liberal opinion would tolerate sado-masochistic behaviour between adults of the same sex (the 'libertarian' principle) in so far as grievous bodily harm was limited (the 'paternalist' restriction). But chains and whips for individuals of different races and sexes might raise problems of racial and sexual stereotyping. A white man whipping a chained black woman, who gives her undeceived consent to this pastime, or even a white woman whipping a chained black man, might be intolerable to some liberals. While most liberals would encourage individuals voluntarily offering the use of their bodies for medical purposes, even Nozick might balk at a proposal for selling or giving one's body for cannibalism or necrophilia. (If readers find my examples far-fetched, let me assure them that only good taste impedes me from commenting on Joel Feinberg's example[21] of coprophiliacs' right to do their thing.) In short, Nozick's position that individuals have a right to do anything to one another under conditions of undeceived consent is an extreme declaration that social manners ought not to condition human rights. Nozick's theory, which is nowhere lived or practised, is that individuals have an unlimited right to be offensive. Nevertheless Nozick's position – that rights stand in a relation of repulsion to manners – is an inherent aspect of liberal doctrine, albeit one side of a synthesis of opposites.

The combined forces of attraction and repulsion between rights and manners is manifest in Herbert Hart's lectures at the Hebrew University of Jerusalem. Hart states that Bentham's and Mill's 'philosophy of law was not a particularist one, but was universal in the sense that the criteria ... proposed for the criticism of law and social institutions were the universal values of human happiness and human liberty and not the de facto morality of particular societies.'[22] While professing his allegiance to a universalist philosophy of law, Hart concludes his lectures with the disclaimer that his remarks are those 'of a liberal reformer in the perspective of English society, in which I live and work. Inevitably the weight given to various considerations must depend on many sociological facts; what seems reasonable law for Piccadilly may not be so for Mea Shearim.'[23] Thus Hart both denies that rights should be conditioned by manners (or what he calls 'the *de facto* morality of particular societies') and asserts that rights must be conditioned by 'sociological facts,' presumably the differing manners or mores of Piccadilly and Mea Shearim.

The relation of individual rights to social manners is thus the relation of the universal to the particular. Human rights are timeless and placeless; manners refer to time and place. Manners may have the fixity of customs or the evanescence of fashions but are, as Hart says, 'sociological facts.' That one *should not* eat meat is not a fact for a positivist; that a practising Jew or Muslim *does not* eat pork is a positive fact. Manners, then, are particular social mores or customs which sociologists and historians can relate to the behaviour of particular groups at particular times and places. Manners are community standards of taste and conduct. Manners may be liberal or illiberal, tolerant or chauvinist – even racist or sexist. Maurice Cranston writes: 'The private individual must 'behave'; that is to say, he must do what is done in the milieu to which he belongs, whether it is the society of the Scottish grouse moors or that of California hippies.'[24] If manners change from place to place, they also change from time to time. Joel Feinberg, who advocates the legal punishment of offensive behaviour, concludes: 'Thus, I am in the uncomfortable position of justifying the punishment of, say, antiwar demonstrators in 1965 for parading a Vietcong flag (shocking!) while denouncing the punishment of other protestors in 1970 for doing the same thing (yawn).'[25]

3 Maurice Cranston points out that while libellous, obscene, blasphemous, and seditious words and deeds may be punishable by law, unmannerly conduct may be subject to a form of social censorship that can make state censorship redundant. 'The existence of a state censor can only be seen as a badge of immaturity – that is, if it is not seen as a mark of servitude.'[26] Thus, while conformity to community standards may seem illiberal, those who do not wish to see the heavy hand of the state interceding in social affairs may, like Cranston, recognize the existence and the authority of social manners. Manners are, as it were, self-policing. One desires to be praised for one's conformity to the standards of taste, consideration, haughtiness, or intolerance that prevail in one's social circle and one desires to avoid the sanction occasioned by non-conformity. Rights, in contrast, impose some sanction beyond social favour or disfavour.

The love-hate relationship between rights and manners is manifest in Mill's *On Liberty*. While Mill deprecated the prevalence of Victorian manners as 'the despotism of custom' or 'the tyranny of public opinion' in the first three chapters, he emphasized a positive role for social manners in chapters 4 and 5. Mill began chapter 4 by asserting that an individual 'may then be justly punished by opinion, though not by law' if he performs acts which 'may be hurtful to others, or wanting in due consideration for their welfare, without going to the length of violating any of their constituted rights.'[27] Mill continues by asserting that 'we have a right, and it may be our duty to caution others against' a base individual 'if we think his example or conversation likely to have a pernicious effect on those with whom he associates. We may give others a preference over him in optional good offices, except those which tend to his improvement.'[28] Mill then thought social sanctions rather than legal punishment may be appropriate for those who do not violate others' rights. 'There is a degree of folly, and a ... lowness or depravation of taste, which, though it cannot justify doing harm to the person who manifests it, renders him necessarily and properly a subject of distaste, or, in extreme cases, even of contempt ...'[29] By harm, Mill meant here legal punishment, not ostracism, social stigma, or denial of employment.

In chapter 5, Mill argued that 'a violation of good manners' or 'offences against decency' may be rightly prohibited by law.[30] He also advocates laws to prohibit marriage between parties who do not have the means to raise children but adds that where 'it is not deemed expedient to superadd legal punishment,' the marriage of improvident parents 'ought to be a subject of reprobation, and social stigma.'[31] Public opinion may then be self-policing in addition to, and distinct from, the state enforcement of individual rights.

Thus, in *On Liberty*, Mill was not consistently hostile to the inculcation of social manners or public opinion that would regulate conduct by the provision or withholding of esteem rather than by coercive law. Indeed, perhaps Mill's hostility to the prevalence of social manners or the tyranny of public opinion in the first three chapters of *On Liberty* was related to his apprehension that democratic majorities may fail to distinguish between the sanctions appropriate to the realm of opinion and those wielded by government.[32] Moreover, in *Utility of Religion*, he welcomed the replacement of divine authority by 'the power of public opinion, of the praise and blame, the favour and disfavour, of their fellow creatures.'[33] Mill would seem to participate in the enlightenment creed that good manners, or as Hobbes put it, the love of virtue from love of praise, could govern conduct as effectively as the constraints of religion. In his *Autobiography*, Mill asserted that 'love of distinction and fear of shame' are 'capable of producing, even in common men, the most strenuous exertions as well as the most heroic sacrifices.'[34]

In his conclusion to chapter 2 of *The Subjection of Women*, Mill thought that, if a family depends upon wages rather than an independent income, the most 'desirable custom' is for women to attend to the children and the household, while her working-class husband earns the wages (to which the wife had proprietary title). 'These things, if once opinion were rightly directed on the subject, might with perfect safety be left to be regulated by opinion, without any interference by law.'[35] Regulation of conduct by opinion, by social sanction or favour, is integral to chapters 4 and 5 of *On Liberty*. The central principle is that legal punishments (as distinct from social sanctions) are inappropriate for self-regarding actions but 'for such actions as are prejudicial to the interests of others, the individual is accountable and may be subjected either to social or to legal punishment if society is of the opinion that the one or the other is requisite for its protection.'[36]

Herbert Hart, as stated earlier, asserted that Mill proposed universal criteria 'and not the *de facto* morality of particular societies' for his philosophy of law and social development. However, Hart concludes with the assertion that 'what seems reasonable law for Piccadilly may not be so for Mea Shearim.' Hart *appears* to revise Mill's universal individualist morality in terms of relativist social mores or manners. Rather, Hart *is* laying out the implicit principle of Mill that public indecency varies from community to community. Relatively modest attire in Piccadilly would seem wildly immodest in Mea Shearim. What Hart appears to ignore is the role of the informal approval or censure of public opinion. The scantily clad young lady in Mea Shearim is likely to be pursued by the derisory hoots of children and the stony stares of adults rather than by a cop

181 The Right to Be Offensive

with a key to a prison. And this failure to provide a role for the informal and non-coercive sway of social manners may leave us with the dictum of *On Liberty* that 'all places of public resort require the restraint of a police.'[37]

4 Ronald Dworkin asserts that 'political liberties have been used ... by social rebels who threaten ideals of social order and public decency that the old liberal did not question.'[38] This statement contains a number of important truths. First of all, an 'old liberal,' such as John Stuart Mill, did not question, or assumed without questioning, standards of gentle conduct or good manners in his celebrated championship of individualistic self-expression in *On Liberty*. Secondly, social rebels challenged the assumption that liberals, such as Mill and Herbert Hart, are keen to defend: namely, that libertarian conduct is appropriate in private but inappropriate in public. One may use the flag of one's country as toilet paper in the privacy of one's bathroom but one must not burn the flag in public. Thirdly, social rebels have used liberal principles, however one-sidedly, to attack a liberal society. Liberalism, as anarchism for gentle society, when universalized as liberal democracy, become anarchism. When one abstracts from the social assumptions Mill held in applying his libertarian principles, *On Liberty* appears to be a hippie tract.

For example, Mill's justly celebrated defence of freedom of speech defends the public utility of the individual right to speak in a manner which is offensive to the other members of his society. Yet this individual right is bound to a code of social manners to which Mill referred but generally took for granted. Mill recognized that 'intemperate discussion, namely invective, sarcasm, personality and the like,' is to be avoided in the conflict of opinion if truth is to be advanced.[39] The progressive clash of opinions has the form of a gentleman's debating society where no expressions such as 'piss off' or 'fuck you' arrest the advance of truth. (It is indeed my opinion that such arresting expressions should be confined to dry scholarly works on rights, for they do arrest, and may be subject for arrest.) These most common forms of the freedom of expression are not, for Mill, to be subject to legal interdiction or restraint on grounds of equity. Orthodox opinions, according to Mill, are likely to be expressed with greater vituperation than heterodox opinions but since only intemperate radical opinions are likely to be legally constrained, Mill thought the interdiction of unmannerly speech to be inequitable. However, he asserts that 'the denunciation of these weapons would deserve more sympathy if it were proposed to interdict them equally to both sides ...'[40]

Joseph Tussman, one of the most thoughtful of contemporary advocates of Mill's doctrine, experienced, in the Berkeley free-speech debates of the 1960s, the facts that free expression does not always conform to the manners of a gentlemen's debating society and that vituperative expression is not the monopoly of conservative or orthodox opinion. Tussman is deeply concerned that public speech avoid such forms of verbal assault as those mentioned above in order to preserve 'the manners of the forum.'[41] He writes: 'Communication ... is hedged by taboos that protect values and sensibilities. A community may insist on good manners, on respect for its verbal and symbolic conventions, and it may even resort to law to control this form of verbal aggression.'[42] Tussman, while departing from the letter of chapter 2 of *On Liberty*, is, I think, faithful to the spirit of Mill's liberalism, and perhaps even to the letter of chapter 5 of *On Liberty*, where Mill justified the limitation of rights by social mores.

Again, there are many acts which, being directly injurious only to the agents themselves, might not be legally interdicted, but which, if done publicly, are a violation of manners, and coming thus within the category of offenses against others, may rightfully be prohibited. Of this kind are offenses against decency; on which it is unnecessary to dwell, the rather as they are connected only indirectly with our subject, the objection to publicity being equally strong in the case of many actions not in themselves condemnable, nor supposed to be so.[43]

Mill's concern with the legislative protection of public decency perhaps pertained more to the realm of actions than speech.

Drunkenness or 'self-abuse' would be examples of acts 'injurious only to the agents' but if done publicly are legal offences. And copulation between spouses might be one of the 'actions not in themselves condemnable, nor supposed to be so' but when performed in public is punishable. The philosopher Hipparchia, who is alleged to have copulated with her hunchback husband in the public market-place in order to prove her natural superiority to the social convention of marriage,[44] is not simply to be censured as a cynic for her canine conduct but is, according to Mill's doctrine, to be locked up.

Nevertheless, the criterion of public indecency has been used to justify limitations to freedom of speech by exponents of Millian liberalism. Maurice Cranston writes: 'But however the word "obscenity" is interpreted, a reasonable case can be made for limiting the freedom of speech in the interests of public decency and of protecting vulnerable persons from the kind of utterance which stirs up base and ignoble passions.'[45] Joel Feinberg defends the jailing of a Californian youth who in 1971 wore a jacket emblazoned with the slogan 'Fuck the Draft.' Paul Robert Cohen violated section 415 of the Penal Code by 'engaging in tumultuous and offensive conduct.' The judgment against the youth declared that his slogan was 'clearly offensive' and below the 'minimum standard of propriety and the accepted norm of public behavior.'[46] Feinberg says that, on Mill's principles, one can express any opinion, including one on draft regulations, 'in the imperative or exclamatory moods. But to forbid the public display of the sentence "Fuck the draft" is not to ban the expression of a political opinion because *it* (the opinion) is offensive; rather it is to ban the public use of a single word whose offensiveness, such as it is, has nothing to do with political opinion.'[47] Feinberg's opinion, to which we shall return, is that the sentence 'Down with the draft' conveys an equivalent message to the more offensive expression, and that the offensive word by itself would constitute an equivalent legal offence as it did in combination with 'the draft.' Section 260 of the Canadian Criminal Code exempts from the crime of blasphemous libel any person 'expressing in good faith and in decent language, or attempting to establish by argument used in good faith and conveyed in decent language, an opinion upon a religious subject.' Not the substance but the form of utterances about the draft or a god is what is legally an offence.

5 Public indecency is then considered by liberals to be properly a criminal offence. Herbert Hart asserts that Mill's acceptance of punishable acts of public indecency does not fully accord with his other strictures that punishable acts must hurt an 'assignable individual' and must not be 'merely contingent' or 'constructive' injuries.[48] Hart is keen to argue that the punishment of public indecency is not a departure from the liberal principle that the law is not to be used to enforce or promote morality. 'The Romans distinguished the province of the Censor, concerned with morals, from that of the Aedile, concerned with public decency, but in modern times perhaps insufficient attention has been given to this distinction.'[49] In making this distinction, Hart overlooks the really crucial point, that the Roman censors governed conduct by means of the conferring or withholding of status or honour, whereas the aediles were armed with the powers of legal coercion. Hart's philosophy of law systematically ignores a role for non-coercive sanctions applied to unmannerly conduct. Moreover, Hart is so keen to defend an aedilic rather than censorial function of law that he makes the far-fetched argument that bigamy is prohibited, not because it is immoral but 'in order to protect religious sensibilities from outrage by a public act.'[50] Mill, of course, believed polygamy to be morally offensive (not merely a public indecency) but counselled against using the law to repress polygamy. However, despite their difference on this matter, Mill and Hart are both concerned to distinguish private immorality from public indecency, and to establish a private space for moral choice and experimentation free from legal interference.

Hart thinks that there is no proof of conservative claims that private immorality 'is something which, like treason, threatens the existence of society.'[51] To be sure, conservatives often mistake symptoms for causes. But is Hart's tacit assumption that treason threatens the existence of society grounded in solider proofs than conservative allegations? To be sure, Hart does not discuss treason, subversion, dissent, and advocacy of violent transformation of society. But could one draw the implication from Hart's distinction between what is tolerable in private and what is tolerable in public that a tolerance for private immoralities may complement a tacit intolerance of public offensiveness? Hart does not seem to wish to restrict prosecution for seditious libel or seditious conspiracies with even the moderate zeal of Mill's *On Liberty*. Is the solemn complement of a toleration in the private realm intolerance in the public realm? Is Hobbes' preference for the liberties of subjects over the liberties of citizens, for the possessive individualists who enjoy personal freedoms over the civic humanists who wish to participate in public life, present in the latitude accorded 'private' and 'self-regarding' actions relative to 'public' and 'other-regarding' actions?

The antithesis of Hobbes' possessive individualism is Rousseau's civic humanism. Rousseau's principle of right precludes representative government, entails the direct participation of all citizens in legislation, in establishing the rules that will govern their conduct. The maintenance of public mores, of customs and opinions that are not inconsistent with civic virtue, is the indispensable condition of active citizenship.[52] The censor, who lacks all executive power but who governs public manners by declaring what is honourable or infamous, has a central role in Rousseau's illiberal democracy.[53] It is clear that Hart, and most contemporary liberals, are far closer to the Shylockian principles of Hobbes than to the utopian anti-Shylockianism of Rousseau.

The two great products of the 1960s, political protest and the drug culture, were perhaps ideal types of public and private activities, other-regarding and self-regarding acts. Is it clear, as Hart apparently thinks, that the former (including the burning of flags and draft registration cards, refusal to pay taxes, unlawful assemblies, and 'seditious conspiracies') is more of a threat to the American republic than the latter? Perhaps a drug-induced withdrawal from the 'res publica' depopulates the public realm of all but technocrats. Perhaps a drug-ridden army incapable of fighting conventional wars is a reason for an otherwise unreasonable nuclear escalation. Doubtless, such a view is unprovable but perhaps is as tenable as Hart's view that private immoralities are not as socially destructive as treasonable actions. A liberal democracy has a stake in the reproduction of citizens who will defend liberal democracy.

I have suggested above that current interpretations of Mill's liberalism could be read to imply that, while liberal states have no business in the bedrooms of the nation, they may be used to suppress 'subversive' political activities. In saying this, I do not mean to support Herbert Marcuse's conception of 'the repressive tolerance' of liberal societies.[54] There is no reason to think that societies which are less tolerant of apolitical liberties are more likely to tolerate political dissent than 'repressively tolerant' regimes. Nor is the greater latitude for private over public activities inherent in Hart's liberalism necessarily an advocacy of political apathy. However, there is no reason to assume the contrary: namely, that Rousseauan censorship necessarily limits democratic rights or that maximal toleration of apolitical liberties is necessarily maximal tolerance of political liberties.

A DEFENCE OF POLITICAL RIGHTS OR PUBLIC OFFENSIVENESS

What we have argued in this chapter is that rights and manners are united in opposition to one another, as in the relationships of Shylock and Antonio. Manners are more 'worldly' than rights, more social, less individual, and less universal. Manners require discrimination of the social situation, of the time and place; human rights require the ability to generalize the principles of choice into binding rules and apply the universal principle to individual choices. The individualism and universalism of a rights-based morality – do your own thing as long as you do not interfere with the rights of others – often comes in conflict with social mores. Manners and rights would be at one only on the conditions, first, that the mores prevalent in one's society are held to be rules applicable to all societies and, second, that the mores are owned, are identified as one's own, by the individual members of that society. Whereas manners require discrimination of the social situation, of the time and place, a rights-based morality enjoins forms of individualist self-expression which are offensive (although not a threat to another's body or property). The principles of *On Liberty* clearly suggest that legislation should prohibit smoking in public places but tolerate it in private in so far as tobacco taxes pay for the increased costs to public health. But sensory irritants that pertain only to mental rather than physical well-being, such as gum-cracking, wind-breaking, transistor radios, and exotic attire, are forms of individualist self-expression that do not materially harm others. As such, if one ignores Mill's assumption about social manners, these forms of conduct might be manifestations of the liberal creed. The right to be offensive is a central right of liberal doctrine, not only because asserting one's rights against others tends to be antithetical to good manners but also, and more importantly, that inoffensive rights need no defence and are likely to wither away without repeated offence and defence.

Of course, one could say that offensive conduct properly belongs to the categories of indictable public disturbance or public indecency. Presumably, that is what Herbert Hart means when he says that what is good law for Piccadilly may not be so for Mea Shearim. We pointed out that Hart overlooked the possibility that the principles of law could be the same for both places despite the differences of manners or standards of decent dress if the 'policing' of communities by social favour or censure is effective. We would further like to point out that liberal societies, like illiberal communities like Mea Shearim, have a stake in the preservation of the manners which sustain their society.

Rights are enforced by the state whereas manners hold sway by means of social sanctions rather than legal coercion. Yet Mill, Hart, Tussman, and Feinberg advocate the use of the state to prohibit public indecency. My concern with this view is the possible implication that apolitical offensiveness is to obtain wider toleration than political offensiveness. More broadly, rights doctrines may tend to favour 'possessive individualism' over 'civic humanism,' may 'privatize' the public realm, may consign liberty to the realm of personal 'values' or what is not publicly observable, may restrict citizens' participation by enlarging the consumer choices in private lifestyles. I would like to champion the right to politically offensive conduct, not to forms of apolitical offensiveness that may be prohibited in the name of public decency.

That is, I would distinguish offensiveness with an avowedly political objective from apolitical forms of public indecency. Overtly public dissenters surely belong to a different category than those whose actions only unintentionally and furtively come to public attention. Parading an enemy's flag is different from the covert desecration of public symbols at night. Philosophers who copulate in the public market-place are different from a couple who cannot wait to get off a public beach. The bloody foetuses displayed by the 'pro-life' movement at the University of Toronto in February 1983 belong to a different category than the bloody corpses littering commercial films. Yet the university police, supported by university administrators, closed down the 'pro-life' display because it 'bordered on the obscene' and violated 'the norms of good taste established by social norms.'[55] Like Joel Feinberg, who supported the jailing of a young man with the slogan 'Fuck the draft' written on his jacket, the university authorities asserted that they were merely repressing indecent display rather than enforcing a moral-political position.

My view is that political breaches of public decency should normally be considered as an offence against manners, not against rights, and thus should be subject to social censure rather than state enforcement. Thus, contrary to Feinberg, I do not think 'down with the draft' conveys the same force or meaning as the more offensive variant, and I do not think writing 'fuck the draft' to be the same as simply writing 'fuck.' (To simplify, I would not be as worried if the jails were filled with individuals writing obscene words or making obscene movies if they could not convincingly claim some 'redeeming social' or political purposes.) But a more appropriate response than jail to the slogan 'fuck the draft' is surely 'young man, how exactly can one do that?' or 'I would not have thought you manly enough even to do that.' To the extent that neither gentle manners not macho codes can shame the youth off the streets, then he has probably registered his point about the obscenity of conscripting youth into an illegitimate war.

According to Hobbes, passionate and honour-loving youth, whether rebels or conformists, are governed by custom (that which brings esteem or praise from one's peers) rather than a profitable calculation of personal comforts and discomforts. To adapt Montesquieu's typology of climate and regime to Hobbes' typology of age, what Mill calls the despotism of custom is appropriate to youth. Liberal rationalism, in abstracting from the ardour of youth, tends to ignore a mode of the governance of youth. The repulsion of manners from the reign of rights leaves the youth with the manners of old Shylock.

We have said that liberals, such as Herbert Hart, tend to ignore the role of social sanction in regulating human conduct. Other liberals, such as Joel Feinberg, obliterate the difference between political and apolitical forms of public offensiveness. Feinberg thinks the law should suppress public displays of Nazi insignia on the same grounds that it should suppress public coprophilia – both are intolerably disgusting.[56] While it could be argued that ostracism or the social stigma against coprophilia would render police action unnecessary, I have no objection to aediles descending to suppress apolitical forms of public offensiveness. I wish to defend something both more disgusting and more political than coprophilia, namely, Naziism. More exactly, I wish to subject Nazis to the domain of the censor, its censure of public infamy, rather than the aedile, or the weapon of coercive law.

To be sure, there may be circumstances in which the flaunting of Nazi emblems or the expression of racist slogans may be suppressed on liberal grounds of prohibiting incitement to violence or suppressing public disorder. However, the charging and conviction of Ernst Zundel for violating section 177 of the Canadian Criminal Code for his Nazi propaganda and the trial of James Keegstra under section 281.2 (Hate Propaganda) do not conform to the liberal reasons for restricting free speech in that the garbage Zundel and Keegstra had been spewing forth for many years was not linked to any incident of violence. Indeed, had Keegstra not preached against other groups besides Jews, it is unlikely that the citizens and school board of Eckville, Alberta, would have removed him from the professional position for which he is lamentably unqualified.

Under both sections 177 and 281.2 of the Canadian Criminal Code, the Crown must prove not only that the defendants have expressed odious falsehoods but that they knew that the propaganda they advanced was false. However section 177 (under which Zundel was tried) seems to me to safeguard political liberties better than section 281.2 (under which Keegstra is appealing his conviction). Not only is section 177 much shorter (and less subject to qualifications and loopholes) than section 281.2 but also it refers to 'one who wilfully publishes a statement, tale or news that he knows is false and that causes or is likely to cause injury and mischief.' Zundel published, and made money, from his anti-Semitic lies whereas Keegstra did not profit from his anti-Semitic falsehoods. Whereas Zundel is readily exposed as someone who knew what he wrote, and what he published of others, was not true, there is some doubt whether Keegstra is sufficiently captain of his soul to be able to distinguish truth from falsity. Keegstra may be a sincere Christian Nazi, that is, one who sincerely believes that a Christian Nazi is not a contradiction in terms. While the jailing or deportation of Zundel does not appear a grave violation of justice, I would like to argue that both Zundel and Keegstra belong first in the domain of the censor, and only subsequently in the hands of the aedile, if the public declaration of infamy does not suffice to shame them from a public forum.

Ernst Zundel asserted that his trial gave him 'one million dollars of free publicity.' Researchers have reported that only 2 per cent of Canadians declared that they had less sympathy with Jews as a result of the trial, while 24 per cent declared that they have more sympathy with Jews.[57] However, the figures do not completely prove that the trial was, from Zundel's point of view, a failure. The audience for the evening news received, without comment, Zundel's statements that all the lawyers and judges at the Nuremberg trial were Jewish, that *The Diary of Anne Frank* was written in 1951, and so on. In Robert

Fulford's view, 'The enormous uncritical publicity which Zundel received from the trial was a direct result of the rigid conventions of journalism, which hold that the press should report only what happens in public. Extremists are able to gain exposure for repeated lies because their lies are not evaluated for their truthfulness. As journalism is practised, the task of the reporter is to convey what a newsworthy person has said in public and not transmit information which might help evaluate the truthfulness of what is said.'[58]

Zundel's cretinous lies and Keegstra's evil lunacy should be exposed to public opinion for what they are, rather than filtered through press conventions designed not to jeopardize malefactors' chances of going to jail. That is, if Zundel and Keegstra were not subject to legal punishment, the press would be free to educate the public on the truth or falsity of their allegations. Perhaps liberal democracies need censorial tribunals which lack executive power so that the truth and falsity of dangerous and offensive political positions can be exposed to public opinion. Such tribunals would be empowered only to declare political beliefs nefarious or infamous. Individuals, once censored, who continue to profess in a public forum opinions proved by competent judges to be false and defamatory might then be turned over to the aedile and subjected to coercive law. Censorial tribunals would be primarily educative, for the people of Eckville and the Canadian people are as responsible as James Keegstra for the fact that he preached anti-Semitic nonsense in the public schools for many years. Such a tribunal would allow the lawyer for Zundel and Keegstra, Doug Christie, an opportunity to explain his inconsistent utterances to the effect that the Nazi position is wrong but his clients have a right to express their views and that his clients are right and have a duty to present their views to a needy public.

The conclusion to this chapter is that if rights exist, offensiveness exists. The right to be offensive is not one of many human rights. Rather it is the condition for the assertion of any rights. Political rights entail public offensiveness. However, standards of public decency may be, and have been, used to limit political liberties. In arguing that enforceable standards of public decency may be waived for overtly political actions, I am not championing Shylockian rights over Antonian manners. Shylock is above all not a citizen, not someone who participates in public life.

What we have argued is that a current trend in contemporary rights-doctrines is to privatize individuals, to drive citizens from the public realm, to favour the apolitical possession of individual rights over the public cultivation of political competence. The state enforcement of public decency does not so much limit as reinforce Shylockian right or the private space of the possessive individualist. To bring Shylock into the public realm, to make a citizen of him, would remove the opposition between him and Antonio on which rights-doctrines are based. Shylock's rights would dissolve into manners, the virtues of a commercial civilization.

CHAPTER NINE

Conclusion

This book has interpreted the tradition of rights-discourse as a commentary on Shakespeare's *The Merchant of Venice*. Shylock personated the typical rights-claimant who emerged on the stage of European history in opposition to imperial Christian charity, personated by Antonio. The religious, political, and economic implications of Shylock's position (as the possessive subject rather than the virtuous citizen, as someone with claims against, rather than contributions to, the community) were given philosophic expression, in the English-speaking world, in the writings of Thomas Hobbes. If there is to be a hero of our narrative, it is the philosopher Hobbes – rather than the more influential exponent of Shylockian doctrine, John Locke.

The question that remains to be asked is whether rights-discourse is, as Hobbes put it, 'insignificant speech.' We introduced our reflections on rights with Adam Ferguson's observation that every peasant knows he has his rights but cannot explain what he means by the word 'rights.' If pressed, the peasant will 'substitute a less significant, or less proper term, in the place of this ...'[1] Ferguson implied that the fault lies with peasant ignorance rather than the insignificance of the term 'rights.' Perhaps a litmus test of the significance of 'rights' would be the ability to substitute appropriate synonyms for the various usages of 'rights.' We have suggested throughout the book that the most appropriate synonym for 'rights' is 'properties,' that is, something belonging to or possessed by individual subjects or persons, something which is one's own as distinct from what is common, something claimed against fellow members of one's community which one is entitled to possess and which one has an option of exercising or waiving.

We rejected the description of rights as moral properties in that the adjective 'moral' is either redundant or misleading. Ferguson, who deprecated peasant ignorance with respect to the grammar of rights, asserted that 'a right to do wrong ... is an abuse of language, and a contradiction in terms.'[2] But, despite his thoughtful study of the post-Grotian rights tradition, Ferguson here confused rights with obligations. Rights as properties are conceptually distinct from obligations to do what is morally right. Ferguson's moralizing of rights-discourse, excluding the rights to do wrong which are so central to the liberal heritage, eliminates the choices or options of rights as properties. That is, if one has no right to do wrong, then one has no option but to do what is right, no claim to do or say things which are commonly taken to be wrong. One's obligation to secure the common good overrides individual autonomy. But rights (and properties) function to safeguard choices rather than to direct one to what is choiceworthy or morally right. To call rights moral properties is then misleading if it suggests that the condition of having a right is doing right. To have a property is to permit its use or abuse. To possess a right is to have the option of abusing what is one's own, of exercising or waiving the power to dispose of one's own.

However, we often call welfare entitlements rights when provision of welfare is mandatory and recipients are unable to refuse to accept the benefit proffered. That is, such rights are not permissive options or personal properties. For example, article 26 of the Universal

Declaration of Human Rights stipulates '(1) Everyone has the right to education ... Elementary education shall be compulsory.' Thus, we perhaps have a right to education that we are unable to waive or exercise at our discretion. However, after asserting the compulsory right to education, article 26 continues: '(2) Education shall be directed to the full development of the human personality and to the strengthening of respect for human rights and fundamental freedoms.' The article concludes: '(3) Parents have a prior right to choose the kind of education that shall be given to their children.' It is not clear whether the option or proprietary right of parents to educate their children as they see fit is 'prior' to (1) the children's compulsory right to education or just (2) the educational objective of inculcating respect for human rights. I suspect that what article 26 means is that nation-states have a duty to educate children, at least at the elementary level, and they should do this in a spirit of tolerance and mutual respect for different groups, that parents are obliged by law to send their children to school but they reserve the choice of sending their children to qualified alternatives to public or state schools. However, in this construction we have replaced the language of compulsory rights (of children) with that of duties or obligations (of states and parents). By translating the language of rights into duties in this case, we have replaced insignificant with significant speech.

Article 25 refers to the right of health and well-being. If immunization against disease is compulsory rather than voluntary, is the person inoculated against his will for reasons of public health exercising his right to health when he has no option of waiving it? According to our interpretation, the language of needs and duties, rather than compulsory rights, is appropriate to the mandatory provision of education, health, and welfare. However, to say the language of rights is inappropriate to mandatory welfare entitlements is a far cry from saying that it is not right to provide compulsory education, public health, and nutrition. Indeed, the argument of this book is that the reasonableness of measures of universal education, public health, safety, and welfare is impaired by the employment of the vocabulary of rights. By employing rights as ideological weapons to justify practical proposals to extend welfare facilities, we uproot rights from its historical context of significations. Compulsory rights are forms of insignificant speech. The significant context of rights-discourse is the mighty Leviathan whose blood is money, the representative state constructed for market society. To fight the mighty Leviathan, we had better stay on land. That is, to argue for social justice, we would do well to avoid the murky waters of rights in which the Leviathan flourishes.

But it is not the task of great poets, like Shakespeare, or great philosophers, like Hobbes, to tell citizens or statesmen how to conduct their business. Poets and thinkers, as distinct from applied scientists and statesmen, have, as their craft and raw material, words not things. Shakespeare saw this even more clearly than Hobbes. Through the mouth of Theseus, in *A Midsummer Night's Dream*, the poet declared:

> The poet's eye, in a fine frenzy rolling,
> Doth glance from heaven to earth, from earth to heaven;
> And, as imagination bodies forth
> The forms of things unknown, the poet's pen
> Turns them to shapes, and gives to airy nothing
> A local habitation and a name.

What appears to practical men as the night of madness and of love's frenzy is the element of the wordsmith. The daylight of cool practical reason, in which things are visible and in which Theseus is active, depends on the night of divine madness. Hobbes may be 'the greatest, perhaps the sole' political philosopher in the English-speaking world, as Michael Oakeshott asserts,[3] not because his doctrines or political opinions (on monarchy, on undivided sovereignty, or whatever) represent a more accurate view of things political than those of subsequent thinkers. The specific care of the political philosopher is political words, not political things. Thus the unique charge of political theorists is not to direct political activists but to safeguard political language. With the language of rights ascending to a monopoly position in articulating matters of right and wrong (supplanting the language of classical justice, of Christian charity, of classical, Christian, and renaissance virtues, of the Rousseauan principle of right, of utility, of humanity, or of decency), a night of rights-blindness descends, a night without the warmth of divine madness, a night of cool practical reason employing the discarded husks of philosophic words.

At the American Congressional Committee of Human Rights and International Organizations, meeting on 15 September 1983, expert witnesses asserted that while murder and torture have decreased in the present (relative to the previous) regime in Nicaragua, and while murder and torture are much less prevalent in Nicaragua than in neighbouring states, the human rights record of Nicaragua is worse than that of Guatemala, Honduras, and El Salvador (which have less rationing, restrictions on mobility, etc.).[4] Amnesty International, in its submission to the congressional committee, asserted that Nicaragua's human rights record is better than that of its neighbours because of the relative absence of political murder and torture.[5] While it might appear that American witnesses, rather than Amnesty International, were employing insignificant speech, I shall argue the converse (although, as a citizen rather than a theorist, I approve of virtually all of the activities of Amnesty International). The question here is not whether Nicaragua is more or less liveable than its neighbours. Doubtless, as the economic and military pressure from the empire of human rights builds up, not only the human rights record but also any other standard of human achievement will deteriorate in Nicaragua. The question I want to consider is why murder, torture, political detention, press censorship, emigration restrictions, and food rationing are all equated as human rights violations. Why are atrocities and irritating wartime restrictions subsumed under the one category? Is there a pricing system to equate as discommodities various forms of human rights violations and to weigh the value of the discommodities relative to one another?

Simone Weil demonstrated how atrocities are trivialized and routinized by means of the language of human rights. Weil wrote:

If someone tries to browbeat a farmer to sell his eggs at a moderate price, the farmer can say: 'I have a right to keep my eggs if I don't get a good enough price.' But if a young girl is being forced into a brothel she will not talk about her rights. In such a situation the word would sound ludicrously inadequate.

Thus it is that the social drama, which corresponds to the latter situation, is falsely assimilated, by the use of the word 'rights,' to the former one.

Thanks to this word, what should have been a cry of protest from the depths of the heart has been turned into a shrill nagging cry of claims and counter-claims, which is both impure and impractical.[6]

By 'the social drama,' Weil meant the mundane and undramatic sale of productive abilities for wages. A youth forced by the absence of alternatives to work on an assembly line or as a piece-worker in a factory is like a young girl coerced into a brothel. Weil stated that to claim one's rights in such a situation is tantamount to demanding a better price for one's person, rather than refusing to submit one's being to the commodity market. Weil meant that to assert one's rights is tacitly to consent to the framework of a commercial transaction. One's rights are alienable properties or the negotiable items in a commercial contract. That is, one's rights are limited to what one is permitted to sell. Anything which is inviolable, inalienable, sacred, or constitutive of one's being is not one's right, that is, is not subject to one's disposition. Violation of the inviolable is an atrocity; violation of human rights is merely a failure to get fair market value for one's person, to have one's economic demands recognized, one's claims validated. Human rights violations, on this interpretation, are to be understood as arising from barriers to the open bargaining situation of the free market. The framework of the free market reduces atrocities to human rights violations.

Rights as properties have a commercial character; they constitute the legal and moral basis of market societies. Political intervention in Adam Smith's system of natural liberty violates human rights. For this reason, Jan Narveson argues that political rights cannot be considered human rights. Narveson asserts that political rights presuppose 'a right to counteract the workings of the free market' but because 'the right to a free market is established, the right to political processes cannot be. We must choose between them and ... it is clear we must prefer the market to politics.'[7] Human rights

199 Conclusion

constitute a standard for imperial expansion. The Canadian Charter of Rights and Freedoms, which Canadians received as if it were a welfare benefit allotted to them and which terminated their tradition of parliamentary supremacy, will facilitate the northern expansion of the empire of human rights.

The tradition of rights-discourse began in a clear-sighted opposition to imperial charity. The fact that the clarity of the discourse has been clouded by the indiscriminate extension of the language to inappropriate subjects of rights does not mean that rights-discourse is coming to an end. Rather, talk about rights has become idle chatter, insignificant speech, the small talk of the powerful and the big talk of the weak. While words and deeds have experienced an amicable divorce, the unremitting commericialization of life hangs over us as fate or fortune. That the empire of human rights is not an empire of Christian charity is not an unqualified triumph of Shylockian principle. For the great founders of rights-discourse were not just possessive individualists. To be sure, Grotius, Hobbes, Spinoza, and Locke saw in market society a liberating force. Commerce was a vehicle not only to material progress but also to enlightened tolerance. Their clear-sighted opposition to imperial charity was more a detestation of 'imperium' than contempt for charity. The same spirit might animate an opposition to an empire of human rights.

Rights-discourse, we have argued, arose and flourished with the expansion of commerce. However, precisely because of the integral connection between rights-discourse and commercial expansion, the language of rights is inappropriate to assess the desirability of an expansion or contraction of the commericalization of life. Rights-discourse has become a major barrier to unclouded communication and to a reasonable and cautious approach to the invitations (demands, dictates) of justice. The bold philosophic justification of Shylock's rights descends into the public market-place as the amoral moralism and the rationalized unreason of the Shy-Lockian 'I have a right to ...'

NOTES

INTRODUCTION

1 C.B. Macpherson, *The Political Theory of Possessive Individualism* (Oxford: Clarendon 1964)
2 An elaboration and interpretation of Shylock's person based on the text of *The Merchant of Venice* and on secondary literature will be provided in chapter 1.
3 J. Locke, *A Letter Concerning Toleration*, in *Works* (London: Thomas Tegg 1823), 6: 17
4 A review of the literature contrasting Locke's *Essay* and his *Two Treatises* may be found in P. Laslett's introduction to J. Locke, *Two Treatises of Government* (Cambridge University Press 1964), 82, and in G. Parry, *John Locke* (London: Allen and Unwin 1978), 11–14.
5 Macpherson, *Possessive Individualism*, 197–222; L. Strauss, *Natural Right and History* (University of Chicago Press 1953), 202–51; R. Cox, *Locke on War and Peace* (Oxford: Clarendon 1960)
6 J. Tully, *A Discourse on Property: John Locke and His Adversaries* (Cambridge University Press, 1980); J. Dunn, *The Political Thought of*

John Locke (Cambridge University Press 1969); J. Dunn, *Rethinking Modern Political Thought* (Cambridge University Press 1985)
7 J. Locke, Bodleian Manuscript, cited in Dunn, *Rethinking Modern Political Thought*, 24, 61
8 R. Nozick, *Anarchy, State and Utopia* (New York: Basic Books 1974), 9, 58
9 J. Rawls, *A Theory of Justice* (Oxford: Clarendon 1972)
10 J. Rawls, 'Kantian Constructivism in Moral Theory,' *The Journal of Philosophy*, 77 (1980): 515–72
11 St Thomas Aquinas, *Summa Theologica*, trans. Fathers of the English Dominican Province (New York: Benziger Brothers 1947), II.ii.Qu.10–11
12 Ibid, II.ii.Qu.32.Art.5; Qu.58.Art.12; Qu.66.Art.7
13 Ibid, II.ii.Qu.66.Art.7–8
14 Ibid, II.ii.Qu.58.Art.12
15 J. Finnis, *Natural Law and Human Rights* (Oxford: Clarendon 1980), 206
16 D. Hume, *The Philosophical Works*, ed. T.H. Green and T.H. Grose (Aalen: Scientia Verlag 1964), 2: 296–7
17 H. Grotius, *The Rights of War and Peace, Including the Law of Nature and of Nations*, trans. A.C. Campbell (Washington: Walter Dunn 1901), I.i.3
18 T. Hobbes, *Leviathan*, ed. M. Oakeshott (Oxford: Blackwell 1960), 103; *Philosophical Rudiments Concerning Government and Society*, in *The English Works*, ed. W. Molesworth (London: John Bohn 1839), 2: 45, 62; *Elements of Law*, 4: 107
19 All references to *The Merchant of Venice* are taken from the Arden Edition, ed. J.R. Brown (London: Methuen 1964).
20 J.S. Mill, *Three Essays,*, ed. R. Wollheim (Oxford: University Press, 1975), 302
21 H.L.A. Hart, 'Are There Any Natural Rights?' *The Philosophical Review*, 64 (1955): 182
22 H.L.A. Hart, 'Positivism and the Separation of Law and Morals,' in R.M. Dworkin (ed.), *The Philosophy of Law* (Oxford University Press, 1977), 21–2
23 M. Cranston, *What Are Human Rights?* (London: Bodley Head 1973), p. 47
24 A. Ferguson, *An Essay on the History of Civil Society*, ed. D. Forbes (Edinburgh University Press 1966), 34

25 H.L.A. Hart, 'Between Utility and Rights,' in A. Ryan (ed.), *The Idea of Freedom: Essays in Honour of Isaiah Berlin* (Oxford University Press 1979), 90
26 Hart, 'Are There Any Natural Rights?' 175, 181
27 Cranston, *What Are Human Rights?* 81
28 J. Feinberg, *Rights, Justice and the Bounds of Liberty* (Princeton University Press 1980), 151
29 K. Marx, *On the Jewish Question*, in K. Marx and F. Engels, *Collected Works* (New York: International Publishers 1975), 3: 153

CHAPTER ONE

1 H. Berger, 'Marriage and Mercifixion in *The Merchant of Venice*: The Casket Scene Revisted,' *Shakespeare Quarterly*, 32 (1981): 155–62
2 Aristotle, *Politics*, ed. E. Barker (New York: Oxford University Press 1962), 1258b
3 Ibid, 1256b
4 Ibid, 1256b–1258a
5 J.R. Pennock, 'Rights, Natural Rights, and Human Rights – A General View,' in J.R. Pennock and J.W. Chapman (eds.), *Human Rights, Nomos XXIII* (New York University Press 1981), 2
6 Ibid, 3
7 J.W. Jones, *The Law and Legal Theory of the Greeks* (Oxford: Clarendon 1956), 151
8 Ibid, 201–3, 298
9 J.G.A. Pocock, 'Virtues, Rights and Manners,' *Political Theory*, 9 (1981): 360
10 Aquinas, *Summa Theologica*, II.ii.Qu.77.Art.4
11 Ibid, Qu.78.Art.1
12 B. Tierney, *The Medieval Poor Law* (Berkeley: University of California Press 1958), 37
13 Aquinas, *Summa Theologica*, II.ii.Qu.32,Art.5
14 Ibid, Qu.66.Art.7
15 Ibid, Qu.32.Art.5; Qu.58.Art.12; Qu.66.Art.7
16 Ibid, Qu.66.Art.7
17 Ibid, Qu.10.Art.8
18 Grotius, *Rights of War and Peace*, II.xx.48
19 J. Selden, *Table Talk* (London: Smith 1689), 38–9, 57
20 Ibid, 23–4

21 W. Cohen, 'The Merchant of Venice and the Possibilities of Historical Criticism,' *English Literary History*, 49 (1982): 770
22 J.W. Draper, 'Usury in *The Merchant of Venice*,' *Modern Philology*, 33 (1935): 46
23 Cohen, 'The Merchant of Venice,' 767–9; R. Arneson, 'Shakespeare and the Jewish Question,' *Political Theory*, 13 (1985): 85–110
24 P.N. Siegel, *Shakespeare in His Time and Ours* (University of Notre Dame Press 1968), 249
25 R.H. Tawney's introduction to T. Wilson, *A Discourse uppon Usurye* (New York: Augustus Kelley 1963), 35
26 B. Nelson, *The Idea of Usury: From Tribal Brotherhood to Universal Otherhood* (University of Chicago Press 1969), chs. 2, 3
27 R. Filmer, *Quaestio Quodlibetica* in L. Silk (ed.), *The Usury Debate in the Seventeenth Century* (New York: Arno Press 1972), 111
28 F. Bacon, *Works*, ed. J. Spedding, R.L. Ellis, and D.D. Heath (London: Longmans 1861), 6: 474
29 Ibid, 475
30 G.L. Haskins, *The Growth of English Representative Government* (New York: Barnes 1960), 10, 78; A.F. Pollard, *The Evolution of Parliament* (London: Longmans 1964), 49; W. Stubbs, *The Constitutional History of England* (Oxford: Clarendon 1896), 2: 127, 289, 558–60
31 For a review of the literature linking the hanging of the Jew Lopez to *The Merchant of Venice*, see J.R. Brown's introduction to the Arden Edition of *The Merchant*; also A. Quiller-Couch and J.D. Wilson's introduction to W. Shakespeare, *The Merchant of Venice* (Cambridge: University Press, 1968).
32 M. Shell, *Money, Language and Thought* (Berkeley: University of California Press 1982), 73
33 A. Bloom and H.V. Jaffa, *Shakespeare's Politics* (New York: Basic Books 1984), 16
34 H.B. Charlton, *Shakespearean Comedy* (London: Methuen 1969), 154
35 B.K. Lewalski, 'Biblical Allusion and Allegory in *The Merchant of Venice*,' in S. Barnet (ed.), *Twentieth Century Interpretations of the Merchant of Venice* (Englewood Cliffs, NJ: Prentice-Hall 1970), 50
36 Ibid, 51
37 H.A. Deane, *The Political and Social Ideas of St. Augustine* (New York: Columbia University Press 1963), 200–2
38 Charlton, *Shakespearean Comedy*, 138
39 S. Barnet, 'Prodigality and Time in *The Merchant of Venice*,' *Proceedings*

of the Modern Language Association, 87 (1972): 26–30; Lewalski, 'Biblical Allusion and Allegory in *The Merchant of Venice*'; J.R. Brown's introduction to the Arden Edition of *The Merchant*.
40 The Arden Edition of *The Merchant of Venice*, 150
41 Ibid, 170
42 J.L. Palmer, *Political and Comic Characters of Shakespeare* (London: Macmillan 1962), 413
43 L.W. Hyman, 'The Rival Lovers in *The Merchant of Venice*,' *Shakespeare Quarterly*, 21 (1970): 109–11
44 M. Luther, *Von Kaufshandlungen und Wucher*, in Nelson, *The Idea of Usury*, 152

CHAPTER TWO

1 B. Spinoza, *A Theologico-Political Treatise*, in R.H.M. Elwes (trans.), *The Chief Works* (New York: Dover 1951), 1: 264
2 Ibid, 237
3 Ibid, 76
4 Selden, *Table Talk*, 24
5 J. Hastings (ed.), *Encyclopaedia of Religion and Ethics* (New York: Scribner 1925), 6: 683
6 See note 18 of introduction.
7 Hobbes, *The English Works*, 2: 62
8 Ibid, 6: 99–103
9 Grotius, *Rights of War and Peace*, I.i.3
10 Ibid, II.xx.48–50
11 Ibid, II.xx.49
12 Ibid, II.xx.48
13 H. Grotius, *The Jurisprudence of Holland*, trans. R.W. Lee (Oxford: Clarendon 1953), I.xiii.3
14 Cited in R. Tuck, *Natural Rights Theories* (Cambridge University Press 1979), 60
15 Grotius, *Jurisprudence*, III.x.9
16 B. Mandeville, *The Fable of the Bees: Or Private Vices, Publick Benefits*, ed. P. Harth (Harmondsworth: Penguin 1970), 358
17 Hobbes, *Leviathan*, 57, 98
18 S. Pufendorf, *Of the Law of Nature and Nations*, trans. B. Kennet (London: Sare 1717), II.vi.6
19 Ibid

20 Ibid, I.ii.8
21 Ibid, 21
22 Hobbes, *The English Works*, 2: 46; 6: 26
23 Pufendorf, *Of the Law of Nature*, I.i.16
24 Ibid; cf. IV.iv.11
25 Ibid, IV.v.1
26 Hobbes, *The English Works*, 2: ii
27 Locke, *Works*, 3: 296; 9: 176
28 J. Locke, *Two Treatises of Government*, ed. P. Laslett (New York: Mentor 1965), I.42
29 Ibid, II.27
30 Macpherson, *Possessive Individualism*, 199–221
31 J.J. Waldron, 'Enough and as Good for Others,' *Philosophical Quarterly*, 29 (1979): 321
32 I. Barrow, *The Theological Works* (Cambridge University Press 1890), 1: 34–5
33 K. Chetwood, *A Sermon before the Lord Major, Alderman, Sheriffs and Governors of Several Hospitals* (London: Jonah Bringer 1708), 29
34 J. Locke, *A Report of the Board of Trade to the Lord Justices*, in *An Account of the Origin, Proceedings, and Intentions of the Society for the Promotion of Industry* (Louth: Lindsey 1789), 102–3
35 Ibid, 104–5
36 Ibid, 106
37 Ibid, 107–15
38 Ibid, 134–5
39 M. Seliger, *The Liberal Politics of John Locke* (London: Allen and Unwin 1968), 114–24
40 Laslett, in Locke, *Two Treatises*, 325–6
41 Locke, *Two Treatises*, II.43
42 Ibid, II.42 (my emphasis)
43 Locke, *Works*, 3: 87–8
44 M. Cranston, *John Locke: A Biography* (London: Longmans 1957), 474–5
45 Mandeville, *The Fable of the Bees*, 263–325
46 Ibid, p. 142
47 Ibid, p. 202
48 C. de Montesquieu, *The Spirit of the Laws*, trans. T. Nugent (New York: Hafner 1962), I.xx.7
49 See T. Pangle, *Montesquieu's Philosophy of Liberalism* (University of Chicago Press 1973), 30–4, 114–7.

50 A. Smith, *Lectures on Jurisprudence 1762–3*, cited in I. Hont and M. Ignatieff, *Wealth and Virtue: The Shaping of the Political Economy in the Scottish Enlightenment* (Cambridge University Press 1983), 24
51 B. Spinoza, *Ethics*, trans. A. Boyle (London: Dent 1963), 175
52 Ibid, 176

CHAPTER THREE

1 Cranston, *John Locke*, 107, 331
2 Locke, *Works*, 6: 52
3 Ibid, 102
4 Ibid, 46–7
5 Cranston, *John Locke*, 391–2, 409, 429–30; Strauss, *Natural Right and History*, 202–51; Cox, *Locke on War and Peace*, 22–5, 50–62
6 Laslett, in Locke, *Two Treatises*, 86–7
7 Locke, *Works*, 9: 167, 191
8 Ibid, 3: IV.xii.11
9 Ibid, 7: 150
10 Ibid, 157
11 Ibid, 150
12 Ibid, 5: 6
13 Hobbes, *English Works*, 4: 350
14 Ibid, 294
15 Spinoza, *A Political Treatise*, in *The Chief Works*, 1: 369
16 Ibid, 296
17 Hobbes, *Leviathan*, 96
18 Hobbes, *English Works*, 2: 31; *Leviathan*, 86
19 Hobbes, *Leviathan*, 19
20 Ibid, 5
21 Ibid, 18
22 *English Works*, 5: 197
23 Ibid, 442
24 Ibid, 4: 211
25 Ibid, 5: 178
26 Ibid, 180
27 *Leviathan*, 220
28 Hume, *The Philosophical Works*, 3: 456
29 A. Smith, *Lectures on Justice, Police, Revenue and Arms*, ed. E. Cannan (Oxford: Clarendon 1896), 253

30 Mandeville, *Fable of the Bees*, 201–2; also 96, 230
31 Hume, *The Philosophical Works*, 2: 310
32 A. Smith, *The Theory of Moral Sentiments*, ed. D.D. Raphael and A.L. Macfie (Oxford: Clarendon 1976), 330
33 I. Kant, *Perpetual Peace and Other Essays*, trans. T. Humphrey (Indianapolis: Hackett 1983), 127
34 Hume, *The Philosophical Works*, 2: 265
35 Kant, *Perpetual Peace*, 124
36 I. Kant, *The Metaphysical Elements of Justice*, trans. J. Ladd (New York: Bobbs-Merrill 1965), 39–40
37 I. Kant, *The Metaphysical Principles of Virtue*, trans. J. Ellington (New York: Bobbs-Merrill 1964), 136
38 Ibid, 137
39 Ibid, 130
40 Ibid, 90
41 I. Kant, *Critique of Practical Reason and Other Works on the Theory of Ethics*, trans. T.K. Abbott (London: Longmans Green 1889), 362
42 Ibid

CHAPTER FOUR

1 Grotius, *The Jurisprudence of Holland*, II,i.42
2 Ibid, II.i.43
3 Ibid, II.i.44
4 Ibid, II.i.45
5 Ibid, II.i.48
6 Ibid, III.xix.8
7 Grotius, *The Rights of War and Peace*, I.iii.8
8 Hobbes, *Leviathan*, 142
9 Ibid, 91–2
10 Hobbes, *The English Works*, 6: 88
11 Hobbes, *Leviathan*, 84
12 Ibid, 48–9
13 Ibid, 57
14 Ibid, 87
15 *The English Works*, 5: 180
16 Ibid, 2: xxii
17 Ibid, 4: 169
18 Ibid, 2: 140

Notes

19 Hobbes, *Leviathan*, 105-6
20 Hobbes, *The English Works*, 6: 122
21 Ibid, 227
22 Ibid, 2: 186
23 Hobbes, *Leviathan*, 139
24 J. Narveson, 'Human Rights: Which, if Any, Are There?' in Pennock and Chapman, *Human Rights*, 194
25 Hobbes, *Leviathan*, 116
26 Ibid
27 Hobbes, *The English Works*, 4: 387-408
28 Ibid, 172
29 Spinoza, *The Chief Works*, 1: 118
30 Ibid, 245
31 Ibid, 258
32 Ibid, 259
33 B.A. Richards, 'Inalienable Rights: Recent Criticism and Old Doctrine,' *Philosophy and Phenomenological Research*, 29 (1969): 403-4
34 Locke, *Two Treatises*, II.23
35 Cited in J. Farr, '"So Vile and Miserable an Estate": The Problem of Slavery in Locke's Political Thought,' *Political Theory*, 14 (1986): 269
36 Locke, *Two Treatises*, I.30, 52-4, 85-7; II.6, 23, 135, 149, 172
37 Ibid, II.193
38 Ibid, II.123
39 Ibid, II.27
40 Ibid, II.28
41 Macpherson, *The Political Theory of Possessive Individualism*, 197-222
42 J.P. Day, 'Locke on Property,' *Philosophical Quarterly*, 16 (1966): 207-21
43 Locke, *Works*, 5: 36
44 Locke, *Two Treatises*, I.92
45 Ibid, II.65
46 Ibid, 116
47 Ibid
48 R. Polin, 'The Rights of Man in Hobbes and Locke,' in D.D. Raphael (ed.), *Political Theory and the Rights of Man* (London: Macmillan 1967), 24
49 Ibid, 25

50 A.J. Simmons, 'Inalienable Rights and Locke's *Treatises*,' *Philosophy and Public Affairs* 12 (1983): 192
51 Nozick, *Anarchy, State and Utopia*, 58
52 L.D. Becker, 'The Labour Theory of Property Acquisition,' *Journal of Philosophy*, 73 (1976): 660; H. Steiner, 'The Natural Right to the Means of Production,' *Philosophical Quarterly*, 27 (1977): 49

CHAPTER FIVE

1 Locke, *Two Treatises*, II.57
2 Marx and Engels, *Collected Works*, 11: 104–5
3 Locke, *Two Treatises*, II.6
4 Ibid, II.149
5 Ibid, II.6; also I.42–54, 85–6
6 Ibid, II.23
7 Ibid, II.172
8 Ibid, II.119
9 Locke, *Works*, 6: 129
10 Ibid, 129–31, 135–40, 154–5
11 Ibid, 137
12 Ibid, 128–9, 154–5
13 Ibid, 128
14 Locke, *Two Treatises*, II.168
15 Ibid, II.240
16 Ibid, II.168
17 Ibid, II.135
18 Hobbes, *Leviathan*, 142–3
19 N. Tarkov, 'Locke's *Second Treatise* and "The Best Fence against Rebellion,"' *The Review of Politics*, 43 (1981): 198–217
20 J. Umbeck, 'Might Makes Rights: A Theory of the Formation and Initial Distribution of Property Rights,' *Economic Inquiry*, 19 (1981): 39
21 Locke, *Two Treatises*, II.20, 21, 87, 91, 94, 168, 176, 241–2
22 J. Dunn, *Locke* (Oxford University Press 1984), 28, 55; Dunn, *The Political Thought of John Locke*, 48, 50, 52, 124, 183–6, 196–7, 240; Tully, *A Discourse on Property*, 173; M. Seliger, 'Locke's Theory of Revolutionary Action,' *Western Political Quarterly*, 16 (1963): 548–68; J.W. Gough, *John Locke's Political Philosophy* (Oxford: Clarendon 1973), 128; R. Ashcraft, 'Revolutionary Politics and Locke's

Two Treatises of Government; Radicalism and Lockean Political Theory,' *Political Theory*, 8 (1980): 429–86
23 J. Locke, *Two Tracts on Government*, ed. P. Abrams (Cambridge University Press 1967), 160
24 Locke, *Two Treatises*, II.223; c.f., II.225
25 Dunn, *Locke*, 55
26 P. Laslett, 'The English Revolution and Locke's *Two Treatises of Government*,' *Cambridge Historical Review*, 12 (1956): 55
27 J.P. Kenyon, *Revolutionary Principles: The Politics of Party 1689–1720* (Cambridge University Press 1977), ch. 7
28 Laslett, 'The English Revolution,' 52
29 Laslett, in Locke, *Two Treatises*, 43–4
30 Cranston, *John Locke*, ch. 14; Ashcraft, 'Revolutionary Politics and Locke's *Two Treatises*,' 440
31 Laslett, in Locke, *Two Treatises*, 43–5; Ashcraft, 'Revolutionary Politics,' 431; J.G.A. Pocock, *Virtue, Commerce, and History* (Cambridge University Press 1985), 226
32 Locke, *Two Treatises*, II.196
33 Laslett, 'The English Revolution,' 55
34 Locke, *Two Treatises*, II.168
35 Ibid, II.208
36 Ibid, II.240
37 Ibid, II.158
38 Ibid, II.240
39 Ibid
40 Ibid, II.34
41 Ibid, II.31
42 Ibid, II.123
43 Locke, *Works*, 5: 71
44 Locke, *Two Treatises*, II.221
45 Ibid, II.211
46 Ibid, II.222
47 W. Nelson, *The American Tory* (London: Oxford University Press 1961), ch. 5
48 E.R. Wolf, *Peasant Wars of the Twentieth Century* (New York: Harper and Row 1969); E. Andrew, *Closing the Iron Cage* (Montreal: Black Rose 1981)
49 Nozick, *Anarchy, State and Utopia*, 9

212 Notes

CHAPTER SIX

1 Mill, *Three Essays*, 380–8
2 C.D. MacNiven, 'Utilitarianism and Abortion Policy,' *Canadian Forum*, 62 (June/July 1982): 30
3 G.F.W. Hegel, *The Philosophy of Right*, trans. T.M. Knox (Oxford University Press 1979), 235
4 Hobbes, *Leviathan*, 101; *English Works*, 2: 40, 57; Spinoza, *Chief Works*, 1: 208
5 Grotius, *The Jurisprudence of Holland*, I.i.1–I.xiii.3.
6 Grotius, *The Rights of War and Peace*, I.i.4
7 Pufendorf, *Of the Law of Nature and of Nations*, I.i.16
8 Hobbes, *Leviathan*, 105
9 Hegel, *Philosophy of Right*, 39
10 S. Weil, 'Human Personality,' *Selected Essays 1934–43*, trans. R. Rees (London: Oxford University Press 1963), 21
11 Ibid
12 Finnis, *Natural Law and Human Rights*, 205
13 Ibid, 225–30
14 Ibid, 214
15 Ibid, 207
16 Ibid, 208
17 Ibid
18 Ibid, 173
19 Ibid, 172
20 Ibid
21 Ibid, 210
22 For an account of the reasons why Weil thought rights and justice to be antagonistic idioms, and why she thought rights were secondary to duties to relieve suffering, see E. Andrew, 'Simone Weil on the Injustice of Rights-Based Doctrines,' *The Review of Politics*, 48 (1986): 60–91.
23 R. Wasserstrom, 'Rights, Human Rights, and Racial Discrimination,' *The Journal of Philosophy* 61 (1964): 629, 632
24 Ferguson, *An Essay on the History of Civil Society*, 84
25 Hobbes, *The English Works*, 2: 188
26 Hobbes, *Leviathan*, 83
27 Hobbes, *The English Works*, 4: 84
28 Ibid, 6: 154
29 Locke, *Two Treatises*, II.194

213 Notes

CHAPTER SEVEN

1 C. Wilson, *England's Apprenticeship 1603–1763* (London: Longmans 1975), 224
2 No one after Burke has so wonderfully exploded Burke's ancient code of chivalry or gentlemanly honour as Mandeville. *The Fable of the Bees*, 230, wittily demonstrates Mandeville's historical sense: 'But the Wings of all the Dragons being clipt, the Gyants destroy'd, and the Damsels every where set at liberty, except some few in *Spain* and *Italy*, who remain'd still Captivated by their Monsters, the Order of Chivalry, to whom the Standard of Ancient Honour belong'd, has been laid aside for some time. It was like their Armours very massy and heavy; the many Virtues about it made it very troublesome, and as Ages grew wiser and wiser, the Principle of Honour in the beginning of the last Century, was melted over again, and brought to a new Standard; they put in the same weight of Courage, half the quantity of Honesty, and a very little Justice, but not a Scrap of any other Virtue, which has made it very easie and portable to what it was.'
3 Locke, *Two Treatises*, II.36,50
4 Ibid, II.36–51,108–11
5 Ibid, II.41
6 A. Smith, *An Inquiry into the Nature and Causes of the Wealth of Nations* (Edinburgh: Stirling and Slade 1819), 1: 167
7 H.T. Dickinson, *Liberty and Property: Political Ideology in Eighteenth-Century Britain* (London: Methuen 1977), ch. 7
8 T. Paine, *The Life and Works*, ed. W.M. Van der Weyde (New Rochelle: Thomas Paine National Historical Association 1925), 5: 222
9 Ibid, 228
10 Ibid, 213
11 Ibid, 212
12 E. Burke, *Works* (New York: Harper 1853), 2: 437
13 E. Burke, *Reflections on the French Revolution* (London: Dent 1955), 45, 46, 52, 81, 101, 188, 237, 246, 254–5; *Works*, 2: 335
14 G. Holmes and W. A. Speck (eds.), *The Divided Society* (New York: St Martins 1968), 72, 94, 142; J.G.A. Pocock, *The Machiavellian Moment* (Princeton University Press 1975), 447–8
15 Holmes and Speck, *The Divided Society*, 135
16 Ibid, 137–8

17 Locke, *Works*, 5: 60
18 Ibid, 61
19 I am grateful to Joanna Innis for this information. In the subsequent section, we shall see that Hume argued (with misgivings) against the position that landowners were not the sole source of taxation.
20 J.O. Appelby, *Economic Thought and Ideology in Seventeenth Century England* (Princeton University Press 1978), 223
21 Ibid, 235–6; Wilson, *England's Apprenticeship*, 219–21
22 Wilson, *England's Apprenticeship*, 221
23 Appelby, *Economic Thought and Ideology*, 235–6
24 Locke, *Works*, 5: 28
25 Ibid, 69
26 Ibid, 74
27 Ibid, 28, 60–1, 71
28 Appelby, *Economic Thought and Ideology*, 236–7
29 Ibid, 237
30 Ibid, 271
31 Hume, *The Philosophical Works*, 4: 190
32 Ferguson, *An Essay on the History of Civil Society*, 34; *Principles of Moral and Political Science* (New York: Garland 1978), 194–7, 267–71; Smith, *Lectures on Justice, Police, Revenue and Arms*, 8. Also Hume, *The Philosophical Works*, 4: 276
33 D. Forbes, *Hume's Philosophical Politics* (Cambridge University Press 1975), 89
34 Ibid, 88
35 J. Dunn, 'From Applied Theology to Social Analysis: The Break between John Locke and the Scottish Enlightenment,' in Hont and Ignatieff, *Wealth and Virtue*, 119–35. S. Hollander, 'Historical Dimension of the Wealth of Nations,' in G.P. O'Driscoll (ed.), *Adam Smith and Modern Political Economy* (Ames, Iowa: Iowa State Press 1977), 71–84, asserts that Smith's theoretical system combines a speculative rationalism with historical empiricism.
36 Dunn, 'From Applied Theology to Social Analysis,' 130
37 Hume, *The Philosophical Works*, 2: 273, 293, 318; 4: 192, 277
38 Ibid, 3: 372
39 Ibid, 2: 326; 3: 450; 4: 194; Smith, *Wealth of Nations*, 1: 167; 2: 424; *Theory of Moral Sentiments*, 330
40 Hume, *The Philosophical Works*, 4: 5
41 Ibid, 2: 245–6

42 Ibid, 326
43 D. Hume, *The History of England* (London: Millar 1767), 2: 90
44 Hume, *The Philosophical Works*, 2: 105; 4: 151
45 Ibid, 1: 475
46 Ibid, 2: 273, 293, 308, 318; 4: 192, 277
47 Ibid, 2: 201
48 Ibid, 247
49 Ibid, 3: 83
50 Ibid, 2: 329; 3: 113; 4: 182–5; Smith, *Wealth of Nations*, 2: 186
51 Hume, *The Philosophical Works*, 2: 311
52 Ibid, 3: 445
53 Ibid, 444–5; also 113
54 Ibid, 446
55 Ibid, 447
56 Ibid, 2: 312
57 Ibid, 2: 280–1
58 Ibid, 3: 451
59 Smith, *Lectures on Justice, Police, Revenue and Arms*, 8
60 Hume, *The Philosophical Works*, 3: 110
61 Ibid, 2: 328
62 Ibid, 319
63 Ibid, 3: 450
64 Ibid, 451
65 Ibid, 2: 314
66 Ibid, 325–6; 3: 372, 458, 461–3
67 Ibid, 2: 310, 315–16
68 Ibid, 3: 461–2
69 Ibid, 359
70 Ibid, 364
71 Ibid, 370
72 Ibid, 373–4
73 Ibid, 488, 491
74 Ibid, 110
75 Ibid, 112
76 Ibid, 2: 293
77 Smith, *Wealth of Nations*, 2: 186
78 Ibid, 1: 64
79 Ibid, 66
80 Ibid

81 Ibid, 2: 156; *Lectures on Justice, Police, Revenue and Arms*, 124
82 Smith, *Wealth of Nations*, 1: 64
83 Ibid, 167
84 Ibid, 350–1
85 *Lectures on Jurisprudence, 1762–3*, cited in D. Winch, *Adam Smith's Politics* (Cambridge University Press 1978), 58
86 Smith, *Wealth of Nations*, 1: 2
87 Ibid, 12
88 Smith, *Theory of Moral Sentiments*, 184
89 Ibid, 85
90 Smith, *Lectures on Jurisprudence, 1762–3*, cited in Hont and Ignatieff, *Wealth and Virtue*, 24
91 Smith, *Wealth of Nations*, 2: 363
92 Ibid, 350
93 Ibid, 363. J. M. Buchanan, 'The Justice of Natural Liberty,' in O'Driscoll, *Adam Smith and Modern Political Economy*, 117–31, argues that Smith's theory is based on rights rather than utility.
94 Smith, *The Wealth of Nations*, 2: 340
95 Ibid, 486–7
96 Ibid, 3: 194–7
97 J. Cropsey, *Polity and Economy* (Westport, Conn.: Greenwood Press 1977), 26–35, demonstrates the affinity between Smith's ideas and those of Hobbes.
98 Burke, *Reflections on the French Revolution*, 57
99 I. Kramnick, *The Rage of Edmund Burke* (New York: Basic Books 1977)
100 Strauss, *Natural Right and History*, 296; B.T. Wilkins, *The Problem of Burke's Political Philosophy* (Oxford: Clarendon 1967), 26, 66
101 A. Cobban, *Edmund Burke and the Revolt against the Eighteenth Century* (London: Allen and Unwin 1962), 37–8
102 Note 13 of this chapter
103 Wilkins, *The Problem of Burke's Political Philosophy*, 111
104 Burke, *A Letter to a Member of the National Assembly*, in *Reflections on the French Revolution*, 254–5
105 Burke, *Thoughts on French Affairs*, in *Reflections on the French Revolution*, 292
106 Paine, *The Life and Works*, 6: 98
107 Ibid, 235–6
108 Burke, *Reflections on the French Revolution*, 10
109 Burke, *Works*, 2: 183

110 Ibid, 188
111 Ibid, 180
112 Ibid, 188
113 Ibid, 183
114 Ibid, 184–5
115 Burke, *Reflections on the French Revolution*, 241
116 Burke, *Works*, 2: 190
117 Ibid, 190–1
118 Smith, *Wealth of Nations*, 3: 156
119 Burke, *Reflections on the French Revolution*, 31
120 Ibid, 29
121 Ibid, 48
122 Burke, *Works*, 2: 184
123 Burke, *Reflections on the French Revolution*, 123
124 Burke, *Works*, 2: 238
125 Burke, *Reflections on the French Revolution*, 56–7
126 Ibid, 93
127 Ibid
128 Burke, *Works*, 2: 210
129 Burke, *Reflections on the French Revolution*, 104
130 Ibid, 91
131 Ibid, 30
132 Ibid, 31
133 Ibid
134 *Works*, 2: 18–19
135 Burke, Speech on 11 April 1794, cited in Wilkins, *The Problem of Burke's Political Philosophy*, 198
136 Burke, *Works*, 2: 192
137 Ibid, 1: 229; 2: 270
138 Ibid, 2: 213–359
139 Dickinson, *Liberty and Property*, 300
140 Burke, *Works*, 2: 437
141 Ibid
142 Paine, *The Life and Works*, 5: 230
143 Hegel, *The Philosophy of Right*, 216
144 Marx and Engels, *Collected Works*, 6: 150
145 Paine, *The Life and Works*, 5: 226
146 Ibid, 6: 305
147 Ibid, 7: 78

148 Burke, *Reflections on the French Revolution*, 264
149 A.D. Lindsay, *Karl Marx's Capital* (London: Oxford University Press 1925), 107

CHAPTER EIGHT

1 Hegel, *Philosophy of Right*, 235
2 Hobbes, *The English Works*, 6: 467
3 Ibid, 468–9
4 Burke, *Works*, 2: 238
5 A. Hamilton, J. Madison, and J. Jay, *The Federalist*, ed. J.E. Cooke (New York: Meridian 1965), 580
6 Kant, *The Metaphysical Principles of Virtue*, 140
7 Ibid
8 Ibid, 129
9 Ibid, 15
10 Ibid, 129–30
11 Ibid
12 J.S. Mill, *Essential Works*, ed. M. Lerner (New York: Bantam Books 1961), 344
13 D. Lyons, 'Human Rights and the General Welfare,' *Philosophy and Public Affairs* 6 (1977): 127
14 Feinberg, *Rights, Justice and the Bounds of Liberty*, 151
15 J. Narveson, 'Commentary on Feinberg,' *Journal of Value Inquiry*, 4 (1970): 259
16 H.L.A. Hart, *Law, Liberty and Morality* (Stanford University Press 1963), 5, 33, 42–3; P. Devlin, *The Enforcement of Morals* (London: Oxford University Press 1965), 104, 128; H.L.A. Hart, *Essays on Bentham* (Oxford: Clarendon 1982), 101; C.L. Ten, *Mill on Liberty* (New York: Oxford University Press 1980), 52, 106, 110, 117–19; D. Lyons, 'Human Rights and the General Welfare,' 114–17; D.G. Brown, 'Mill on Harm to Others' Interests,' *Political Studies*, 26 (1978): 395–9; Feinberg, *Rights, Justice and the Bounds of Liberty*, 70; B. Barry, *The Liberal Idea of Justice* (Oxford: Clarendon 1976), 37; Cranston, *What Are Human Rights?* 43
17 Nozick, *Anarchy, State and Utopia*, 58
18 Mill, *Essential Works*, 341
19 Hart, *Law, Liberty and Morality*, 33, 38–9
20 Ibid, 33

21 Feinberg, *Rights, Justice and the Bounds of Liberty*, 103
22 H.L.A. Hart, *The Morality of the Common Law* (Jerusalem: Magnes Press 1964), 37
23 Ibid, 54
24 Cranston, *What Are Human Rights?* 39
25 Feinberg, *Rights, Justice and the Bounds of Liberty*, 105
26 Cranston, *What Are Human Rights?* 40–1
27 Mill, *Essential Works*, 322
28 Ibid, 325
29 Ibid, 324
30 Ibid, 344
31 Ibid, 354
32 Ibid, 262
33 Ibid, 410
34 Ibid, 138
35 Mill, *Three Essays*, 484
36 Mill, *Essential Works*, 340
37 Ibid, 347
38 R. Dworkin, 'Liberalism,' in S. Hampshire (ed.), *Public and Private Morality* (Cambridge University Press 1978), 116
39 Mill, *Essential Works*, 303
40 Ibid
41 J. Tussman, *Government and the Mind* (New York: Oxford University Press 1977), 110
42 Ibid, 92
43 Mill, *Essential Works*, 344
44 G.H. Tavard, *Women in the Christian Tradition* (Notre Dame University Press 1973), 73
45 Cranston, *What Are Human Rights?* 44
46 R.A. Wasserstrom (ed.), *Morality and the Law* (Belmont, Cal: Wadsworth 1971), 134
47 Feinberg, *Rights, Justice and the Bounds of Liberty*, 101
48 Hart, *Law, Liberty and Morality*, 42–3
49 Ibid, 44
50 Ibid, 41
51 Ibid, 50
52 J.J. Rousseau, *On the Social Contract*, ed. R.D. Masters (New York: St Martin's 1978), bk. II, ch. xii
53 Ibid, bk. IV, ch. vii

54 H. Marcuse, 'Repressive Tolerance,' in R.W. Wolff, B. Moore Jr., and H. Marcuse (eds.), *A Critique of Pure Tolerance* (Boston: Beacon 1969)
55 *The Varsity*, 103 (7 February 1983), 1
56 Feinberg, *Rights, Justice and the Bounds of Liberty*, 69–109
57 G. Weimann and C. Winn, *Hate on Trial: The Zundel Affair, The Media and Public Opinion* (Oakville, Ont: Mosaic Press 1986), ch. 3
58 Ibid, 30

CHAPTER NINE

1 Ferguson, *An Essay on the History of Civil Society*, 34
2 Ibid, 64
3 Hobbes, *Leviathan*, viii
4 House of Representatives, Committee on Human Rights and International Organizations, *Human Rights in Nicaragua*, 15 September 1983: 108–10
5 Ibid, 120–32
6 S. Weil, 'Human Personality,' 21
7 J. Narveson, 'Human Rights: Which, if Any, Are There?' in Pennock and Chapman, *Human Rights*, 193

INDEX

Abortion, 11, 119–20, 188
Anti-semitism, 4, 32, 34, 61, 140, 157–8, 161, 171. *See also* Naziism
Antonio, 24–7, 36–50, 80, 82, 92, 119–20, 157, 169–70, 192; opposition to Shylock, 8, 18, 67, 140, 186; personification of Christian charity, 8, 21, 34, 35, 67, 93, 159; representative of Thomistic doctrine, 8, 32, 96; unreliability of his word, 43–4, 47–8, 68, 73, 75
Appelby, Joyce, 141–4
Aquinas. *See* Thomas Aquinas, Saint
Aristotle, 4, 9, 27–8, 72, 77–8, 103

Ashcraft, Richard, 111
Augustine, Saint, 17, 31
Autonomy: moral, Hobbes on, 73–5, 83–5; Locke's repudiation of, 5–6, 102–3. *See also* Dworkin; Kant; Rawls; Rousseau

Bacon, Francis, 33–4
Bank of England, 30, 135, 140, 142
Baptism, 28, 40, 64; as circumcision of the heart, 37
Barbeyrac, Jean, 58
Barrow, Isaac, 61
Bentham, Jeremy, 91, 177
Bible, 34, 37, 38, 41–2, 44. *See also* New Testament; Old Testament; Torah

222 Index

Bolingbroke, Henry Saint-John, 1st Viscount, 136, 140, 143, 147
Bonds: in *Merchant of Venice*, 36–7, 45–50; of commercial society, 67–78, 86
Bramhall, Bishop John, 74
Burke, Edmund, 116, 136–7, 139–40, 156–67, 171–2

Canadian Charter of Rights and Freedoms, 20, 199
Capital, 135–8, 153–6. *See also* Commerce; Interest, moneyed; Money
Censorship, 184–92
Charity: and compulsory conversion, 8, 31–2; as obligatory or just, 8, 30–1; as optional, 56–8, 77, 155; opposition to, characteristic of liberalism, 4, 8, 21, 53–65, 199; repressed by rights-discourse, 127; separation from justice, 7–9, 53–65, 160–1. *See also* Antonio; Christianity
Charlton, Henry, 37–8, 42
Chetwood, Knightley, 61
Christianity, 26, 28, 30–2, 34, 39–40, 42, 68–9, 73, 89–90, 101, 159–61, 190, 197; Locke's use of Christian natural law, 5, 68–9, 92–7
Circumcision, 37, 44–5, 48, 50, 64
Citizenship, 27–30, 35, 150, 192. *See also* Virtue: civic
Civil rights. *See* Historicization of right

Civil war, 147–8; English, 4, 89, 100, 170. *See also* Revolution
Class conflict, 113–16, 141–3, 154
Class perspectives on history, 135–40
Cobban, Alfred, 157
Cohen, Walter, 32
Commerce, 5, 8–9, 147, 150–6; and toleration, 35, 53–6, 63–8, 199; in Athens, 27–30; in medieval Europe, 30–1; in relation to civil law, contractual fidelity, rights, 9, 20, 28–30, 50, 67–8, 75–6, 198–9; in relation to nation-state and representative government, 30, 32, 34, 85. *See also* Capital; Economy; Trade
Commercial revolution, 135, 140, 143
Conquest, 115, 132–3
Conscience: rights of, 90–1, 105–6
Contractual fidelity, 47–8, 50, 67–78
Conversion, 36–40, 69, 93; compulsory, 31, 39–43, 50, 54–5
Cox, Richard, 5
Cranston, Maurice, 15, 19, 173, 178, 183
Credit, 135, 137, 150, 163

Day, John Patrick, 94
Discrimination, 18–19, 121–6
Division of labour, 136, 153, 156
Dunn, John, 5, 108, 145
Duty, 20, 131, 155, 160, 191, 195. *See also* Obligation
Dworkin, Ronald, 16, 17, 74, 124, 173, 181

Economy: natural and commercial, 27–8, 59, 96; moral and political, 33, 156
Empire: Holy Roman, 39; of rights, 22, 96, 197, 199
Equal rights, 97, 126, 163; redundancy in, 16–17, 21, 124
Equity, 10, 29, 34, 57–8, 77, 114, 182

Feinberg, Joel, 19, 173, 175, 177–8, 183, 187–9
Ferguson, Adam, 16, 31, 136–7, 144–5, 149, 153, 193–4
Filmer, Sir Robert, 33
Finnis, John, 9, 127–31
Forbes, Duncan, 145
Freedom of thought and speech, 53–5, 89–91, 104–5, 172–3, 181–5, 189–92
Friendship: in relation to rights, 35–40, 77–8; in relation to usury, 35–40
Fulford, Robert, 190–1

Gewirth, Alan, 10
Grammar, 3, 14, 22. *See also* Language
Grotius, Hugo, 4, 8, 11, 21, 31, 55–7, 62, 65, 68, 80, 82–3, 86, 92–3, 122–4, 128, 194, 199

Hamilton, Alexander, 172–3
Harm, 175–7, 179, 186–7
Hart, Herbert Lionel Adolphus, 14–18, 124, 173, 176–8, 180–1, 184–7, 189
Haskins, George Lee, 34
Hegel, Georg Wilhelm Friedrich, 7, 29, 73, 101–2, 121–4, 126, 146, 166, 169–71
Hillel, 55
Historicization of right, 135–67. *See also* Manners
Hobbes, Thomas, 4–9, 11, 16, 21, 47, 55–6, 58, 62, 65, 68–9, 92, 100–3, 107, 111, 114–16, 121–3, 126, 146–7, 169–74, 180, 185, 189, 199; boldest exponent of Shylockian doctrine, 6, 71; moral constructivism, 70–5; on property, 132–3, 143–5; on representative government, 86–7, 89; relation of law and liberty, 87–9; right to life and liberty, 83–90; *the* political philosopher of the English-speaking world, 21, 66, 74, 193, 196
Honour, 10, 28, 30, 82, 84, 103, 120, 184–5
Hooker, Richard, 97
Hume, David, 10, 75–6, 134, 136–8, 144–51, 153, 160, 166

Il Pecorone, 38, 45
Innis, Michael, 122
Inheritance: right of, 148, 161, 166; and tacit consent, 136, 148, 162; and tradition, 136, 148, 162–5
Interest: and rights, 54, 65, 76, 105–7, 156, 161, 181; as advantage, benefit, profit, 65, 69, 76, 113, 117, 149, 181; as money paid for use, 35–6, 39, 65, 142–3; landed versus

moneyed, 135–66; Locke's charges on loans to friends, 30; Locke's union of, to Christian virtue, 69–70. *See also* Usury; Utility

Jesus, 11, 28, 38–9, 41–2, 55. *See also* Christianity
Jews, 4, 26, 30, 32–4, 39–40, 42, 53–4, 157–8, 190. See also Anti-semitism; Naziism; Shylock
Jones, John Walter, 29
Judaism. *See* Jews
Justice: absolute, incompatible with rights, 127–31; 'diké' and 'jus' distinguished from rights, 9, 28–9; disrespect of, by Lockian majority, 114; relationship to charity, 7–10, 21, 42, 53–65, 127, 160–1; social, versus rights, 20, 167, 195–9. *See also* Natural justice; Rights

Kant, Immanuel, 6, 10, 47, 73–4, 76–8, 88, 91, 115, 169–73
Kramnick, Isaac, 157

Labour, 69, 94, 97, 101–2, 114, 136, 140–4, 150, 153–6, 160, 198. *See also* Person
Land, 113, 135, 140–4, 147, 150, 153–6, 161–3
Language, 20, 71–2, 74–5, 127–31, 196–9. *See also* Grammar
Laslett, Peter, 62, 94–5, 109–11
Law, 6–7, 13, 74, 87–9, 102, 132; in relation to Love, 35, 37–42, 47–50. *See also* Moral Law; Natural Law; Principle of Right; Torah
Lewalski, Barbara, 38
Liberalism, 3–5, 21–3, 89–91, 120, 171–3, 181, 185–9; enemies of, 22; religious dimension, 4–5, 21, 53–6. *See also* Locke; Mill; Shylock
Liberty: civil versus political, 88–9, 174, 185–8, 191–2; commercial, 153–6; right to, 81–97, 100–7, 145
Life: right to, 81–97, 100–7, 145. *See also* Necessity: right of
Locke, John, 4–5, 14, 21, 30, 58–65, 68–71, 77, 92–7, 99–117, 119–21, 129, 136–7, 142, 144–51, 153, 155, 157, 162, 193; and Bank of England and Great Recoinage, 140–3; anti-Catholicism, 68, 109–11; as commissioner on Board of Trade, 61–2; as mercantilist, 63, 144; compared with Shylock, 3, 13, 59, 61; lack of philosophic grounding to his politics, 5–6, 14, 102–3, 117, 146; on armed resistance to government, 107–17; on charitable duty versus property right, 58–63; on contractual fidelity, 69–70; on inalienable right and alienable property, 73, 82, 92–7, 102–7, 131–3; on money, 59, 96, 137, 143–4; on ownership of one's person, 93–7, 103, 113, 120–1, 126, 131, 138, 167; on toleration,

68, 199; shy, contrasted with bold Hobbes, 5–6, 70–1; tension between individual rights and majority rule, 112–16
Love: in relation to Law, 37–40, 47–50
Lowndes, William, 141
Luther, Martin, 33, 46–7
Lyons, David, 175

Macpherson, Crawford Brough, 4–5, 59, 94, 96, 99. *See also* Possessive Individualism
Machiavelli, Niccolo, 40, 63, 70, 112
Mandeville, Bernard, 56, 63–5, 75–6, 78, 136–7, 157, 213
Manners, 11, 21, 137, 146, 169–92. *See also* Virtue: commercial
Marcuse, Herbert, 186
Market morality, 5, 21, 198. *See also* Possessive Individualism; Virtue: commercial
Marx, Karl, 17–18, 71–2, 99–103, 114, 116, 126, 139, 156, 166–7
Mill, John Stuart, 11, 14–15, 119–20, 154, 168, 173, 175–87
Money, 59, 96, 137, 143–4. *See also* Capital; Interest, moneyed; Locke
Montesquieu, Charles de, 64, 189
Moral law, 7, 10, 88, 132, 172. *See also* Kant

Narveson, Jan, 88–9, 175, 198
Natural justice, 9, 11, 197

Natural law, 5, 7, 9, 10, 21, 61, 74, 83, 93, 96, 102–3, 107, 117, 128–9, 132, 146, 151. *See also* Antonio; Christianity; Locke; Thomas Aquinas, Saint
Natural rights, 9, 10, 21, 30, 35, 67, 81–97, 102–7, 145, 151, 167. *See also* Hobbes; Paine; Shylock; Spinoza
Naziism, 22, 189–91
Necessity: right of, 56–9
New Testament, 34, 37, 38, 41–2, 49
Newton, Isaac, 141
Nobility: versus self-preservation, 103–7, 111–12, 117
Nozick, Robert, 6, 72, 88, 96–7, 102, 106–7, 117, 175–7

Oakeshott, Michael, 196
Obligations, 6, 131, 195, moral and legal, 10; moral and prudential, 86–7; relationship to rights, 6–7, 10, 127, 131, 194–5
Old Testament, 34–5, 37–8, 44, 49

Paine, Thomas, 136, 138–9, 157, 159, 163, 166–7
Palmer, John Leslie, 45
Paternalism, 39–40, 50, 93, 96, 173, 175–6
Pennock, James Roland, 29
Person, 16, 101, 117, 119–33, 175–6, 198; as ability to labour, 94, 97, 138–9, 167–8, 198; as abstraction from social differences, 19, 121–6; as subject

or bearer of rights, 102, 120–33, 146
Plato, 17, 27, 67–8, 102
Pocock, John Grenville Agard, 29–30, 99, 111
Polin, Raymond, 95, 131
Possessive Individualism, 4–5, 99–101, 185, 187, 192, 199. *See also* Macpherson
Poverty, 8, 30–1, 57, 61–3, 69, 113–16, 142, 148, 155–6, 160–1
Power: in relation to rights, 12, 19–20, 91, 112–13, 116–17, 121–7, 132
Principle of right, 10, 185, 197. *See also* Rousseau
Property, 145–51, 161–7; lack of clear title in Greece and medieval Christendom, 29–31, 67; origins of exclusive property right, 56–63, 132–3, 144–5; private property versus common good, 129–30
Protestantism: elimination of prohibition on usury, 33, 47
Pufendorf, Samuel, 4, 56–8, 65, 101, 122–4, 129

Rawls, John, 6, 10, 16, 74, 124
Rebellion, 107–17, 139, 181; American, 116, 136, 149–50, 165–89; Monmouth, 111
Religion, 4, 35, 39, 53–6, 68, 89–90, 111, 155, 159–61, 170, 172, 176, 179–80, 184. *See also* Christianity; Conversion; Judaism; Protestantism; Toleration

Rembrandt, Hermanszoon Van Rijn, 4, 122
Resistance: right of armed. *See* Rebellion: Revolution
Revolution, 99–117, 139; American, *see* Rebellion; French, 102, 115–16, 124, 135–6, 157, 165–6; Glorious, 4, 109, 111, 146, 162, 165. *See also* Civil war
Richards, Benjamin, 92
Rights: and negative form of the golden rule, 11, 55; and power, 12, 20, 91, 112, 127, 151; and power of lawyers, 17, 175; antonym obligations, not wrongs, 7, 10, 20; as amoral moralism, 6, 14, 21, 199; as claims *against* or entitlements *to*, 14, 19–20, 194; as distinct from law, 'droit', 'Recht', 6–7, 9–10, 84, 88, 128–9; as distinct from *the* right, 6, 9–10, 12, 21, 120, 132, 194; as good things or necessary evils, 17–19, 34–5; as inalienable possessions or alienable properties, 16, 81–97, 102–7, 126–33, 198; as moral properties, 14–16, 21, 120, 194; as permissive, protecting choices, options, 6–7, 11, 18, 34, 117, 119, 129–30, 194; as personal possessions or properties, 7, 10–11, 13, 15, 20, 56, 94–5, 120, 126, 132, 145, 151, 194; as privatization of right, 7, 10, 120, 127–31; as privileges or as equal rights, 16, 21,

121–6; as unclaimed claims, 18–19; as unreasonable rationalism, 13–14, 21, 199; confusion about, 14–17, 22, 95–6, 193–4, 196; expression of will, not reason, 12–14, 72–5; genesis in separation of justice and charity, 4, 7–10, 53–65, 199; inappropriate between friends, lovers or fellow communicants, 35–6, 49–50; in conflict with manners, 171–92; of armed resistance, rebellion, revolution, 107–17; option, versus welfare, 20, 194–6; to be offensive, 171–92; to do wrong, 11–12, 15, 114–15, 119–20, 129, 131–2, 191, 194; violations of, and atrocities, 197–8. *See also* Charity; Commerce; Conscience; Freedom of thought and speech; Historicization of right; Inheritance; Justice; Liberty; Life; Natural rights; Necessity; Person; Power; Property; Shylock; Strangers; Taxation; Toleration; Virtue

Rousseau, Jean-Jacques, 10, 73–4, 83, 86, 88–9, 101, 104, 131, 155, 167, 174, 185–6, 197

Selden, John, 31–2, 54–5
Seliger, Martin, 62
Shakespeare, William, 21, 193, 196; *The Merchant of Venice*, 3, 8, 21, 25–50, 53, 67, 72, 75, 77, 169, 175, 193
Shylock, 24–6, 36–50, 57, 64, 70, 73, 75, 80, 82, 85, 91–3, 97, 111–12, 119–20, 140, 151, 155, 157, 161, 186, 189, 192; antagonist of Antonio or compulsive Christian charity, 8, 18, 34, 67, 193, 199; archetypical rights-claimant, 8, 13, 33, 35–6, 50, 62, 169, 193; as pluralist, 38, 71–3, 78; compared with John Locke, 3, 13–14, 59, 69, 103, 117; exponent of liberal doctrine, 4, 21, 67, 96, 185; his mercifixion, 26, 36, 39
Simon, Saint, 24, 45
Simmons, Alan John, 95–6
Slavery, 27–8, 62, 81–3, 92–3, 101–2, 104, 176
Smith, Adam, 64–5, 75–6, 136–8, 144–5, 147, 152–7, 159–61, 198
Spinoza, Benedict, 4, 8, 21, 52–5, 62, 65, 68–71, 75, 77–8, 90–2, 121, 126, 199
Strangers: bearers of rights in the relationship of, 35, 71, 73
Strauss, Leo, 5, 9, 96, 157
Suarez, Francisco, 128
Swift, Jonathan, 136–7, 140, 143, 147

Taxation: and Representation, 113, 116, 129, 138, 140–2, 149–51, 156
Thomas Aquinas, Saint, 7–9, 30–1, 33, 128–9, 131
Thompson, Edward, 156
Tierney, Brian, 30
Toleration, 4, 21, 35, 55–6, 68, 89, 127, 157, 199

Torah, 35, 37, 45
Trade, 30, 56, 63, 68, 75, 150
Trudeau, Pierre Elliott, 20
Tully, James, 5
Tussman, Joseph, 173, 182, 187

Universal Declaration of Human Rights, 130, 194–5
Usury, 8, 27, 30–6, 41, 56, 65
Utility, 10, 75–7, 147–8, 150, 156, 161, 181, 197

Virtue: Christian, 7, 69, 137, 160, 197; civic, 7, 27–30, 137, 185, 193, 197; commercial, 70, 76, 78, 160, 180, 192 (*see also* Manners); imprecision of, relative to language of rights, 10, 58; union of interest to, 69–70, 76

Waldron, Jeremy, 59
Wasserstrom, Richard, 131
Weil, Simone, 127, 131, 197–8
Wilkins, Burleigh, 157
Wrong, 11–15, 77, 114–15, 119–20, 129, 131–2, 191, 194, 197–8